# MODERNIST QUARTET

*Modernist Quartet* offers a sweeping new assessment of the four most influential poetic presences embraced by American modernism: Robert Frost, Wallace Stevens, Ezra Pound, and T. S. Eliot. Seeking out the origins of modernism in the intellectual and cultural milieu from which the movement drew its strength, *Modernist Quartet* probes the ideological inheritance shared, if differently invested, by the four poets. Frank Lentricchia reads through the lens of various historical environments (literary, philosophical, gender relations, the business of capitalist economics) the texts now recognized as central to the era, as they at once reflect and shape, through their surprising language, our understanding of those very environments. From the poems thus emerge the stories, sometimes only implicit, of poets seeking to sustain a life in noncommercial writing, in a culture that is for the most part hospitable only to commercial art. Offering a synoptic vision of the lives and literary careers of the four poets in question, *Modernist Quartet* presents a rich and new literary history of an era in American letters whose explosive effect on subsequent generations has never been disputed.

# MODERNIST QUARTET

FRANK LENTRICCHIA

*Duke University*

CAMBRIDGE
UNIVERSITY PRESS

Published by the Press Syndicate of the University of Cambridge
The Pitt Building, Trumpington Street, Cambridge CB2 1RP
40 West 20th Street, New York, NY 10011-4211, USA
10 Stamford Road, Oakleigh, Melbourne 3166, Australia

First published 1994

*Library of Congress Cataloging-in-Publication Data*

Lentricchia, Frank.

Modernist quartet / Frank Lentricchia.

p.    cm.

Includes bibliographical references and index.

ISBN 0-521-47004-8 (hc). – ISBN 0-521-46975-9 (pb)

1. American poetry – 20th century – History and criticism.
2. Modernism (Literature) – United States. 3. Frost, Robert,
1874–1963 – Criticism and interpretation. 4. Stevens, Wallace,
1879–1955 – Criticism and interpretation. 5. Pound, Ezra,
1885–1972 – Criticism and interpretation. 6. Eliot, T. S. (Thomas
Stearns), 1888-1965 – Criticism and interpretation. I. Title.

PS310.M57L46    1994
811.5209–dc20        93-50239
CIP

A catalog record for this book is available from the British Library.

*Cover photographs (clockwise from top):*
Robert Frost, Ezra Pound, T. S. Eliot, and Wallace Stevens.
Courtesy of the Bettmann Archive (Pound, Eliot, and Stevens)
and the Dartmouth College Library (Frost).

ISBN 0-521-47004-8 hardback
ISBN 0-521-46975-9 paperback

Transferred to digital printing 2003

For
Anthony DeCurtis
Dan O'Hara
Don Pease

# CONTENTS

# PREFACE AND ACKNOWLEDGMENTS

Early in 1983, Sacvan Bercovitch asked me, and I agreed, to write a contribution of some reasonable length (200 manuscript pages) on modern American poetry for the new *Cambridge History of American Literature*. That contribution, too many years in the making, has grown to twice its stipulated length and narrowed drastically in focus, from "modern American poetry" to my "modernist quartet": Robert Frost, Wallace Stevens, Ezra Pound, and T. S. Eliot. I have learned some things in the process; one of the most important is that my taste is hopelessly canonical. And for this taste of mine I offer no apologies. I regret only not being able to write with seriousness about two other American poets whom I like almost as much as my quartet: Marianne Moore and Hart Crane. The reasons I have not written about those two are obscure to me. The fault may lie with insufficient love.

The American literary culture that my poets grew to know, and despise, as young men of great literary ambition was dominated by values that hostile commentators characterize as "genteel." The names of the genteel literary powers are now mostly forgotten: R. H. Stoddard, Bayard Taylor, G. H. Boker, Thomas Bailey Aldrich, E. C. Stedman, Richard Watson Gilder (Boston, Philadelphia, but mainly New York); at Columbia, Harvard, and Princeton, the academic reflectors G. E. Woodberry, Barrett Wendell, Henry Van Dyke. These were the men who shaped and ruled the literary culture of modernism's American scene of emergence. They represented, in their prime, the idea of poetry and true literary value. What Willard Thorp said about them more than forty years ago still cuts to the heart of this matter of literary politics: "As the years went by, connections which the group formed with magazines and publishing houses multiplied until their names were spoken and seen everywhere, and they formed a kind of literary interlocking directorate." In other words, they policed Parnassus by capturing and controlling the modes of literary publication. And not only did they "represent" the idea of poetry ("represent" is too weak, and they would have said *ideal* of poetry): they enforced that representation from the 1880s through the first decade or so of the twentieth century, in particular, they enforced it by editing, in those pre–little magazine times, the period's dominant magazines of culture – *Scribner's,* the *Atlantic,* and the *Century.*

America's looming genteel directorate unleashed a culture-saturating wave of literature and criticism: appreciations, recollections, histories of English and American poetry, numerous volumes of their own verse, some novels, one major translation (Taylor's of Goethe), travel books of considerable popularity, social reflections and criticism (most often under the mask of literary reflections and criticism), decisive taste-making anthologies of American literature, coffee-table books of photos, illustrations, and light essays on great American writers "at home," including one such volume which featured one of the group's own, E. C. Stedman. The volume on Stedman ensured that his face, as well as his name, would be seen everywhere. And when his poems, like those of his "Fireside" predecessors, finally made their way into a Houghton Mifflin "household" edition, Stedman's cultural power received its ultimate enhancement.

"Household": there's a key word, an index to a culture that modernist writers would bury in scorn. "Fireside" poets, "schoolroom" poets (Bryant, Whittier, Longfellow, Holmes, Lowell): poets for the whole family, to be read around the fireside, sometimes out loud, with children and grandparents in comfortable attention. "Genteel" poets, successors to the Fireside group: nothing abrasive to family values here, either, but probably not much read around the fireplace. For bad reasons, they were difficult of access.

These genteel poets and critics formed our poetic nineties, not to be conflated with the Paterian nineties of British aestheticism. Our aesthetes valued purity above all, the rigorous evacuation from poetry of sensuousness and the sensual, and of any tendencies to social representation. Our aesthetes were ascetics of the circumambient gas. They flew from the world that capital was making (but so would the modernists), from what one of them called the "modern industry of prose fiction" (the metaphor reveals almost everything), a denigrating reference to the (then) avant-garde presence of realist and naturalist fiction and all the repulsive social references of this new writing: the classes, middle and lower, in uneasy relation and movement, America's new (and swarthy) immigrants, business, money, power, sex, divorce, and other distinctly nonideal preoccupations of a postaristocratic literary world. The new fiction carried the news of radical social change, and Thomas Bailey Aldrich, editor of the *Atlantic,* poet and novelist, took notice:

> The mighty Zolaistic movement now
> Engrosses us – a miasmatic breath
> Blown from the slums. We paint life as it is,
> The hideous side of it, with careful pains,
> Making a god of the dull commonplace.

Of course, they were attacked – from Twain and Howells to Santayana, Van Wyck Brooks, and Mencken – for being out of touch: hopelessly nostalgic, prudish, feminine, all enervated lyric inwardness. In Santayana's unfair phrase for Emerson: they digested vacancy. A great lyric poet, Wallace Stevens, could make such an act the poignant and persistent substance of his work, a lyric drama of inwardness. The genteel poets maybe digested vacancy. In fact, it's hard to say what they digested. They would have agreed, at any rate, that they were out of touch: they intended to be out of touch; it was the nature and function of poetry to be out of touch. Thus: "Language is colloquial and declarative in our ordinary speech, and on its legs for common use and movement. Only when it takes wing does it become poetry." Invested with the Swinburnean "trinity of time-beat, consonance, and assonance," language manages to "rise to the upper air," free of the vernacular voice in worldly situation, afloat over a dimly perceived pastoral terrain. Genteel poetry was a poetry of happily dissociated sensibility; its odor was distinctly one of mildewed and dusty old books. The library needed proper ventilating, but these poets didn't know it, and would never know it:

THE WOODS THAT BRING THE SUNSET NEAR

The wind from out the west is blowing
The homeward-wandering cows are lowing,
Dark grow the pine-woods, dark and drear, –
The woods that bring the sunset near.

When o'er wide seas the sun declines,
Far off its fading glory shines,
Far off, sublime, and full of fear –
The pine-woods bring the sunset near.

This house that looks to east, to west,
This, dear one, is our home, our rest;
Yonder the stormy sea, and here
The woods that bring the sunset near.
                                    – Richard Watson Gilder

The first chapter of this book, on the Harvard philosophers, offers an American link in the philosophical conversation that stretches from

## Preface

Kant to Marcuse: American philosophical modernism before the fact of the much discussed continental phenomenon. The second chapter, through the examples of Pound and Frost, offers a view of a key inaugural moment: the founding of the little magazines in the setting of emergent mass culture. Then follow four chapters on the poets, intended to give four angles of vision on modernist experiment. In the setting of four "modern" lives, these chapters present four individual efforts to create a new poetry against the restrictive standard established by the poetics that encouraged the practice of a writer like Richard Watson Gilder. These chapters on the poets, though multi-intentioned, are united in the purpose to evoke the genteel environment as cultural origin of modernist reaction, one important (though not the only) historical ground of experiment.

I understand how odd it must appear to include Robert Frost in modernist company. One of the reasons for the oddity is that we have forgotten the heterogeneous character of modernist literature: Ibsen, Strindberg, Chekhov, Hardy, Shaw, the Joyce of *Dubliners*, and Frost, as well as the usual (and glorious) suspects who knew how to ventilate the library.

Earlier versions of parts of this book appeared in *South Atlantic Quarterly*, *American Literary History*, *American Literature*, *Critical Inquiry*, and *Ariel and the Police* (Madison: University of Wisconsin Press, 1988).

Special thanks are due to Sacvan Bercovitch, Melissa Lentricchia, Luke Menand, William Pritchard, Tom Ferraro, Cary Wolfe, and the three gentlemen named in my dedication.

# 1

## PHILOSOPHERS OF MODERNISM
## AT HARVARD, CIRCA 1900

WHEN GEORGE SANTAYANA was appointed to the philosophy department at Harvard in 1889, just a year after finishing his doctorate there, he became the junior colleague of William James and Josiah Royce, and the three together, over the next two decades – in relationships supportive, competitive, and critical – collectively defined the shapes and limitations of what would come to be understood as modernism in the United States: its desires and values, its literary, social, and philosophical genesis and ground, and the sometimes stinging antithetical force of its cultural and social commentary. In different ways, Santayana, James, and Royce each addressed the future of philosophy and poetry as if, at the same time, they were addressing the future of society, as if the shape of things to come in some crucial part depended on the way writers and intellectuals conducted themselves. The landmarks of modernism established by the group are easy to identify: James's *The Principles of Psychology* in 1890, a work which among its other accomplishments gave us both the term and the theory of "stream of consciousness"; Santayana's *The Sense of Beauty* in 1896 and his pivotal *Interpretations of Poetry and Religion* in 1900; James's *Pragmatism* in 1907; and, finally, in 1913, one year after Harriet Monroe founded *Poetry: A Magazine of Verse*, modernism's inaugurating little magazine, Royce's *The Problem of Christianity*.

If the years between 1890 and 1913 mark the most energetic

period of American philosophical modernism, that same period also represents, as more than one historian of American literature has deceptively implied by word and by silence, the big blank of American poetic history. Bryant died in 1878, Longfellow in 1882, Lowell in 1891, Whittier in 1892, and Holmes in 1894. When we correlate these end-dates with their respective beginnings – Bryant was born in 1794, the other "Fireside" presences early in the nineteenth century – in other words, when we add the fact of biological endurance to the fact of unprecedented popular acceptance, we are pressed to conclude that the dominance of America's Fireside poets, who were published in the later nineteenth century by Houghton Mifflin in "household" editions, is a literary reality of long and oppressive reach. (Imagine, if you can, a "household" edition of *The Cantos.*) The Fireside poets were among the chief cultural powers of our nineteenth century: they stood for poetry. By their lives as well as by their practice as writers they defined, however conservatively, a broad-ranging cultural (educative) function for the man of letters: they translated Homer and Dante; they held chairs in romance languages at Harvard; they edited influential newspapers; they were foreign diplomats; they gave well-noted and well-attended speeches on the controversial affairs of the day. Whitman, a visible dissenter from Fireside forms and morals (though not from its cultural ambition), died in 1892, a year after the publication of the tenth edition of *Leaves of Grass.* Emily Dickinson, another qualified dissenter, died without fame in 1886.

Looking back at the early days of his poetic development, in the first decade of this century, T. S. Eliot reflected on the literal truth of his poetic origins when he said that there was not "a single living poet, in either England or America, then at the height of his powers, whose work was capable of pointing the way to a young poet conscious of the desire for a new idiom." Long after the fact, Eliot was rationalizing his interests in continental literatures and in older periods of English literature. (American literary history would, however, eventually exact its revenge: Eliot would become the high

2

modernist representative of the traditional New England poets.) Wallace Stevens added a concurring and decadent note to Eliot's testimony when he wrote that when he was a student at Harvard, "it was commonplace to say that all the poetry had been written and all the paintings painted." Feeling the familiar romantic burden, the embarrassment of tradition, Stevens, after settling himself economically, moved into self-consciously avant-garde styles in an effort to accentuate his difference and originality. But, like Eliot, he was also decisively marked by his American poetic inheritance – hence his self-definition in "The Comedian as the Letter C" as a poet of "disguised *pronunciamento*," a writer of "anecdotes" which he characterized as doctrinal, not in form (no Longfellow or Bryant he), but in intention: Stevens as closet Fireside poet, as it were. On the other hand, Robert Frost, who was never embarrassed by the American literary heritage of popular poetry, paid open tribute to his Fireside predecessor, Longfellow, when he titled his first volume *A Boy's Will*.

E. A. Robinson, Stevens, and Frost were all "special" (nondegree candidate) students at Harvard in the period in question: Robinson from 1891 to 1893, Frost from 1897 to 1899, Stevens from 1897 to 1900. Eliot, from 1906 to 1914, was the genuine article at Harvard, taking a B.A. in 1910, an M.A. in 1911, and doing advanced work for the Ph.D. in languages and philosophy before settling in London in 1914, dissertation completed but, by choice, no Ph.D. in hand. So the apprenticeship of what we know as modern American poetry coincides both with the big blank of American poetic history and the big bang of modernist American philosophy. And the site of emerging modernist poetic idioms and of an authoritative philosophical discourse was Cambridge, Massachusetts, at the turn of the twentieth century. Both in personal ways and in the prescribed academic fashion, Robinson, Frost, Stevens, Eliot, and Radcliffe's modernist, Gertrude Stein, encountered the Harvard philosophers. In the conventional sense of what we mean by the terms, these philosophers were "influences" and "sources." Stevens knew Santayana personally, read and was moved to a lifetime of meditation by

# Modernist Quartet

*Interpretations of Poetry and Religion;* Frost taught the shorter version of James's *Principles;* Eliot took a class with Royce. It is not hard to trace links between sentences in Santayana and James and specific poems and phrases in Stevens, Frost, and Eliot. But those are the footnotes to the text of modern American poetic history. The philosophical works written in Cambridge in the last decade of the nineteenth century and first decade of the twentieth, despite the attitude of traditional literary history, are not background. As more expansive, detailed, and precise expressions of modernist thought than anything written in prose by any of the important American poets, either in that period or thereafter, the key works of Santayana, James, and Royce are themselves collaborative modernist texts, the original metapoetic idiom of the youth of Eliot, Frost, and Stevens – both expressions and criticisms of the ideologies of modernism before the fact.

George Santayana (1863–1952), who was born in Spain and brought by his father to the United States in 1872, will be recalled, if by nothing else, as the author of the maxim that those who will not remember the past are condemned to repeat it; as the archetypal fallen Roman Catholic who is reported to have said that there is no God and the Blessed Virgin Mary is His mother; and, by readers of Wallace Stevens, as the philosopher evoked in Stevens's moving late poem "To an Old Philosopher in Rome," who in fact died in Rome, in a convent. This trivia is relevant to the deeper drifts of Santayana's writing (and to the course of modernism), though it might be impossible to see such relevance in his major publication of 1896, *The Sense of Beauty,* a treatise on aesthetics which can stand as a miniature of the nineteenth-century preoccupation (via Kant and Schiller) with beauty in isolation from knowledge, use, and morality. Autonomous beauty: not an elusive and ascetic spirituality, but a special kind of "play" that certifies our final achievement of human-

4

ity: our civilization, our happiness, and (key word for aesthetic idealists) our "freedom" from all necessities imposed upon us from outside. Aesthetic play in the utopian elaboration of aesthetics developed in the 1950s and 1960s by Norman O. Brown and Herbert Marcuse would nevertheless be sublimely useful: it would abolish the joyless grind known as *work* in the capitalist system and become the sign of a race which does, in Santayana's anticipation of the happy talk of the new left, "spontaneously whatever conduces to its welfare," and which lives "safely and prosperously without external stimulus or restraint." And not only would nature be overcome, in the first act of this aesthetic apocalypse, but so would consumer capitalism – the economy, ethics, and culture of the commodity. Eventually, we would win our freedom from capitalist society, which has displaced nature as the iron law of our destiny. Until the revolution, however, we will have to comfort ourselves with the fore-pleasure provided by proleptic hints of radical social transformation in the beauties of nature and the plastic arts, which (in Santayana's carefully chosen words – Marcuse could not have said it more precisely) "are not consumed by being enjoyed."

The intriguing sense of Santayana's "sense of beauty" lies in its evasion of two powerful trivializations of the literary experience at the end of the nineteenth century, two kinds of aestheticist extremity which signaled two kinds of alienation from the bourgeois life: on our side of the Atlantic, thanks to the genteel cultural critics, the vaporization, in the name of Keats (of all writers) of the aesthetic into the ascetic; on the other side, and also in the name of Keats – Pater's Keats – the conversion of the aesthetic into private sensuous delight, the revelry of sensation cherished in a revery locked behind the thick walls of personality. For Santayana, aesthetic pleasure is a different kind of pleasure, and its difference lies in its teasing invitation to the social being that Pater and genteel America had deliberately turned their backs on. Aesthetic pleasure for Santayana is neither an "impression" imprisoned in an isolated subject, nor a release into the stratosphere of disembodied souls. It is instead the sort of pleasure that is anchored in the immediacy and inviolable integrity of perception.

What Santayana calls the "objectification" of perception is the creation of that special sort of literary effect that a self-conscious modernist poetics would shortly call the "image," and in Santayana it is clear, as it rarely is in the celebrated modernist theorists who followed him, that the image is not only a form of perception but also a form of expression which integrates feeling and object in a public medium. As perception caught and crystallized in language, the image *is* the sense of beauty and it ought not to be an inducement to retreat into an incommunicable inwardness. By virtue of its fluidity, as a shuttle between, and binder of, subject and object, Santayana's "sense of beauty" becomes a necessary condition for collective recovery of our sensuous environment, collective integration of feeling and object: community formed by and for the pleasures of the percept; a community of hedonists, but a community. Santayana cannot, under any circumstances, be charged with having a radical social conscience, but neither can he be charged with the onanism of Pateresque aestheticism.

Santayana's thinking from *The Sense of Beauty* to the later chapters of *Interpretations of Poetry and Religion* prefigures the primary conflict inside poetic modernism between what would be called "imagism," the dream of the percept, and the sustained effort of a number of American poetic modernists to meet the challenge of a post-Miltonic long poem. In the arc of Wallace Stevens's career, it is the long movement between the early modernist perceptual "minutiae" of *Harmonium* and his "grand poem" of the 1940s, *Notes toward a Supreme Fiction*. Similarly, the tendency of *Interpretations of Poetry and Religion* is to argue from isolate sensibility to community, from poems as aids to perception to poems as aids to connection, from the singular image and its support in the lonely imagination to the long poem and its support in a community of interpreters, from a poetry of presence, a poetry of the present tense (Keatsian apotheosis), to a poetics of history and destiny – a poetry of the long shadow and the act whose fruit is futurity.

In the final chapter of *Interpretations of Poetry and Religion*, Santayana moves against the personal retreat inherent in conventional turn-of-the-century Pateresque hedonism as well as the Dionysian community that would be celebrated by the philosophers of the New Left in the 1960s. He begins with oppositions that will soon become clichés in modernist theory, and which had already appeared in American genteel aestheticism: verse is to prose as song is to speech as "jewels" are to "clay"; he begins, in other words, by assenting to the formalist credo that poetry, like stained glass, "arrests attention in its own intricacies" – a double-edged, yearning metaphor that asserts not only the intrinsic nature of aesthetic value but also, in its insistence on arrested attention, holds out the promise of rapturous fulfillment in complete rest, the extinguishing of will and our tomblike encasement (in the pretty rooms of sonnets) from history's world of chronicle and power. When sound and rhythm, perfectly "measured" and therefore distanced from the vernacular voice, produce the stained-glass effect, we are in the presence of a language "redolent" of "objectless passion" indistinguishable from the "sensation of movement and sensuous richness of the lines." Santayana's diction, deliberately overwrought, suggests something of his fin-de-siècle context: poetry in full retreat from the object is free-floating feeling, passion without reference, an exotic flower whose exhalations will satisfy what the chilling prose of thought and reference apparently threaten – the "glow of sense" and the thrills thereof. Santayana's ironic perspective both summarizes and judges (by half scorning) the desire to leave the world unseen and to fade far away to a warm south of orgiastic sensuousness. He says, in so many words, that the idolatry of Keats, whether Pateresque or genteel, is a "tedious vacuity"; it is "unworthy of a mature mind"; it belongs to the "apprenticeship of genius."

Stevens's imagination, in "Sunday Morning," of a socialized hedo-

7

nist sensibility (a "ring of men," chanting in orgy), his community of muscular ("supple and turbulent") nontubercular Keatsian males, is a nice counterpoint to the wispy and wimpy genteel recreation of Keats and to the insipidness of a genteel Christianity that can come only in dreams and in silent shadows. But the vision of community in "Sunday Morning" can be taken seriously only as the desperation of the poet who, like so many high modernists, often felt the need to turn back the clock. The comical impotence of Stevens's Dionysian fantasy of community in the seventh section of "Sunday Morning" is underscored by its exclusive male membership and by its nostalgia for pastoral enclosure. But in such pathos lies another, less conventional critical tale which the social history that surrounded the Harvard of Santayana and Stevens helps us to read by implicitly posing this question for the hedonists of modernist poetics, thereby forcing that poetics to show its rhetorical hand: if it is true that the economically shielded of upper-middle to upper-class background (including their intellectuals) in the youth of Stevens felt themselves distanced from their bodies – neurasthenia in the Harvard days of Stevens, Frost, and Eliot was a privileged illness – then it is also the case that hedonist poetics produces a cult poetry for the successful bourgeois victims of capitalism, that hedonist poetics (despite its romantic heritage) is conceived, not in radical Wordsworthian literary hopes, so that poets could speak to ordinary people, but so that the socially and culturally extraordinary could *in imagination* get physical, become ordinary and ignorant, mating their lives (in Stevens's phrase) with the sensual, pearly spouse, while in reality, nine to five, continuing to serve and enhance the society that had made them ill in the first place.

The privileged implied reader of early modernist literature is not among the exemplary heroes of that literature, and the ordinary people who are often celebrated in modernist texts do not read, or maybe even need, modernist literature. To get in touch with their bodies was not exactly the desire of the immigrants who flooded this country from southern Europe at the turn of the century when

Santayana was publishing *The Sense of Beauty* and *Interpretations of Poetry and Religion*. These people, who became the backbone of our working class – among other things, they dug the subway tunnels of New York – were all too immediately touched by experience; on the parched terrain of neofeudal southern Italy, where many of them were born, they had already experienced the discomforts of the sun; they had long before, and very unhappily, mated with the sensual, pearly spouse. (Or, as Stevens put it in a telling moment of sentimentality, after an especially gruelling period at the office – "I have worked like an Italian.") The ideological irony of early modern American poetry (Frost and Robinson are important exceptions) is that its pervasive sentiment for ignorance and the ignorant can be expressed only by Stevens's "sleight-of-hand man" – the self-conscious coterie poet of dense and difficult substance who pitches his language to those with the most patient critical attention. Intensity and purity of perceptual pleasure is one goal of modernist poetics; the difficult, wistful dream of perception and the absence of pleasure is often its reality.

Wallace Stevens's later career raises other basic questions about the ideology of Santayana's modernism: What shall we do after our supple bodies become brittle? How shall we chant our boisterous devotion to the sun when the pharynx goes bad? And how does a hedonist handle the boredom of repetitious sensation? These are the sorts of questions that Yvor Winters would later raise about modernism in a landmark essay on Stevens. In a letter both amusing and moving, written in his late sixties, Stevens in effect confirmed Winters when he said this: "What I want more than anything else in music, painting and poetry, in life and in belief is the thrill that I experienced once in all the things that no longer thrill me at all. I am like a man in a grocery store that is sick and tired of raisins and oyster crackers and who is nevertheless overwhelmed by appetite."

Santayana, who had more sympathy than Winters for modernist dilemmas, in effect read the hedonist impulse in modern poetry not as it is usually read, as irresponsible decadence, but as first-stage

yearning – a critical impulse for social change from within dominant social groups: the cultivation of the senses as an effort to return
to immediate experience, from which the economically privileged
have been alienated. Alienation, as the condition generated by the
economic mode of production that necessarily displaces the condition of nature, is at once the price of our freedom from nature's force
and the code term of a desire to pierce the veils of capitalist social
torpor and to return to more primal contact with the natural sources
of being.

In an allusive and revisionary play on Aristotle's poetics, Santayana says that poetry "in its primary substance and texture" is
"more philosophical than prose because it is nearer to our immediate
experience," from which we have been exiled by a ruthless economics of perception. In a rhetorical maneuver of some complexity,
Santayana brings the authority of Aristotle, who had nothing good
to say about immediate experience, against the culture of capitalism, about which Aristotle could not have had anything to say.
Santayana would hook his kind of aestheticism into classical authority in order to quarantine the era of capitalism as some strange disease
in the history of Western society, a historical deviation from the
social norm, not the next scene in a teleological drama whose last act
would see the delivered promise of socialism. Aestheticism so posi-
tioned by Santayana becomes mainstream social criticism, not marginal bohemian antithesis to the social center. Santayana conceives
the hedonist pleasures of perception and their literary authority and
vehicle, the image, as the incipient human protest of the ages
against the economic perversion of his time. He is, in this effort, a
later representative of the humanist anticapitalism mounted in the
English tradition beginning with Burke and Coleridge, and not a
closet Marxist. The judgments on perception that he cites – unnecessary, impractical, a waste of labor – and the correlative counter-
judgments on conception – preeminently useful, economical – are
penetrations into the often socially rarefied realms of epistemology
and literary theory of the culture of capital. Santayana's epithets, by

1900, are on the way to becoming the crucial critical conventions of T. E. Hulme, Ezra Pound, and the New Critics. Their occurrence in his writing is all the more interesting for being casual, for in their casualness they represent an ever more central American literary preoccupation with the cultural and economic object of the long-established social criticism in the English literary tradition.

What is not part of Santayana's literary periphery and its ambience of bohemianism and alienation – the mostly dull sword of modern poetry's antisocial reflex – is his historically surprising criticism of perceptualist aesthetic more than a decade before Pound's imagist crusade and the work of Hulme. Alongside Santayana's criticism of modernism, Winters's later judgments – for all their justice – sound imposed from outside and out of touch with the context of social issues within which modernist hedonism grew and became an attractive, therapeutic alternative for all manner of neurasthenics (Prufrock is their literary avatar) who, as economically fortunate reapers of the fruits of working-class labor, became the spiritual victims of capitalism. Against Winters's icier Platonism, Santayana would build reason upon sensuousness because he thought that in the sensuous experience mediated by the measured phonetic and rhythmic microlevels of poetry – the *order* of sound and rhythm – we are given our initial glimpses of the "measure" that may come to be at the macrolevel of poetry's social referent.

But if it is the image which is the authoritative language of immediacy, the image which destroys the bridges of conventional action by making us "halt at the sensation" – for which the world of business, in its preconsumer phase, has no use – if it is the image which restores the intimacy of idea and emotion, thereby unifying a sundered sensibility and reactivating (Coleridge's great hope) the whole soul of man; if the image can do all of this, not engage, not revise, nor in any way transform the horrors of business to which it is a response, but rather take us outside, give us new consciousness without disturbing the world of the old (we now recognize these goals as the aims of early modernist aesthetics), then there is something fundamentally empty about the social goals of literary modernism. Santayana knew this. Perceptual poetry may instigate an imaginative recovery of primitive innocence and vitality for the socially and culturally privileged, but in the same act, he thought, it also returns them to the confusions of nature. "If the function of poetry . . . did not go beyond this recovery of sensuous and imaginative freedom," then, Santayana writes, "poetry would deserve the judgment of Plato." Poets at best could take their place with gourmet cooks, high-priced hair stylists, florists, and other decorators of the economically fortunate. The poetry of "sensation and impulse," which "merely tickles the brain, like liquor, and plays upon our random imaginative lusts," is castigated as "irrational" by Santayana not because it appeals per se to the senses (Santayana, no champion of the sexy pleasures of the text, was also no prude). Nor is such poetry irrational simply because it excites what he calls "imaginative lusts" — Santayana would recuperate lust as desire — but because the lust that is aroused is a form of masturbation: random, disconnected, bound by private self-delight. Part of no world of others, it is merely isolated and a sin against community.

The word that Santayana needs to complete his assault on modernism was supplied much later by Georg Lukács, who described the vast and luxuriant particularity of James Joyce's *Ulysses* as "abstract." Leopold Bloom's iridescent and unforgettable "impressions" (in Pater's sense) are placed by Joyce against the background of a Dublin in relation to which they remain fundamentally alien: they have no past and no future, no time to them; they exist in a discontinuous, autonomous present. They are fragments calling for a historical consciousness of totality to make sense of them. Like the abstract alienation Lukács finds in Kafka, the abstract impressionism of Joyce is static. It refers us to a frozen, passive, and essentialized world of "inner" human nature that lies on the other side of history and will. The abstractions of Joyce and Kafka, argues Lukács, produce narratives not of specific social fate but of a universal *condition humain*. In other words, these are writers who appear to be incapable of political narrative because they cannot imagine social transformation.

With its basis in a Marxist theory of history, the political intention of Lukács's criticism of modernism is specific and reasonably clear. If Santayana's criticism is politically motivated (he would have been horrified to hear of it), then it is a criticism on behalf of a politics neither especially clear nor specific in his writing at the turn of the century. The common ground of Lukács (who shares much with the impatient Winters on modernism) and Santayana lies in the meaning they give to the charge that modernism encourages trivial writing – "pictures" rather than "stories": human reality as bits and pieces of things eternally present. Santayana's antidote is what he calls the philosophical poem, the kind of poem (his major examples are Lucretius, Dante, and Goethe) that not only contemplates "all things in their order and worth" and every single thing "in light of the whole," but in so contemplating would *speak for* the totality envisioned – in order, as it were, to urge it into being. Unlike Lukács, Santayana seems capable of imagining the possibility of a specifically modernist equivalent to the classic, philosophical poem – a poetry that would not negate the modernist tendency to root unity in the fragment, but would subordinate image and character to their "effects and causes," their context and condition, to the "*total movement* and meaning of the scene" (the very sort of "poetry" that would be written by Dreiser in *Sister Carrie*, Fitzgerald in *The Great Gatsby*, Dos Passos in *USA*, and Faulkner in *Absalom, Absalom!*). Santayana's antidote would not do away with the phenomenological fullness and particularity of image and character that Lukács finds in Joyce, because (and this is only hinted at in Santayana) the high cultural nexus of any modernist long poem – weightlessness, neurasthenia, banality, and alienation – demands an anchoring fiction of sensuous presence as its crucial point of departure. Sensuous lyric presence in modernism becomes, or would become, a mechanism or rhetoric on behalf of totality and the larger narrative vision – a theory, a supreme fiction – that any philosophical poetry, whether Dante's or Ezra Pound's, aims for.

Not the image, not character, and not the visible landscape, but the double landscape of nature and history is what Santayana means by "context." Poetries of the image and narratives of character, unlike *The Odyssey,* cannot set perception and character on wide seas, and for that reason their ultimate distinction is measured and deflated by the puny diameters of their respective worlds. The modernist poet of philosophical and historical ambition will therefore need to revivify, in his search for relevance, what Santayana calls the topographical sense. His writing will need to "swarm with proper names and allusions to history and fable" – and we can mark this classical desire in *The Cantos, The Waste Land, The Bridge,* and *Paterson.* But the topographical sense is of little moment unless the passions of characters so "placed" are linked with their "correlative object" (Santayana's phrase, his gift to Eliot), the dramatic plot that would give narrative propulsion to historical panorama: movement with direction, movement with a past, present, and future. When disjoined from the narrative sense, the topographical sense in Pound and Hart Crane will give the feeling of history but not its directed movement: impressions and images writ large, as Pound writes them, remain, as Pound admitted at the end ("it will not cohere") images and impressions – collocations, not order, not story. The "experience imagined," says Santayana, in a passage that epitomizes the social desire of high modernist poetics, "should be conceived as a destiny, governed by principles, and issuing in the discipline and enlightenment of the will. In this way alone can poetry become interpretation of life and not merely an irrelevant excursion into the realm of fancy, multiplying our images without purpose, and distracting us from our business without spiritual gain." What he calls "significant imagination" and "relevant fiction" are an imagination and a fiction that would move continuously from the purity of the image and the lyricism of character to the poetry which disciplines and enlightens the will; from Odysseus passive, weeping alone on the shore of Calypso's dreamy island to Odysseus fully energized and engaged, moving again in the historical world, killing the suitors, reclaiming his home.

Not long after the publication of *Interpretations of Poetry and Religion,* William James (1842–1910) set down his reaction: "how fantastic a philosophy! – as if the 'world of values' *were* independent of existence. . . . Always things burst by the growing content of experience. Dramatic unity; laws of versification; ecclesiastical systems; scholastic doctrines. Bah! Give me Walt Whitman and Browning ten times over. . . . The barbarians are in the line of mental growth." Santayana would not have been surprised; he'd been told earlier by James: "What a curse philosophy would be, if we couldn't forget all about it!" James, who saw himself as "unfit to be a philosopher" because at bottom he "hated philosophy," who was never shaken in his conviction "that it is better to *be* than define your being," and whose adult life was scarred by neurasthenia and "the sense of the hollowness and unreality that goes with it," was Santayana's generous-spirited philosophical antithesis. In another response to Santayana's book, he said: "I now understand Santayana, the man. I never understood him before. But what a perfection of rottenness in a philosophy! I don't think I ever knew the antirealistic view to be propounded with so impudently superior an air. It is refreshing to see a representative of moribund Latinity rise up and administer such reproof to us barbarians in the hour of our triumph."

Santayana's perfection of rottenness lay for James in his "pessimistic platonism." Santayana's world of values seemed to James not only independent of existence; it could claim no metaphysical authority in the classic Greek manner. The world of classical values – order, beauty, wholeness, and truth rational, truth universal, truth binding – is what we crave, not what is. This world of values is the world we give ourselves as fiction; it is the gift of imagination, Santayana's imperial faculty that crosses over, contaminates, and controls even our "understanding," which is no more than an "applicable fiction, a kind of wit with a practical use." It was this last sort of corrosive distinction (between applicable and inapplicable fictions) which led Frost to dismiss Santayana, saying that he believed only in illusions, true ones and false ones, and which led Stevens to celebrate him for his consistent elegance of irony that found the real both inadequate to our needs and yet the constant and necessary corrector and deflator of our visionary projections. Santayana would tell James that they were closer than he, James, would allow, and Santayana's pragmatic claim for our understanding is a compelling case in point.

But James thought that the key essay in *Interpretations of Poetry and Religion* was "The Poetry of Barbarism" and that it told another, deeper truth about Santayana's attitudes. Whitman was the poet of healthy-mindedness: James liked nothing better than to weave quotations from *Leaves of Grass* into his essays, especially in his later work, during his overt political phase. For Santayana, however, Whitman was the exemplary type of the barbarian, a poet of "shreds and patches," with "no total vision, no grasp of the whole reality," "no capacity for a sane and steady idealization," no grasp (unlike Dante) of "beauty, order and perfection" – a writer who made no attempt "to seize the eternal morphology of reality." In his "red-hot irrationality," he instead heaped up an "indiscriminate wealth of images." A poet of the most primitive type of perception, a poet of perception in and for itself, Whitman could not subordinate image to conception: for him, "surface is absolutely all and the underlying structure is without interest." Santayana's sharpest phrases for Whitman describe him as a poet of "images without structure," a poet of sensuous immediacy, who was therefore – his barbarism is its literary expression – also the poet of "absolute democracy," or liberalism at its antinomian edge.

The unsubordinated image that refuses to take its place in reason's organized hierarchy of conception is a political sign that Santayana, with Old World contempt, and James, with American enthusiasm, knew how to read. The unsubordinated image, contra the tradition of philosophy as Santayana knew it, is the very token of being, not the definition of being; the image so unsubordinated, and insubordinate, is the antithesis of structure: it bursts through unities of all kinds because unities are nothing but attempts, James thought, to impose artificially and imperiously – "abstractly," to use one of his key words – out of the desire to dominate. Unities, whether of drama or versification; systems, whether ecclesiastical or other; and doctrines, whether literary, scholastic, or political, all are expressions of impulses that would control by making uniform the variegated world of autonomous individuals, that would destroy individuality, personal and national, by trimming, fitting, and normalizing autonomous individuality, making the world safe for structure (mine, not yours; ours, not theirs). Santayana was a moribund Latin, rotten to the core, because, unable any longer to believe that there was an eternal morphology of the real, he cultivated *fictions* of eternal morphology. James, for whom the metaphysical argument over structure was intellectually and existentially empty, saw structure in pragmatic light as political instrument and force: "The bigger the unit you deal with, the hollower, the more brutal, the more mendacious is the life displayed. So I am against all big organizations as such, national ones first and foremost. . . . System, as such, does violence whenever it lays its hands upon us. The best Commonwealth is the one that most cherishes the men who represent the residual interests, the one that leaves the largest scope to their peculiarities."

James's pragmatist conflict with Santayana's moribund Latinity constitutes an American counterpart and prefiguring of the Lukács and Bloch debate over modernism. Lukács would, without knowing it, replay Santayana's metaphors of surface and deep structure in his excoriation of expressionistic montage, which presents the surface of life "immediately," and therefore as "opaque, fragmentary, chaotic, and uncomprehended" – unlike those major bourgeois realists (Flaubert, Balzac, Mann) who knew how to mediate immediacy, who knew how to make the surface "transparent" in order "to allow the underlying essence to shine through," and who, because they were not barbaric, knew how to show the organic connection of scraps of perception to a totality which for Lukács is no fiction but, rather, the "real" whole formed by what Marx called the "relations of production of every society." James's American kind of modernism rejects all totalities, whether epistemological, metaphysical, or political, Marxist or capitalist. In the preface to his *Talks to Teachers on Psychology, and to Students on Some of Life's Ideals* (1899), James speaks of his desire to revitalize the idea he believes to be the base of the American political experiment: that there is "no point of view absolutely public and universal." It is an idea he loves both for itself and for its consequences, which he presumes to be the sacredness of individuality and the "tolerance of whatever is not itself intolerant." With some embarrassment, he notes that his phrases will sound dead on the ears of those whom he would reach, like a piece of sentimentality. He explains his attempt to resuscitate the American ideal by alluding to the politically urgent occasion of his writing: "Once they [his phrases] had a passionate inner meaning. Such a passionate inner meaning they may easily acquire again if the pretention of our nation to inflict its own inner ideals and institutions *vi et armis* upon Orientals should meet with a resistance as obdurate as so far it has been gallant and spirited." We must not, he argued, in "On a Certain Blindness in Human Beings" (which he thought the central essay of *Talks to Teachers*), presume to narrate anyone else's story – only our own is not a "secret and a mystery." This directive not to presume to narrate for others concludes with this (in context) unmistakable political injunction: "Hands off."

With its animus for the a priori (of all sorts), James's antiphilosophy wages a cultural war on words like "law," "theory," "unity," "structure," "reason," "abstract," "system," "organization," "ideal," "idealization," "universal," and "doctrine," which in different ways both Santayana and America's genteel cultural critics had employed on behalf of a discourse of order and homogeneity in order to obliterate the residual and stubborn particular, the local, the occasional, the individual – history without law and order – and all vernacular differences. In other words, James was at war with a cultural tradition (in many ways his own) that sought to preserve a central, waspy voice as the expression of social purity and keep American literature safe from the collage of subcultures that America was fast becoming under the pressure of immigration and that was making genteel America paranoid. James's siding with the literary barbarians against Santayana is a politically coded thrust out of high philosophical culture, motivated by what he construed as the American social idea and directed against the idea of American foreign policy in the McKinley and Roosevelt administrations. James thought, in 1900, that the barbarians, he among them, were experiencing their great hour of triumph. Politically, he could not have been more wrong; as a forecast of what would happen in a decade or so, in England and America, in literature and other arts, he could not have been more right. In James, modernism was born in America as an anti-imperialist project.

James's effort at the turn of the century to open philosophy to the barbarities of immediate experience is captured in a little tale that is primal for his work: we are lost in the woods, we need to find our way home, but we have no map. Then we see a path, choose to believe (maybe because of what we take to be irrefutable olfactory evidence) that it is a cow path which, if followed, will lead us to the safety of a farmhouse. Surfacing in this representative anecdote of cognitive emergency, which is at the same time an existential emergency, is the temporal character of (key pragmatist word) "belief." As tools for accomplishing the various works of liberation, beliefs are instruments of desire; they are born locally in crisis and have local consequences only. When they do not lead us out of the cognitive woods, we revise them – still in the woods, still in crisis, we remeasure our context – for other beliefs that might work. The triggering emergency (the occasion for belief), the actual (present) work of belief, and the consequences (or future) of belief are always bound to local contexts. All efforts to escape these restraining temporal and geographic localities of our political, epistemological, or literary lives are expressions of a passion that undergirds the traditional philosophical impulse, and whose termination, according to Santayana, is the noble insight of "theory" – the ability to contemplate "all things in their order and worth." The desire to move to theory, according to James, is the desire to move over the arena of work to a place where all possible situations of work can be surveyed in a single glance, gathered up, mastered. Fired by such global self-conception, traditional philosophy's desire eventuates in the practice of trying to convert experience into what it wants to see in the world: an object adequate to its desire for totality. Theory, though history-born, cannot bear to live with history. The project of theory or traditional philosophy turns out to be the big-brotherly project of imposition wherein all local situations are coerced into conformity, and where the future itself (in the form of consequences) would be known and therefore controlled and manipulated in advance.

Expressed even more resonantly and complexly in key metaphoric moments, James's pragmatist vision is irreducibly a vision of heterogeneity and contentiousness – a vision strong for criticism, self-scrutiny, and self-revision that never claims knowledge of a monolithic human narrative because it refuses belief in a monolithic human narrative and the often repressive political conduct resulting from such belief. James's fully committed pragmatism has no way of settling, once and for all, the question it constantly asks: Does the world rise or fall in value when any particular belief is let loose in the world? when we act upon others or when others act upon us? By insisting that the question be posed that way, in nonacademic form (Does the *world* – not literature, not philosophy – rise or fall in value?), James is insisting that the consequences of belief reveal themselves most fully outside the immediate domain (in his case, the discipline of philosophy) of any particular belief's application. He starts with the recognition that others believe differently and just as strongly. James would thereby put us in a world of different and sometimes competing choices and conducts, and of different and sometimes competing stories, a world in which resolution could be achieved only in a final solution of criticism: by the forcible silencing of the competitor.

So the world according to James is a geography of practices adjacently placed: a heterogeneous space of dispersed histories, related perhaps by counterpoint, or perhaps utterly disrelated – a cacophony of stories – but in any case never related in medley. "The world we live in exists diffused and distributed, in the form of an infinitely numerous lot of eaches." Overarching metanarratives, say Marxist or Christian, which would make all the "eaches" cohere – and so eliminate heterogeneous plurality – never tempt James. He is no utopian. He believes that history conceived as teleological union is merely a late and nostalgic expression of classical aesthetics – the proleptic imaging forth, in the rigorous causal perfections of Aristotelian plot, of desired historical order, the harmony of time itself. Better, he believes, to think against Aristotle's preference for drama, better to prefer romance to drama, better to think that the "world is full of partial stories that run parallel to one another, beginning and ending at odd times. They mutually interlace and interfere at points, but we cannot unify them completely."

History for James, as for his master, Emerson, is no monument that demands our mimetic awe. The terror of rationalism (his synonym for mainline philosophy) is that it would force a mimetic role upon us: "On the rationalist side," James writes, "we have a universe in many editions, one real one, the infinite folio, or *edition de luxe,* eternally complete; and then the various finite editions, full of false readings, distorted and mutilated each in its own way." The effort of the rational textualist must be to make all finite editions somehow "correspond" to the *edition de luxe*. But the pragmatist gives us history in a complex metaphor both as text and as the liberation of textual work – a text, James writes, "in only one edition of the universe, unfinished, growing in all sorts of places, especially in places where thinking beings are at work." For the pragmatic textualist, who is the bibliographer's version of the devil, there is only one text: the forever unfinished, decentralized text of history – forever supplemented, new chapters being written in all sorts of places by all sorts of people not especially in touch with one another. There is no work of "correspondence," only of "production." James's textual metaphor is an effort to speak against the political authority which masks itself in rationalist certitude and self-righteousness, which demands mimetic fealty, and which he specifically and frequently evokes after his involvement in the New England AntiImperialist League in royalist, militarist, aristocratic, and papal terms. James's textual metaphor speaks *for* the liberation of the small, the regional, the locally embedded, the underdog: the vernacular voice that refuses the elocutionary lessons of genteel cosmopolitan finishing schools. His unfinished (and unfinishable) text of history, authorized by no single author, is the text of American history as it ought to be – the multiauthored book of democracy in its ideal and wild antinomian form.

The lectures James delivered in Boston and New York in late 1906 and early 1907, and then shortly after published as the book *Pragmatism,* bear the mark of a decisive moment in United States history: our first fully launched imperialist adventure, in the last years of the nineteenth century, in Cuba and the Philippines. Although pragmatism was inchoately present in his *Principles of Psychology,* he began to know his philosophy as pragmatism only after he found the political terminus of his thought in his anti-imperialist activism at the turn of the century. In the New England AntiImperialist League, James experienced a direct and codeterminative connection between his philosophical principles and his political life. It was at that point, after his political turn – and not before, when it was abstractly possible for him to do so — that he began freely adapting from C. S. Peirce; at that point, and not before, that he began to understand empire as theory (as the expression of a kind of traditional philosophical impulse), and theory or traditional philosophy as empire (as the expression of a kind of imperialist impulse). For James, the impulse to theory and the impulse to empire constitute two plots against history — two plots best measured and joined by the effects they produce in trying to cure the world of its diversity.

Against the immediate background of Twain's and Howells's inspiring example, James became the first in a hidden history of oddly connected American refusers of imperialism. The second was Wallace Stevens, in his 1919 "Anecdote of the Jar" as read by a third, Michael Herr, in his 1970 book on Vietnam, *Dispatches,* in which the entire focus of American military power concentrated in the fortification at Khe Sanh was evoked by his citation of Stevens's poem. Stevens is made by Herr to speak directly against the ideology of imposition and obliteration coactive in Vietnam with a strategy of defoliation. The textual expression of that strategy is the literal remapping of a country — "the military expediency," in Herr's ironic reflection on the sometimes deadly relations of sign and referent, "to impose a new set of references over Vietnam's truer, older being, an imposition that began most simply with the division of one country into two and continued . . . with the further division of South Vietnam into four clearly defined tactical corps." Herr concludes by glossing Khe Sanh via the imaginative imperialism that was activated and subtly evaluated in "Anecdote of the Jar." "Once it was all locked in place, Khe Sanh became like the planted jar in Wallace Stevens's poem. It took dominion everywhere."

James had written his own anecdote of the jar in the opening lecture of *Pragmatism:* "The world of concrete personal experiences to which the street belongs is multitudinous beyond imagination, tangled, muddy, painful and perplexed. The world to which your philosophy professor introduces you is simple, clean and noble. The contradictions of real life are absent from it, its architecture is classic. Principles of reason trace its outlines, logical necessities cement its parts. Purity and dignity are what it most expresses. It is a kind of marble temple shining on a hill." The marble temple shining on a hill is James's metaphor for traditional philosophy and its project of representation: mind as elevated, removed observer; thought as reflection of real ontological structure; thought emptied of the messes of social time; thought historically uncontingent. But philosophy so conceived, James says, is not, despite its claim, an "account of this actual world." It is an "addition built upon it": a "sanctuary," a "refuge," a "substitute," a "way of escape," a "monument of artificiality" – "cloistral and spectral." All negative qualities, of course, and quite harmless, until we add one other characteristic which gives ominous point to all the others – James's shining marble temple of philosophy, like Stevens's jar of imagination, like Khe Sanh, is also a "remedy." In this dismantling of the classic project of reason, what James wishes to show is that the product of rationalist method is not cool, contemplative representation – "theory" above the battle: it is *purity in action.* The shining marble temple is "round upon the ground"; it does not give "of bird or bush." Like the defoliating jar in Stevens's Tennessee, or the imposed cartographical references by which military need in Vietnam attempted to recreate the referent, classical reason (the desire for theory) becomes, under James's corrosive scrutiny, a "powerful . . . appetite of the mind," the need for a "refined object." Reason as theory-desire, the desire for refinement, gets expressed as the *will to refine:* a chilling process when considered in the political contexts within which James writes. In an eerie foreshadowing of both Stevens's poem and Herr's reading of Khe Sanh as the "planted jar," James evokes his sense of the perversity of the American presence in the Philippines by describing it as an effort to "plant our order."

I have emphasized, a little misleadingly, James's political period, the late phase of his career when he could with some justice refer to himself as an anarchist. But this late phase represents a substantial change of heart which, if ignored, would obscure by suppressing not the nonpolitics but the more familiar American politics of his earlier career. In the late 1880s James responded to the protests of exploited labor in this country by telling his brother not to be "alarmed by the labor troubles here." Brother William went on to explain, with benevolence toward the working class, that the turmoil of strikes was "simply a healthy phase of evolution, a little costly, but normal, and sure to do a lot of good to all hands in the end." But the Haymarket Riot of May 1886 was another thing. In his response to that violent moment in our labor history, James gave voice to American xenophobia. "I don't speak," he continues in the same letter to Henry, "of the senseless 'anarchist' riot in Chicago, which has nothing to do with 'Knights of Labor,' but is the work of a lot of pathological Germans and poles {sic}."

The long cultural journey from "a lot of pathological Germans and poles," to James's criticism of philosophy's shining marble temple on a hill, to Stevens's criticism of the jar on the hill in Tennessee, to Herr's meditation on Vietnam, Khe Sanh upon a hill, began with John Winthrop's vision of Puritan community as a "city upon a hill" and his unwittingly ugly interpretation of that city when, years after he had coined the phrase, he banished Anne Hutchinson for antinomian heresy. Hutchinson: "I desire to know wherefore I am banished." Winthrop: "Say no more, the court knows wherefore and is satisfied." The city upon a hill, a metaphor of community self-consciously visible and vulnerable, is revised in Winthrop's retort to Hutchinson into a metaphor of the imperial city rigorously and violently exclusionary – a structure of male authority, purity (Puritanism) in action, poised as a "remedy" against a radically individualist principle of resistance whose most famous American representative is female. Winthrop's authoritarian suppression of insurrectionary conscience is the political antithesis of Jamesian pragmatism at its radical edge.

If Anne Hutchinson is the hidden moral and political mother figure behind James's pragmatism, then the not-so-hidden moral and political father figure behind his pragmatist celebration of sovereignty (personal and political) is Emerson (for intellectual and biographical reasons, it could not have been anyone else): the Emerson who wrote that "whenever I find my dominion over myself not sufficient for me, and I undertake the direction of my neighbor also, I overstep the truth, and come into false relations with him. . . . This is the history of government – one man does something which is to bind another." The Emerson that James took to the heart of his pragmatism was the Emerson who proclaimed strict adherence to "private conscience," the "aboriginal reality" of the "present man," the derivative nature of institutions, and the irrelevance of the past man, who is "obliterate for present issues." Faith in and to oneself is the only authentic act, and it is an act that spreads itself, eventually, "from persons to things to time and places." That is the substance of Emerson's radical political vision of the contagion of antinomian individualism, and also its severe limit, which implicitly came under criticism from James when he became an anti-imperialist activist who was apparently unable to believe that, in the natural course of all things antinomian, the stories of the politically powerless would somehow win out over the narrative intolerance of the politically powerful few.

The Emerson/James connection may constitute the most influential enhancement of intellectual force in American literary history, for their own time and for the time of modernism and beyond. The connection, moreover, seems to have derived its power from its mediation in the great interbiography of American literary culture. I refer not only to the interrelations of Henry Jr., William, Alice, and their redoubtable father, easily the first family of American intellectual history, but also to the larger cultural family composed of Emerson and the Jameses, with particular emphasis on Emerson's relations to the novelist, the philosopher, and to Henry Sr. – relations which at different times, both in his lifetime and after, cast

Emerson in roles ranging from older brother, teacher, culture hero, and father, to godfather, priest, and deity.

On 3 March 1842, Henry Sr. heard Emerson lecture in New York and later that evening wrote him a letter which combined the sympathy and honor that can only be bestowed by a cold-sober admirer with the spunky impudence and independence of a younger brother (eight years Emerson's junior) determined to contest his older sibling in a similar vocation and with identical ambition. The same letter warmly invited Emerson to visit; Emerson accepted shortly thereafter. According to James family legend – it became a favorite anecdote – Henry Sr., immediately after Emerson's arrival, with the enthusiasm appropriate to a proud father, ushered his guest upstairs into the nursery to see his infant son, William, then about three months old. Henry Jr. tells us that "it remained a tradition" with William that "our father's friend" gave "his blessing to the lately-born babe." It remains a psychoanalytically resonant fact that only six weeks before his first visit to the New York home of the Jameses and the bestowal of his mythic blessing, Emerson had been decisively devastated by the death of his first son, Waldo. And it remains forcefully significant for American literary and philosophical history that, although Henry Sr. was a central man for his more famous sons, Emerson became for them an alternative, perhaps even a competing father – in Henry Jr.'s memory, a "center of many images."

The most extraordinary of the many provocative expressions of this culturally provocative family romance, from among the participants themselves, came from the novelist, and again from his recollections:

I 'visualize' . . . the winter firelight of our back-parlor at dusk and the great Emerson – I knew he was great, greater than any of our friends – sitting in it between my parents, before the lamps had been lighted . . . affecting me the more as an apparition sinuously and . . . elegantly slim, benevolently aqui-

line, and commanding a tone alien, beautifully alien, to any
we had heard round-about, that he bent this benignity upon
me by an invitation to draw near to him, off the hearth-rug,
and know myself as never yet . . . in touch with the wonder of
Boston . . . just then and there for me in the sweetness of the
voice and the finish of the speech – this latter through a sort of
attenuated emphasis which at the same time made sounds
more important, more interesting in themselves, than by any
revelation yet vouch-safed us. Was not this my first glimmer of
a sense that the human tone *could,* in that independent and
original way, be interesting? It had given me there in the
firelight an absolutely abiding measure . . . the truth of
which I find somehow reflected in the fact of my afterwards
knowing one of our household rooms for the first time . . . as
"Mr. Emerson's room."

This appearance in the fading light of dusk of a benign father, this
parent who sits "between" the actual parents, bears the gift that is
wholly and originally *himself.* It is he who commands the alien yet
beautiful tone, inviting intimacy and the knowledge of the wonder
of his difference, of the "absolutely abiding measure" that set the
standard for what is not subject to standards: the unrepeatable individual self. For the novelist, long after the fact to which his memory,
no doubt creatively, referred, the great Emerson returns in splendid
individual perfection as the apparition who sanctions his art of the
novel.

For James Sr., on the other hand, what Emerson represented
philosophically was simply the curse of selfhood. The "sphere of
redemption" for James *père,* according to son William, was society
with a capital letter, while for Emerson redemption lay precisely in
"resolute individualism" (William's phrase), which could be felt
even in the aesthetic texture of his writing. In a headnote to an essay
written by Henry Sr. on Emerson, but not published (in the *Atlantic*) until long after the death of both (when neither could respond),

William set forth this fundamental dispute between his father and Emerson and then adjudicated it in favor of Emerson; in favor, to be exact, of William's own reading of Emerson. In the sentence which I am about to quote, it is important to see William the adjudicator dramatizing himself as critical audience in the back-parlor theater at 58 West Fourteenth Street: "Emerson would listen, I fancy, as if charmed, to James's talk of the 'divine natural Humanity,' but he would never *subscribe:* and this, from one whose native gifts were so suggestive of that same Humanity, was disappointing." Against his father, William in effect took the side of Henry Jr., who in this family fight over the meaning of Emerson wrote that the heart of Emerson's genius was "for seeing character as a real and supreme thing."

Emerson's intellectual heritage passes through the James brothers and then on to the distinctively American modernists: the low, because nationalist, modernists – the poetries of native ground (Frost, Williams, Crane), and the poetries that yearn ceaselessly for native ground (Stevens and Crane, here, too). It is a heritage that celebrates the vernacular, thought and feeling rooted in and expressed through local contact, and radical individualism (this last most full-throatedly) even as it resists (American style) the denaturing consequences of sophistication. But the Emerson/James connection is also the unlikely engine of high modernism in the person of Ezra Pound, who had nothing good to say about Emerson and who along with Eliot represents modernism's internationalist ideal: a cosmopolitan poetry of tradition, comparative literatures and cultures, strongly propelled by distaste for native ground. Nevertheless, Emerson returns only thinly disguised as the father of Pound's deepest values in Pound's passionate essay on Henry James (1918) and in his (Pound's) poetics of imagism.

Pound describes James as the "hater of tyranny," the author of "book after book against oppression, against . . . sordid petty personal crushing oppression," *the* novelist of "personal liberty" and "the rights of the individual against all sorts of intangible bondage."

What James combats (but certainly no more fiercely than had Emerson himself) is "'influence'" – "the impingement of family pressure, the impinging of one personality on another; all of them in the highest degree damn'd, loathsome, and detestable." And, then, in Pound's most resonant phrasing – which brings to light the embedded Emersonian ideology of the theory of the image – he praises James's "[r]espect for the peripheries of the individual." It is as if in his reading of Henry James he had at last discovered for himself the latent William Jamesian pragmatist politics and ethics of his two key imagist directives – "Direct treatment of the thing" and "Go in fear of abstractions" – because the most important "thing" is human, a unique individual, no thing at all; because abstraction, whether in lyric diction or political organization, is the major symptom of a society's terminal illness, its desire to do psychic murder to the individuality of its constituents – crossing the periphery, violating the boundary of the self – for the presumed good of some presumed whole.

What ran deep in James was a sense of American history and society as severely ruptured from its European origins and from European institutions synonymous with oppression: the Roman Catholic church, the army, the aristocracy, the Crown. James named these institutions as the enemy of his philosophic method, which he sometimes associated with a Whitmanesque, unbuttoned, even anarchic notion of self-determination. It was the American intellectual's duty, he wrote in numerous letters to the *Boston Transcript,* in protest against our imperialist policies, to expose the empty but murderously effective "abstractions" of the party of Roosevelt – like our "responsibility" for Cuba and the Philippines, like the "unfitness" of the Filipinos to govern themselves.

James imagined the American writer as defender of a self that is, or should be, inaccessibly private property; a self that is, or should be, the motor principle of American anti-imperialism. Each of us, he writes in the essay "On a Certain Blindness in Human Beings," is bound "to feel intensely the importance of his own duties and the significance of the situations that call these forth. But this feeling is in each of us a vital secret, for sympathy with which we vainly look to others. The others are too much absorbed in their own vital secrets to take an interest in ours. Hence the stupidity and injustice of our opinions, so far as they deal with the significance of alien lives." The elaborate but symptomatic difficulty in making sense of James is coming to see that his overt commitment to the inalienable private property of selfhood (the "innermost center within the circle," "the sanctuary within the citadel," the freedom felt within in the *"self of all other selves"*) is an inscription of a contradiction at the very heart of capitalism (and theorists of capital like Adam Smith), because property under capitalism, including the property which is our capacity for labor, the basis of private property itself, can *be* property only if it *is* alienable — only if it can be bought, sold, stolen, and, when necessary, appropriated. James's political turn taught him that nothing was inalienable in the coercive world of imperialism, not even the secret self that we think we possess beyond alienation. So he employed the language of private property in order to describe the spiritual nature of persons and in an effort to turn the discourse of private property against itself by making that discourse literal in just this one instance: so as to preserve a human space of freedom, however interiorized, from the vicissitudes and coercions of the marketplace, a theme repeated by all manner of American poets and novelists.

James's anti-imperialism is American anti-imperialism; his philosophical term "pluralism" is an antithetical word signifying not so much what *is*, but rather resistance to the imperialist context of his work in its modernist moment. In other words, pluralism signifies what "is *not*" and what should be in the face of a near universal impulse whose project is the elimination of difference. His major effort is to combat the dominant discourse of a capitalism rooted in a democratic political context by appropriating the cornerstone economic principle of capitalism (private property) to the advantage of his counterdiscourse: a vision of human sanctity central to his pragmatism, to the originating myth of American political history, and to modernist writers on both sides of the Atlantic who assert the complementary values of radical individuality and radical personal freedom, and who often have nothing in common except a commitment to stylistic and formal experiment as the vehicle of selfhood, whose "program" is the belief that programs are the death of authentic literature and the self. What James says in all but words is that if imperialism and capitalism on their own are capable of destroying the self, then in their unified American form they represent a global principle of structure, a world-historical menace of unparalleled proportions. In the name of pragmatism and the American dream, James wanted to turn America against the self-pollution of its foreign policy at the end of the nineteenth century. In such an act of self-criticism, he thought, we would subvert the economic and political directives which treat all human subjects as if they were objects and, therefore, for all practical purposes, convert us into objects who suffer degradations that nonhuman commodities cannot suffer.

James had no vision of a future social arrangement that would insure the safety of the self, no vision of the good collective. His pragmatism was emancipatory — it would lead us out of suffocating and tyrannous theorizations; it had nothing to say about where we should be, only about where we do not want to be. And not least among the various imperial cities that James urged us to free ourselves from is that to which we find ourselves bound *by* ourselves in the need of self-consistency and continuity. The revolutionary spirit he bequeathed to the young modernists at Harvard was the hope for an aesthetic of pragmatism, and the life that ceaselessly begins anew, radically refreshed, when the mind lays by its imperious needs to replicate itself in all that it sees. In its William Jamesian phase, the literary experiment called "modernism" is hard to distinguish from the social experiment called "America" – twin desires (desperate, impossible) to wipe out tradition and history, to experience life as if for the first time, without mediation. Emerson: "Our age is retrospective. It builds the sepulchres of the fathers. It writes biographies, histories, and criticism. . . . Why should not we also enjoy an original relation to the universe?"

In 1900, James was in a mood to measure himself against his two most powerful colleagues. The moribund Latin Santayana seemed too far outside the American formation of his desire. In the end, James could dismiss him rather than engage him. But Josiah Royce (1855–1916) was another, more intimate case – he was James's unavoidable American agonist and lover, and judging by the insistent allusions to James that pepper the second half of *The Problem of Christianity*, Royce thought so too. "You are still the center of my gaze," James wrote Royce:

> the pole of my mental magnet. When I write, 'tis with one eye on the page, and one on you. When I compose my Gifford lectures mentally, 'tis with the design exclusively of overthrowing your system and ruining your peace. I lead a parasitic life upon you, for my highest flight of ambitious ideality is to become your conquerer, and go down into history as such, you and I rolled in one another's arms and silent (or rather loquacious still) in one last death-grapple of an embrace. How then, O my dear Royce, can I forget you, or be contented out of your close neighborhood? Different as our minds are, yours has nourished mine, as no other social influence has, and in converse with you I have always felt that my life was being lived importantly.

James, who had spent a good deal of his energy in partisan and anxious adjudication of his father's socialist debate with Emerson, found himself late in life replaying that contest in debate with Royce. James, who had rebirthed himself out of his genealogy in order to become the intellectual son of Emerson, found himself late in life playing Emerson to the ghost of his father, now newly resurrected as the intellectual spirit of Josiah Royce – that rarest thing in American culture, a philosopher of community.

The spiritual family of Anne Hutchinson, Emerson, and William James, America's first family of self-reliance, periodically experienced nightmares triggered by the memory of "society" and "community." For this family of antinomians, such terms recalled an old European class story of the repression and exile of selfhood. Antinomian stories of inviolate selfhood are stories of the sheerest sentimentality, unless they are seen as parasitic narratives – unless they are seen historically as stories not only set against, but also feeding off the background of bad, European totality; seen against, but also feeding off what must have seemed to Hutchinson, Emerson, and James the betrayals of America figured by social theorists as diverse as John Winthrop, Henry James Sr., and Josiah Royce: authoritarian voices of the law seductively represented in ideals of community.

Royce's later work established a context of social issues in compelling terms for his most famous student, T. S. Eliot, who as poet, dramatist, literary critic, and social theorist brought his own (arguably authoritarian) inclinations and his philosophy teacher's (arguably democratic) preoccupations to the center of literary modernism. The key text, *The Problem of Christianity,* was published almost simultaneously with Eliot's participation in Royce's graduate seminar on comparative methodology and only five years before Eliot's landmark theorization of modernity in "Tradition and the Individual Talent." In the second half of *The Problem of Christianity,* Royce explored in broader terms than Eliot would the difficult proposition that we all, not just the professional writers among us, need (in Eliot's words) to "surrender" our private selves to "something which is more valuable," and that, paradoxically, such surrender will result not in slavish conformity and all loss of selfhood but in the discovery of an enriched and more satisfying self within a "living whole." By "living whole" Eliot meant, in 1919, when "Tradition and the Individual Talent" appeared in the *Egoist,* the Western literary tradition since Homer. After his conversion in 1927, he would embed that literary "living whole" in an idea of Christian community. Emerson asks, "Why should not we also enjoy an original relation to the universe?" and Royce and Eliot reply that Emerson has no right to say "we" because the ground of "we" is history and community, or precisely everything from which Emerson's isolated visionary seeks to sever himself in quest of "original relation."

Royce's starting point — he calls it "social common sense" — is strongly reminiscent both of James's vision of isolate "personal consciousness" and F. H. Bradley's vision of the prison-house of self that dominates Eliot's poetry through *The Waste Land:*

> . . . I have heard the key
> Turn in the door once and turn once only
> We think of the key, each in his prison
> Thinking of the key, each confirms a prison.

In less elegant language, and under Bradley's direct influence, Eliot had uttered similar thoughts in Royce's seminar in December 1913, stressing the impenetrability of one interpretation by another and allowing entry only in the case of common belief — in the case of what would, in effect, be total overlap of points of view. Royce agreed, to a point: "Each of us lives within the charmed circle of his own conscious willing and meaning . . . hopelessly beyond the direct observation of his fellows." What Royce would eventually argue is that though we are locked away, hopelessly, from direct (empirical) *observation* of another self, the process of *interpretation* is not so imprisoned, because it is not constrained by the canons of empiricism.

Royce defined his ideal community as a collective historical consciousness whose any given temporal present is an intersection of memory and expectation; the psychological unity of "many selves in one community is bound up . . . with the consciousness of some lengthy social process which has occurred, or is at least supposed to have occurred." Whether historically real or mythical, a community needs a distinct and concrete past, but just as significantly it needs a future. Such collective historical consciousness is founded upon the historical character of the individual, precisely the sort of being which, he writes, in terms that betray his desire, "needs and is a history." To be a self is to be aware that what I am at "present" is the expression of a process that flows from a double source: from the memory of an extended past and from an expectation, the hope that the process whose past I extend myself into will eventuate in a future, that the historical process of selfhood, in other words, is intentional, that it possesses "sense and coherence." A self, therefore, is an "interpretation," in effect an invention of storytelling; a way of extending one's "present" sense of one's life backward and forward into temporal areas which are not "directly observable." When many sundered selves (according to social common sense) achieve, by interpreting (narrating) an identical past and future, a community is born. Royce argued that, contrary to what his student, the soon-to-be-modernist guru, thought, interpretation might be a community-making event.

The rich variety of individual "selves who are the members of the spiritual body" of a community is neither negated nor slighted in Royce's understanding of community; he believed that true community liberates and sustains human variety. In the words of John Dewey: "Liberty is that secure release and fulfillment of personal potentialities which takes place only in rich and manifold association with others. . . . Equality denotes the unhampered share which each individual member of the community has in the consequences of associated action. . . ." Dewey's idea of equality stresses the economic base of liberated selfhood and therefore the economic obligation of a community to be a just, democratic society actively engaged in the work of supplying its members' requirements for sustenance. Dewey's emphasis as a social theorist, unlike Royce's, is on the present and on all those inhibitions of long institutional lineage that pressure the present and defer equality. Like James and Emerson before him, Dewey does not encourage the American Adam and Eve to look back, for if they do so they put their capacity for freedom and equality at the peril of the crushing habits of history and its oppressive models of human association. Emerson's moving directive, in "Self-Reliance" (1844), to stop looking backward and forward, to be wholly for and in the present, with no time in us, is the radical American hope to begin again that American pragmatists took to heart in their idea of the good life.

But it is precisely the present that is elided in Royce's idea of community as a historical process. If Dewey's tendency is to envision the ideal of community realized — at work in real time — by imagining the work of such community in its actual material functions as being democratic in goal (an association dedicated to providing a sustaining context for both the material and the cultural needs of its members), then Royce's drift is toward idealization and the repression of the present. It is never clear in Royce whether what he calls, in a magnificent oxymoron, the "spiritual body" of community has, or can have *material* body, whether the values of communal association actually shape our political and economic lives, whether community is necessarily cut off from an active social function in the present. The implication of Royce's oxymoron is that community can have nothing but *spiritual* body, that the values he associates with community can keep their integrity only in the inner life's realms of nostalgia and hope, memory and imagination: "It is, in fact, the ideally extended self, and not, in general, the momentary self, whose life is worth living, whose sense outlasts our fleeting days. . . . The present self, the fleeting individual self of today, is a mere gesticulation of self." The present and material status of a community, it turns out, is the major threat to its existence as a community. Royce's insistence that it is the extended self, in individual and collective form, whose life is most worth living, implies

37

his evaluation that ongoing life in our society — Royce has specifically in mind the life of a complex industrial society — is not much worth living. A community can keep itself whole and can sustain itself through time only if it can "keep the consciousness of its unity through the vicissitudes of an endlessly shifting and often dreary fortune." In the "present" of a community, memory and hope function with great difficulty, and the life of the community is revealed in crisis for the fragile thing that it is: "The individual members cannot always recall the sense in which they identify their own lives and selves with what has been, or with what is yet to come."

The antidote to this imminent collapse of a common consciousness, within the diseased context of our shifting and dreary present, is nothing less than collective work: "[T]he true common life of the community," Royce argues in that phase of *The Problem of Christianity* in which community is imagined as active society, "consists of deeds which are essentially of the nature of the processes of cooperation." And the example of cooperative labor that comes first and most repeatedly to him is the example of workmen in a factory, "side by side." In such cooperative activity, we presumably produce not only the material life of the community but also its consciousness *as* a community. But just as soon as Royce opens this key topic of social criticism since Edmund Burke, he finds himself — literally within a few sentences — at the symbolic crossroads where romantic critics of capitalism (and the American modernists are no exception) have always found themselves. He is faced with the choice of taking either the path of conservative English social critics — the path of nostalgia that longs for the recapturing of small artisan cultures — or the path of socialism that would fully humanize modernization, urban life, and the big organizations of human beings so despised by Emerson and James. In example after example, the major modernist poets in English tend to take the first path — the path of conservation and sometimes of reaction. Royce refuses both nostalgia and Marxism. The idea of community at his most interesting moments is neither desire for a golden age of community that never was nor desire for a socialist end to domination and inequality that may never be. Royce's idea of community is critically useful: it gives us a way to face without being engulfed by the present – a way to judge the distance between an attractive ideal of human association and the actual modes of association that encumber, clog, and demean our relations.

In a central statement, as tactful as it is moving, Royce says it this way:

> . . . our ideal extensions of the self, when we love the community, and long to realize its life with intimacy, must needs take the form of acting *as if we could survey,* in some single unity of insight, that wealth and variety and connection which, as a fact, we cannot make present to our momentary view. Since true love is an emotion, and since emotions are present affections of the self, love, in longing for its own increase, and for its own fulfillment, inevitably longs to find what it loves as a fact of experience, and to be in the immediate presence of its beloved. Therefore, the love of a community (a love which, as we now see, is devoted to desiring the realization of an overwhelmingly vast variety and unity of cooperation), is, as an emotion, discontent with all the present sunderings of the selves, and with all the present problems and mysteries of the social order. Such love, then, restless with the narrowness of our momentary view of our common life, desires this common life to be an immediate presence for all of us.

In his deft play on the "presence" of community which is not present and the "present" that is, Royce begins to unfold the idea of community not only as historical consciousness, anchored in a faraway past and future, but also as a kind of imaginative consciousness that can be engaged with the actual deficient state of the social order. Community as *that* kind of collective critical consciousness knows not only its origin and its destiny; it also knows its present discontent, and presumably it knows why. A collective critical consciousness that can know so much might know more. It might know that the wholeness of its "spiritual body" is not enough; it might know that memory and expectation must motivate work, not revery; it might know what Emerson knew in his most activist mood: "Your goodness [or "love"] must have an edge to it – else it is none."

The modern social order, though it features a "highly organized social life," is nonetheless far from identical with "the life of a true community." The modern social order is in the throes of its own special kind of original sin: in the "dreary complexity of mechanical labor" it breeds "cooperation at the expense of a loss of interest in the community." In the looser sense of the word, which is not Royce's sense, the modern social order is a community because masses behave as if they were a unit. And in fact they are a unit, just as (crucial metaphor for Royce and the romantic anticapitalists) a machine is a unit. Individuals in the unit cooperate "as the cogs cooperate in the wheels of a mechanism," and this social mechanism is oiled and greased by imitation, rivalry, greed, business, pleasure, war, and industry. And worse: the physical and technological process of modern cooperative labor is so intellectually complex as to make it hopeless for any given individual at work in this process to understand in what sense the process is cooperative – we work together, but few or perhaps even none of us know how we cooperate, or what we should do. Not to mention that few or none can feel a firm and comfortable linkage between individual activity and the ends of the entire cooperative enterprise, or a firm and comfortable relationship between collective desire for community and the actual products (and by-products) of our labor. But in the collective labor of a true community, Royce argues, "individuals who participate in these common activities understand enough to be able, first, to direct their own deeds of cooperation; secondly, to observe the deeds of their individual fellow workers; and thirdly, to know that without just this combination, this order, this interaction of the co-working selves, just this deed could not be accomplished by the community.

So, for instance, a chorus or an orchestra carries on its cooperative activities." Royce does not shrink from his analogy: a community so formed is essentially a community of those who are "artists in some form of cooperation, and whose art constitutes, for each artist, his own ideally extended life."

Royce's true community is like the orchestra of utopia, within which each player freely contributes his individual yet cooperative effort and at the same time is in the position of the conductor who hears the amassing harmony and precise tonality of the whole, of which he approves. The achievement of true community (so imagined) within the "hopelessly complex" modern social order seems farfetched, even to Royce. The modern social order produces individuals, he believed, who feel themselves to be involved not in self-directing human activity but in the "mere process of nature." When on those rare occasions the individual worker can break out of the consciousness that prevents questioning of the social order of things — when he becomes conscious of the effects of his alienated efforts — then he understandably wishes to deny any relationship between himself and the destructive ends of the activity in which he "cooperates." Like James, Royce could feel the pressure of a negative (life-denying) whole. His numerous depressed allusions to the contemporary economic order are significant because they are so casual: negative social totality is Royce's given. But his inability to imagine a contemporary community that does not attempt to turn back the technological clock to villages of artisans reveals Roycean, and many other modernist, images of community as the creation of desperate vision.

Interpretation, a community-making act, the essential activity of human association, is repeatedly repressed in the history of philosophy, which Royce characterizes as the history of a debate over the respective virtues of perception and conception. The antithetical traditions of Plato and Bergson represent, he argues, two sides of the same coin. Philosophers as different as Kant, James, and Russell can understand each other only because they agree on what is at stake in the choice of one faculty over another; what they always know, though do not always say, is that one faculty and its object of knowledge is the nightmare of the other. The object of perception is a datum – etymologically, a gift: a sensuous thing-for-itself, the intuition of a unique temporal event. The object of conception, on the other hand, is a universal, or type, or quality – a static, eternal thing, beyond temporal contingency: ontology's gift – an eternal form of the real; after Kant, the mind's gift of deepest structure – an eternal and necessary form of cognition. Neither perception or conception requires a mediating social context, neither is trained upon a social being: they are acts of consciousness functioning in social isolation. Royce's point is that the activity of interpretation takes no object for its object – nothing is "given to" interpretation. The interpretive act is focused on a self – on my neighbor's mind, in Royce's example, on the process that goes on in my neighbor's mind, his intentions, which we "know" only by the "signs" which express it.

Conception, Royce says, is "sterile," and perception "intolerably lonesome." But perception rather than conception is his consistent target because the philosophical tides of modernism appeared to him to be running in its favor. "Let the philosophers . . . endeavor to avoid 'sterile' conception. Let them equally avoid those wanton revels in mere perception which are at present the bane of our art, of our literature, of our social ideals, and of our religion." Royce felt the modernist pulse of his time – he heard the new and insistent cultural voices on behalf of the aesthetic fragment and the private pleasures of the percept, set against the tradition of reason. He saw that the ancient quarrel between philosophy and poetry had in effect been resolved, that philosophy and poetry had joined forces, that socially isolating *perception* was the ground of agreement, and that imagism and Bergsonism were its key contemporary cultural signs, and he wondered out loud what would become of us if, in cultivating the modern, we ceased to care about what connects us. But Royce's disparagement of the percept ("a wanton revel") is not the simple negation of the body that we conventionally associate with puritanical and idealist sensibilities; he has no use for the disembodied pleasures of conception. Conception and perception are equally lonely operations for Royce because they take *nature* as both object and terminus: nature abstracted for its essences by the categories of reason, or nature cherished and preserved in its sensuous, unreasoning particularities. What Royce wants is that kind of cognitive activity whose locus of work is society and whose object is neither the type, nor the random sensuous particular, but a mind, especially my neighbor's mind: an "object" which is a "subject" encountered only through its signifying manifestations. In C. S. Peirce's definition, which Royce accepted, a sign is the sort of linguistic phenomenon that requires giving rather than receiving, because a sign is an "object to which somebody *gives* or should *give* an interpretation." Royce's thesis is that interpretation is "the great humanizing factor in our cognitive processes" because interpretation demands response; it therefore "makes the purest forms of love for community possible."

To call interpretation "cognitive activity," however, is at once to say too much and too little about it; it is to miscast it as a separate but equal partner of conception and perception. Royce thinks of interpretation not as one among equals but as our most valuable act as human beings, not because it produces a profounder knowledge – it is not especially clear in Royce what interpretation knows, if anything. If interpretation knows at all, it cannot know with the precision and certitude usually claimed for perception and conception; if it knows, then it is hard to formulate what it knows because what it desires to know (the self) is by definition unformulable. Interpretation is our most valuable activity, so Royce argues, because it makes community by producing intimacy and cohesion. We engage in interpretation, not so much because we seek a cognitive object beyond the act of interpretation, but because we love the relations that are created by the activity. In a sense, we love interpretation, we seek the act itself, because it is the psychic substance of solidarity that would turn a social collection into a community.

Royce on interpretation is at his most tantalizing and most disturbing when he works through three metaphors: interpretation as *exchange, translation,* and *giving counsel.* For the metaphor of exchange, Royce's example is a traveler who crosses a border into a foreign country, with the gold and bank notes of his own country in hand but with no letter of credit. At the border a new process quickly becomes indispensable: one of exchanging the coin of one realm for that of another on the basis of a third process (interpretation) which is the application of a standard of value through which to bring together on a mutual basis of comparison the coins of two realms. Royce is interested in exchange as a solution to the spiritual problem of the Jamesian prison-house nature of personal consciousness. He wants to know what will permit us "to pass any of the great boundaries of the spiritual world," and he is convinced that neither conception nor perception will serve. On the social borders of consciousness, conception and perception are nature's unmediable bank notes and gold. But interpretation is the process through which, at the border, isolating foreignness is overcome without, presumably, destroying the human differences that make mediation so necessary and so socially satisfying.

Interpretation in the metaphor of exchange appears as an innocent process of communication whose basis is shared value; interpretation in the metaphor of translation is an unintended deflowering of the metaphor of exchange. What the process of translation brings forth strongly is the triadic structure of any interpretive act. In Royce's specific and uncanny example: the Egyptian text, the Egyptologist who translates, and the possible English reader form a triad necessary in order that an English interpretation of an Egyptian writing should exist. Moreover, the triadic relation is always nonsymmetrical – the terms are "unevenly arranged" into a "determinate order": interpreter, object, and person to whom the interpretation is addressed. But if the terms are unevenly arranged, it would follow that the interpreter, who knows both languages, does not have knowledge of equivalencies. Interpretation as translation is a form of human betrayal – and what is betrayed is one culture for another. West reads East for West. Interpretation, as James had predicted, begins its horrible slide toward imperial conception and imposition. The determinate or uneven character of any translating act, or any act of exchange, means that interpretation is irreducibly rooted in history and in culture, and that the act of reading – now the metaphor of exchange might be read as the *current* rate of exchange – manipulates relations of domination.

Interpretation gives political power an expressive language and a cultural habitation. In all acts of translation and exchange there are winners and losers. So metaphors which are offered to clarify the community-making character of interpretation move toward subversion of Royce's intention and at the same time tell the counterstory of imperialism. The interpreter, to whom Royce gives a privileged place in his community because he exemplifies the love of community, exemplifies as well (as exchanger and translator) the cooperation of the intellect with the conflicts of material interests. The underside of Royce's metaphors of interpretation makes community's foundation (shared value) appear to be a utopian mirage. So what does Royce's interpreter really know? Nothing at all, James might have answered, except his own desire to give the gift of himself by extending himself into his neighbor's mind. So much the better to obey his first and only commandment: Know thy neighbor as thyself.

An interpretive act for Royce, like belief for James, like the philosophical poem for Santayana, is above all else a deed, and like all deeds it is done to and for the future: "deeds once done are irrevocable; and every deed echoes throughout the universe." The present-as-deed, Royce says, is the interpretation of the past to the future. Hence, "just as what is cannot be undone, just so what is truly or falsely counselled by any concrete and practical judgment remains permanently true or false. For the deed which judgment counsels remains forever done, when once it has been done." If interpretation is *giving counsel,* then we inescapably engage to undertake the direction of our neighbor; we find ourselves thrust back into the moral and political arena that Emerson and James had set forth before Royce.

The cardinal sin in Royce's kind of world – Eliot teased out a career as a poet in meditation upon it – has come to be known, thanks to Eliot, as the cardinal modernist sin: the refusal of commitment, the sin of refusing altogether *to act.* It is not so much the badness or the goodness of one's deeds, Eliot wrote in his essay on Baudelaire; good or bad deeds are at least deeds – they occur in a world of redemption and damnation that we inhabit with others, for their and our betterment or detriment, whatever, but undeniably a world in which it is not possible not to say *we, us.* In this world it is possible to be saved. It is also possible to be condemned (as in one of Eliot's favorite passages in the *Inferno*) to a deep level of Hell with Guido de Montefeltro, who counseled a pope falsely. But in the world of refusal to act – where like Prufrock we counsel ourselves into paralysis, thereby earning only the contemptible, shallowest level of Hell – we sin against community directly because we deny that we exist together, that we work upon each other. We refuse human contact by deluding ourselves into thinking that it is possible not to give counsel; we become absorbed in the prison of ourselves. Eliot, in *The Waste Land,* describing the living dead, gives us, via Dante and Baudelaire, a definitive modernist image: "each man fixed his eyes before his feet." The writers who move in Royce's world – Eliot, Pound, the first generation of American New Critics are the major instances – do not suffer from the anxiety of triviality thrust upon modernism by imagist theory, and its dream of the percept, because they see themselves as interpreters who understand that the deed is done for history's sake. Insofar as they are self-conscious interpreters, they must suffer the anxiety of responsibility. The Roycean sort of modernist knows very well that very little, maybe nothing at all, depends upon a red wheelbarrow.

# 2

## LYRIC IN THE CULTURE
## OF CAPITAL

RITING IN SELF-WILLED EXILE to an ex-student
from a cottage in Beaconsfield, England, which he
called "The Bung-Hole"; still deep in literary obscurity – though not quite as deep as the obscurity he had experienced
in America in the previous twenty years; writing in November
1913, with his first book out and warmly reviewed by the right sort
of people, Ezra Pound among them, and with a second and maybe
even a third book waiting in the wings, Robert Frost hatched the
plot of his return to the United States as the first step in his cunning
pursuit of the fame that would eventually become the means of
supporting himself and his family. And more: he would court fame
because it would provide the material base for the realization of a
desire he publicly announced in the 1930s and to which critics on
the Left might have responded sympathetically – but didn't. (Frost
came up through some pretty joyless conditions.) That desire, at
once induced by and mainly prohibited in Frost's American culture,
Yeats – who never earned Frost's right to it – called the desire for
"unity of being." Other high modernists would weigh in with other,
equally romantic, phrases for a need that represented not only longing for another and better – because integrated – kind of life, but
also criticism of the social ground on which they stood. With crafted
American homeliness, Frost called it his "object in living" to unite
"My avocation and my vocation / As my eyes make one in sight":
pleasure, play, doing whatever you want – in 1913, at thirty-nine

47

years old, Frost had done little of the latter – fused with work, what you had to do if you were someone like Frost. The object of Frost and many other twentieth-century American writers was to sustain a commitment to their art in the daunting knowledge that their lives would be pressured by relentless economic need to which their art could bring no surcease.

So the definition of modern American poetry demanded by its economic circumstances is just this: the craft of nonremunerative writing pursued by those who cannot afford to pursue the craft of nonremunerative writing. The American literary dream in the twentieth century is to reconcile aesthetic commitment and economic necessity beyond the storied opposition that had more or less inescapably haunted writers ever since the eighteenth century, the more or less of nightmare depending on the more or less of cash a writer might lay easy claim to from an inheritance, say, or possibly a patron. But where was an American writer going to find a patron? And how many American writers in the twentieth century inherited leisure-class conditions?

Reflecting on the strong critical reception that his first book, *A Boy's Will,* had just won for him, Frost, in November of 1913, wrote his ex-student John Bartlett:

> You mus[t]n't take me too seriously if I now proceed to brag a bit about my exploits as a poet. There is one qualifying fact always to bear in mind: there is a kind of success called "of esteem" and it butters no parsnips. It means a success with the critical few who are supposed to know. But really to arrive where I can stand on my legs as a poet and nothing else I must get outside that circle to the general reader who buys books in their thousands. I may not be able to do that. I believe in doing it – don't you doubt me there. I want to be a poet for all sorts and kinds. I could never make a merit of being caviare to the crowd the way my quasi-friend Pound does. I want to reach out, and would if it were a thing I could do by taking thought.

This ambition of Frost's to stand on his legs "as a poet and nothing else" – he had been barely standing as a teacher and reluctant farmer – is an outrageous ambition inside the emerging context of literary and social ideals that would be codified as "modernist" in the 1950s, and that Pound was doing so much to help bring into existence in the year that Frost wrote this letter.

In 1913, Pound was pursuing his intention to shape a career that would violate the literary values incarnated in the guise of contemporary poetry, which many young American writers, who (like Pound) would become important modern poets, were reading and despising while still youths in the first decade of this century. In so violating established literary culture, Pound would inaugurate another intention, not separable from his literary desire, to make social change: the transformation of the economic structure itself, which (Pound was convinced) had produced the literature he would displace – the very literature that was, he would argue, nothing less than his society's symptomatic expression, in the realm of culture, of its totalitarian direction. In 1913, Pound and his friends were imagining revolt against what another writer about thirty-five years later would call *1984*. In 1913, Frost was imagining turning the social system Pound hated to economic and literary advantage.

Inside Pound's context of avant-garde literary production and manifesto, Frost's desire – represented in his figure of economic sustenance (oh, for a parsnips-buttering poetry!) – can hardly help but be read as contemptible evidence of complicity. By virtue of its deliberate strangeness of structure and discourse and its flaunted hostility to everyday life in capitalist culture, emerging high modernist literature was finding its honor precisely in its economic unviability, and in the distance that separated it from the tradition of popular verse which Frost had in mind when he entitled his first book in echo of Longfellow. Frost would woo that tradition's mainstream audience – the "general reader who buys books in their thousands," even books of poetry; a reader who is no figment of Frost's fame-hungry imagination but the material force that had made the books of Longfellow and other Fireside poets, as well as a number of women poets, best-sellers in nineteenth-century America.

Life at the edge of economic disaster in Greenwich Village, Kenneth Burke once explained in autobiographical reflection, was the choice of serious writers of his generation who hadn't already chosen the route of expatriation altogether, a social rejection out of *La Bohème:* Greenwich Village as expatriation from within. Within Pound's and Burke's avant-garde context, Frost's desire to make it economically as America's poet – he chose neither form of expatriation – places him outside the pale of modernist company, unless literary memory recalls that Frost was the oldest of the American poets with whom he is usually compared, commonly to the denigration of his reputation with those university intellectuals who invented and sustained the official phenomenon called modernism. Frost was formed in the 1890s and early years of the twentieth century when, in the United States, no poetic company existed outside the mainstream. His letter to Bartlett is not the inauguration of an ambition against what would be called modernism, nor, finally, what it most immediately is, an expression of enmity born in his important and difficult relationship with Pound. The letter reiterates, in the face of new opportunities for literary publication – the recently launched little magazines – an ambition generated in him by a poetry scene exclusively controlled by mass-circulation magazines (like the *Atlantic, Harper's,* and *Century*), which were actually supporting the lives of a few genteel poets well known in the young manhood of Frost and Pound, though now passed from canonical memory, and models for poetic success after the examples of Bryant, Longfellow, and Whittier.

For the young Robert Frost, popular success in the mode of the Fireside poets did not represent "mainstream" literary life (a term that presupposes an avant-garde margin of opposition) but the only "stream." In 1892, at eighteen, while contemplating marriage to Elinor White, Frost won his first kind of parsnips-buttering success when he was accepted by the *New York Independent,* a weekly in which the then well-known Richard Hovey appeared frequently — Hovey, a poetic celebrant of red-blooded manhood and our imperialist move toward Cuba, whom the young Frost admired. For a single poem the *Independent* paid Frost nine dollars, a sum that bought considerable groceries in 1892, especially for those, like Frost, whose idea of groceries did not include caviar. Those same mass-circulation magazines that Frost tried with virtually no success for the first twenty years of his career were also well known to Pound (and briefly tried by him, too): together with the writers they published, Pound thought these magazines represented everything that was wrong with his country.

But Frost wanted it both ways ("I want to be a poet for *all* sorts and kinds"). His literary identity was in some part shaped by the critical ideals of the emerging avant-garde. He wanted to get to those who read the *Atlantic* with pleasure, but he also wanted to get to Pound himself, whose approval he painfully sought, who reviewed Frost's first two volumes with guarded admiration, who pushed Frost to Harriet Monroe in Chicago and to editors of new-wave literary magazines in London, and who once punned the *Ladies' Home Journal* right into the *Ladies' Home Urinal.*

Frost returned to the United States in early 1915 in part because he thought he could work within its dominant commercial system of literary production. Making it at the level Frost wanted to make it would, however, require more than the ideal action of his intellect thinking its thoughts, writing its poems; he would have to do more on his own behalf than "take thought." He would have to become practical in a way long forbidden by the anticapitalism of romantic literary models. He would have to become his own best public relations adviser, the first broad-scaled poetic media star, the ordinary man's modernist. And even better, if he could actually become a poet for all sorts and kinds, then he would succeed not only in making the commercial system work on his economic behalf but also in having his literary way with it. Pound saw it otherwise: he saw no

way of living here and boring from within, no way of slyly subverting, much less seizing, the system of literary publication, so he
expatriated himself to a place outside, from which he hurled at his
native country relentless charges of human betrayal, finally to return
after World War II, against his will as fascism's brightest modernist
star.

In modernism's scene of emergence and triumph in America,
"Frost" and "Pound" may turn out to be not so much names of
authors who quarreled over basic issues as they are signs of cultural
forces in struggle, whose difference presented itself to Frost in 1913
as a choice between mass circulation and avant-garde little magazines, forces whose persistent difference would constitute the scene
of what would be called modernism. "Frost" against "Pound" as the
American way of making it new against the European avant-garde,
those producers of aesthetic caviar so culturally inaccessible to the
American masses; "Frost," then, as bearer of a democratic rhetoric,
suspicious of everything from the wrong side of the Atlantic, including and perhaps most especially the political radicalism of the aesthetic vanguard. Frost's 1913 letter to John Bartlett is a prefiguring
of an aesthetic and social argument within modernism that would
shape the movement of the new poetry from its official date of birth,
1912, when the inaugural issue of *Poetry* appeared, to 1930, the
close of its most fertile phase of literary innovation and negative
political critique. By 1930, the major documents of modern American poetry – *North of Boston*, "The Love Song of J. Alfred Prufrock,"
"Hugh Selwyn Mauberley," *Spring and All, The Waste Land, Harmonium, A Draft of XXX Cantos*, and *The Bridge* – had not only all been
published but also, with unpredictable speed, had become the textual conscience of our poetry and a controversial, internally con-
flicted core of social reimagination whose most radical question had
to do with the political experiment called "America," and whether
or not that experiment was a qualified success or a sham and a
failure. The aesthetic arguments within modernism were simul-

taneously arguments over what shape the American social future
should take.

In 1929, with the literary revolution won, modernism fully in
place, and Ezra Pound its widely hailed entrepreneur and guru,
Pound told, in the *New York Herald Tribune,* the story of his moment
of awakening. It was to become the representative anecdote of his
literary career, the substance of the larger tales that his poetry and
his literary and social criticism would ceaselessly tell and retell of
epiphanic revelation: the dawning upon him that aesthetic and economic production were insidiously related. Literary expression in
America and England was the effect of an economic cause deadly to
all individual identity (whether political or literary), a cause whose
aesthetic products were not different in kind from those we conventionally know as commodities. Pound had had his definitive encounter with the culture of capital and had emerged a badly bruised
romantic – poetry, he learned, was an expression of the marketplace,
not its critique, as idealists since Kant had desired – badly bruised,
but more than ever a romantic whose will was newly steeled for
social change.

It struck him that if "the best history of painting in London was
the National Gallery," then the best history of poetry "would be a
twelve-volume anthology in which each poem was chosen not merely because it was a nice poem or a poem Aunt Hepsy liked, but
because it contained an invention, a definite contribution to the art
of verbal expression." With this idea in mind, he approached a
respected agent who was impressed by his plan for an anthology but
apparently too indolent to recast Pound's "introductory letter into a
form suited to commerce." The agent made contact with a "long-
established publishing house"; two days later he summoned Pound
in order to ask him, in astonishment, if he, Pound, knew what he

had said about Palgrave, the editor of the most famous anthology of poetry in the English language. Pound: "It is time we had something to replace that doddard Palgrave." The agent: "'But don't you know that the whole fortune of X & Co. is founded on Palgrave's *Golden Treasury?*'" From that day on, Pound wrote, no book of his received a British imprimatur "until the appearance of Eliot's castrated edition of my poems. I perceived that there were thousands of pounds sterling invested in electro-plate, and the least change in the public taste, let alone swift, catastrophic changes, would depreciate the value of those electros. . . . against a so vast vested interest the lone odds were too heavy."

Pound's anecdote clusters together, at the site of literary production, issues that shape the larger story of his career, as well as (they are not easy to separate) the career of modernism. If a poetry anthology ought to function like the National Gallery — as a space for exhibits — then who or what will provide the economic wherewithal to sustain such space? Who or what will play the role of patron of the arts? And why should the patron, whether national agency or private agent, agree to underwrite a culture of invention ("swift catastrophic changes") implicitly at odds with an economic system so heavily invested in aesthetic repetition, not change, precisely the system that sustains the would-be patron? A specific anthology of poetry, Pound learns — Francis Palgrave's *Golden Treasury of the Best Songs and Lyrical Poems in the English Language* — in fact functions not as the space for the exhibition of original literary talents and their inventions but as a commodity requiring heavy investment in electroplates, the sole purpose of which is to help make the fortune of those who control the means of its production, Macmillan Company, whose goal is best realized by monopolizing the market and thereby avoiding the costly production of new plates.

Palgrave had hoped that his anthology, the poems themselves, would assist in liberating the spiritual life of the capitalist subject (across the classes, but especially "labor and poverty") from the everyday life of getting and spending. Instead, contrary to his

hopes, his anthology would actively reenforce the life of capital at
the cultural level by normalizing (in this order), first taste (this is a
poem), then taste's appetite (this is what I want more of), and finally
taste's evaluative purpose (this is what a poem should be like). From
out of its material economy – the mass-produced object, the system
of its distribution – Palgrave's widely circulating text performs the
cultural ("civilizing") work of a capitalist society. *The Golden Treasury* inaugurates and sustains taste immune to competitive versions,
to other ideals of poetic shape and function. The major economic
enemy of Palgrave's anthology, whether small or catastrophic, is
therefore change; and not economic change, but change of the cultural sort, aesthetic change of the kind indicated and longed for by
those hallmark words of modernist critical vocabulary, "originality"
and "creativity," what Pound calls "invention" and what Eliot, in a
simple but telling phrase, calls "the individual talent."

Pound's idea of where he actually lives corresponds to Orwell's
dystopian imagination of where we might live. We remember Julia,
in *1984*, who works in the fiction-writing department, telling the
sentimental Winston that fiction is just another commodity, like
"jam or shoe laces," a controlled substance of consumption produced
for the better manipulation of its consumers, so that (Orwell's not
Julia's point) they might become more like what they consume –
normalized (pseudo) individuals, repetitions of one another, so
much easier to dominate. For Pound, social actuality has the feel of
dystopian nightmare. And all of it, the culture and economics of
capitalism, is mixed up, for him and other modernists, with the
feminization of culture. Poems that Aunt Hepsy might like, that
symbolic reader and consumer of Palgrave – she is Pound's figure for
a mass audience hostile to real invention – are uncomfortably close
to the edition of Pound's poems that Eliot brought out under the
aegis of Aunt Hepsy's cultural dominance, with Eliot as her ironic
agent: Eliot's edition being an image of Pound castrated. Against
such vast vested economic interests, the lone (male) odds were too
heavy. What the time cried out for to make things right was not

what his words about lone individuals might imply – a solidarity of individuals – but an epic hero to combat conspiracy; and Mussolini was just over the horizon.

Pound's revelation was double: Palgrave's anthology was transformed into a commodity by a publishing firm of necessity interested in dominating the cultural marketplace; the literary contents of the book-as-commodity, thanks to Palgrave's perfectly deployed theory of the lyric, were similarly transformed, in their standardized literariness, into replications of each other, commodities of lyric sameness, literature reduced to the verbal sweetness you could fit uncut onto a page or two of a collection simply filled with things you could fit uncut onto a page or two. The unprecedented dominance of Palgrave's little book in the last four decades of the nineteenth and the first two decades of the twentieth century – it was the rarest of things poetic, an actual best-seller in the United States – coupled with the rise there of the popular magazine as an outlet for what those magazines demanded, had the effect of equating poetry in this period of the earliest stirrings of modernist literary activity with lyric itself, in the traditional song-mode practiced from the mid-sixteenth century through Wordsworth and Shelley. In the scene of modernism's emergence, the poetry anthology, the mass-culture magazine, and the avant-garde little magazine made a single demand: that poets write poems of traditional lyric length or not be published.

Palgrave's intention was to shape a lyric canon, a list for all seasons, embodying the measure of literary value. So he rejected chronological arrangement and refused entry to living poets, including his inspiration and ghost editor, Tennyson, to whom his book is dedicated. He thought of all poems (he got this from Shelley) "as episodes to that great Poem which all poets, like the cooperating thoughts of one great mind, have built up since the beginning of the world." If a canon is by definition for all seasons, it is similarly by definition for all audiences (readers of "all kinds and sorts," as Frost would say). Palgrave's intention was partly to teach those who already loved the poets "to love them more," but predominantly it was popular, class-crossing, with a bias toward the working class: to provide "a storehouse of delight to labour and to Poverty," to provide "better reading" than what usually fills the "scanty hours" that most men (who mainly work and do not have time for it) "spend for self-improvement"; as if in the world of capital a "self" were exactly the sort of thing that one attended to only in leisure time, as if one had no "self," or held it in abeyance, when one worked the jobs that one worked if one were one of those referred to under Palgrave's rubric of "labour and Poverty." Palgrave's aim was to turn such men away from an exclusive preoccupation with the self-precluding grind of work, turn them toward the ideal plane of poetry and the "one great mind" which knows no time – toward poetry's special treasure of selfhood. Hating the economic, Palgrave yet draws his title metaphor from it: treasures "more golden than gold" that lead us in "higher and healthier ways than the world." Lyric will provide consolation for those scanty hours when we are released from our unhappy "work," not insight, nor the spur of intervention, but therapy for all those impoverished who labor because they must, who inhabit a world they never made and perhaps believe they can never change, and whose belief is tacitly bolstered by lyric disengagement.

In a passage in his preface that represents considerable antithetical motivation for emergent high modernist thinking on the lyric, Palgrave defended his choices by defining lyric as writing by exclusion. No narrative allowed, no intellect at meditation, no description of local reference, no didacticism, no personal, occasional, or religious material, no humor (the very antithesis of the "poetical"), no dramatic textures of blank verse because the speaking voice is alien to song lyric (a redundancy: Palgrave recognized no dramatic lyric, no Donne, no Blake). Certainly nothing that might show up in a realist novel: no details of faint smells of beer or of steaks cooking or of cats

licking rancid butter or of dirty fingernails or yellow soles of feet—
no details, in other words, drawn, as T. S. Eliot draws those I've just
cited, from naturalist fiction.

Palgrave's effort to define lyric is representative of mainline Kanti-
an aesthetics and nineteenth-century literary commonplaces about
poetry's noble role. Like Kant's aesthetic mode of attention, lyric is
defined by what it is not, even by its emptiness, by poems that do
not – this is why Palgrave selected them – touch down on determinate historical terrain, a poetry benignly neglectful of the social
space, late-nineteenth-century England and America, in which it
was received. As negative poetic being emptied of the world's interest, lyric discourse turns on the homogeneity of the *isolate,* unmixed
feeling: no ironists need apply. In a very few paragraphs, Pound's
enemy had managed not only to set forth an idea of lyric sensibility
as dissociated sensibility, an idea that virtually every modernist
would combat, and in virtually the same terms, but at the same
time sounded some of the keynotes of the romantic anticapitalism
worked so deeply through the modernist aesthetic: poetry as an
alternative, special kind of discourse, whose values are a would-be
repudiation and transcendence of Mammon at a powerful moment in
the late Victorian life of capital.

Young poets growing up in the United States at the end of the
nineteenth century (Pound, Frost, Eliot, and Stevens all fall into the
category), in search of models of literary change and innovation,
found instead literary models of continuity and repetition. The best-
seller power of Palgrave (in the 1860s alone it sold almost 300,000
copies in the U.S.A.) must have felt repressive. Palgrave wanted to
promote the continuance of the old lyric tradition and had obviously
succeeded by reaching exactly the audience he had posited as his
aesthetic target – a popular readership eager for the lyric pause that

refreshes the long workweek: Shakespeare and Herrick at once as escape from labor and labor's worldly gold and as civilizing contact with a transcendent culture, above time, "more golden than gold," which Americans feared they would never produce. Worse, Palgrave spawned even more continuity by provoking economic competitors (and therefore aesthetic imitators) in America. F. L. Knowles's *Golden Treasury of American Songs and Lyrics* (1898) saw seven editions in about fifteen years, and Jessie Belle Rittenhouse's 1912 *Little Book of Modern Verse* – a book Frost hated, which featured a table of contents of American poets almost all now unknown – sold 100,000 copies in its first edition.

E. C. Stedman's *An American Anthology, 1787–1900*, published in 1900 (this is an *American* anthology), reflects in the first sentence of its introduction ("The reader will comprehend at once that this book was not designed as a Treasury of imperishable American poems") both economic and cultural anxiety over the presence of what Stedman calls, in the third sentence of his introduction, "Palgrave's little classic." And anxiety over Palgrave is just the tip of the iceberg of Stedman's anxiety for American poetry in its American setting. His introduction is a compendium of issues just barely under the control of expository procedure, a legacy of problems that modern poets would spend careers working at but never through. The books of the popular Fireside poets in their "homiletic mood," as Stedman phrased it, "lay on the center-tables of our households" as tangible manifestations of the success with which they had conceived and played out their roles as cultural ministers of a new society, in moral mediation of English romantic forms: literary counterparts and enforcers of America's most powerful engine of cultural ministration in the nineteenth century, the Protestant clergy. But now, in Stedman's America, the Fireside poets were fast becoming cultural dinosaurs, and their roles of cultural ministry usurped by realist writers whose values seemed, in genteel perspective, to be infected by what their narratives were representing – the materialist values of the Gilded

Age. The ever-increasing cultural centrality of the realist novel was pushing poetry into a cultural "twilight"; in response to its marginalization, poetry should renounce the world of Howells, Twain, and the capitalist devils by resisting all temptations of history (the Civil War, after all, had motivated no "little classics of absolute song"). The pure aesthetic note needed to be recovered and sounded fullthroatedly; the lyric voice in its vernacular-free universal cast, its origin a world elsewhere, was to be sought, and the historicizing voice in local color, the new voice of prose fiction, with its temporal and regional contamination, was to be negated.

But with the (realist) novelization of literature virtually achieved, could poetry of lyric grace and feeling make any difference, or could it function only as a haven in a dirty world? Was poetry, as Howells argued to Stedman's horror, a dead genre? Could a lyric poet become a professional, lyric letters a means of subsistence? The growth "of American journals, magazines, and the book-trade" clearly coincided, Stedman understood, "with a wider extension of readers than we had before." Fiction writers could now cash in; but could poets do so without compromising their social rejection of Howells's America? "Poets, in spite of the proverb," Stedman wrote, "sing best when fed by wage or inheritance." But poetry was only rarely paying wages, and he, a representative American man of no inheritance, had turned to Wall Street. Was Stedman the poet, by the terms of a cruel logic, less of a man? His rhetoric tells us that he was uneasy about the answer: "It cannot yet be said of the Parnassian temple, as of the Church," he wrote in response to the phenomenon of the popular American women poets, "that it would have no parishioners, and the service no participants, if it were not for women. The work of their brother poets is not emasculate, and will not be while grace and tenderness fail to make men cowards, and beauty remains the flower of strength." The question that Stedman posed in all but words is: What profits it a man to write a history-free autonomous lyric if he thereby lose his economic viability, and so his manhood and his historically honored role in America of cultural minister – a role that encourages nothing if not acts of social intervention?

POET

Out of a Job

Specialties: incisive speech, sarcasm, meditation, irony, (at special rates), ze grande manair (to order). Will do to travel, or stand unhitched while being fed. Price 1 E per hour. Special rates for steady customers.

In February 1908, after a brief and comically disastrous teaching stint in middle America, Ezra Pound essentially left the United States for good. In February 1910, however, with his first volume of poems, *A Lume Spento,* behind him, and his first American volume, *Provença,* about to be published by a Boston house, he responded to the pressures of his parents to return to Philadelphia, where he might survive without periodically having to hit his father up for loans, and where he might relocate himself in college teaching, for which his graduate training in romance languages and literatures had so well prepared him. Pound was sending his poems to magazines like *Harper's,* because in America in 1910 there were no other kinds of magazines to send them to, and they were sending them back. Like Frost, though in somewhat easier financial circumstances – his background was comfortably middle-class, his father had modestly indulged his requests to support his literary life – he needed to find a way to sustain himself while pursuing his economically unresponsive first love. Like Frost, he tried to write fiction in the hope of securing his material base. And, again like Frost, he was not successful. The advertisement that he had written in Italy and then sent to his father with instructions that he actually place it in a major

Philadelphia daily would suggest, in the words of his most recent biographer, "a certain crisis of confidence," with the socially sarcastic tone of the young aesthete's advertisement for himself compromised by the necessities that impinge even on an aesthetic radical as uncompromising as Ezra Pound. Pound's pun on his own name betrays not only what was constraining his hopes for a life in art, but also what would become a lifelong obsession with what he imagined as the conspiracies of money: "Price 1 E per hour."

He stayed home for about a year. In that period he witnessed the publication of what he regarded as the unethically overpriced American edition of *The Spirit of Romance* and spent much time in New York City, where he gathered his thoughts for one of the most decisive pieces of social and literary criticism he would compose, the monograph-length essay whose Italian title, "Patria Mia," simultaneously reflects his attachment and longing and – in his refusal to state it in English – his distance and alienation.

Pound's divided feelings are expressed in "Patria Mia" in his hopes for what he called an "American *risorgimento*" and in his savaging of our foremost literary disease, that "appalling fungus" which is the commercial system of magazine publishing and circulation, "dry rot, magazitis." But the stakes in Pound's criticism of America were not primarily literary; the suppression of all potentially "original" and – Pound's synonym for "original" – potentially "free" artistic talent does not cover the field of the suppressed. The suppression of idiosyncratic artistic impulse was for him symptomatic of a more general extinguishment in America of all possibilities for human "individuality" (yet another and perhaps Pound's key synonym for freedom). The tyrant was an economy whose ends were, even then, as he wrote "Patria Mia," being assured by the chief theorist and technician of capitalist discipline in the early century, Frederic Taylor, and the process baptized in honor of his time and motion studies: "Taylorization," a term that named the method of transforming the factory into a site of maximum efficiency by the manipulation of laborers into mindless mechanisms of repetition, so much the better for producing the standardized products called commodities.

Writing out of his deepest anti-imperialist mood in 1917, Pound saw democratic society drifting toward totalitarianism and the violation, as he phrased it in Blakean reminiscence, of "all outlines of personality" and "all human variety." The most shocking evidence he found was culturally ingrained in Germanic ideals of higher education that unwittingly turned students into "impotent" and "pliable" tools of the state by keeping them ignorant of all connections between the minute particulars of their philological research and the larger process of the social whole within which they carry on their scholarship. In 1910, in "Patria Mia," Pound believed he could see the drift toward political slavery vividly on display in what passed for poetry in the mass-circulation magazines. For if Germanic scholarly ideals, as he came to think, were an educational forerunner of economic Taylorization, then the popular magazines of his time were its aesthetic realization, the perfection of the cultural division of labor and the poem as commodity: "As the factory owner wants one man to make screws and one man to make wheels and each man in his employ to do some one mechanical thing that he can do almost without the expenditure of thought, so the magazine producer wants one man to provide one element, let us say one sort of story and another articles on Italian cities and above all, nothing personal."

Pound's extended comparison insists on the equivalence of cultural and economic production, not in order to make some roughly Marxist point about the determined relations of culture to the economic base of American society (though he does in effect make that point) but in order to decry the economic condition that transforms cultural agents into mindless and selfless producers who turn out poems, articles, and stories as their factory counterparts turn out screws and wheels, virtually without thought, certainly without personality, all in the service of the magazine-factory's finished product. The economic setting of capitalist culture is the index of cultural degradation under capitalism and our severely diminished capacity in such conditions – here Pound's idealism comes ringingly through – to be human. And by "human" he means something other than an economic being. But his criticism of capitalism is not issued nostalgically on behalf of some other social context, historically now out of reach, where it was once presumably easier to be human ("individual") rather than some cog in a machine. It is a criticism directed against capitalism for what subversion it had done to the promises of freedom in his country, especially the freedom of writers.

All who choose to write within the American system of literary circulation, and Pound knew from personal experience that it was hard to choose otherwise, tend to become its faceless expression and faceless productive agents. All urges to invention tend to be shut off because when writers discover the formulas that pay, they produce repetitions in the normalized style demanded by the system. As agents of a mode of literary production Pound considered unimaginable outside capitalism, these poets write the poems of capitalism, not by didactically singing its praises, but by shaping the discourse of lyric according to the productive ideals of its cultural economy and the captains of lyric industry – Palgrave, Stedman, Knowles, Rittenhouse, and especially R. W. Gilder, R. U. Johnson, and Henry Van Dyke, genteel cultural powers whose names Pound liked to name in 1910, men, as he liked to say, who if not born base were made so by the literary system in which they worked. In a capitalist cultural setting, repetition is a permissible and even encouraged sort of literary forgery with no authentic original standing in silent accusation, the mechanical reproductive technique of choice for those editors ultimately responsible for getting out the conventional lyric of the mass-culture magazine.

But in "'San Zeno' at Verona, one finds columns with the artisan's signature at the base. Thus: '*Me Mateus fecit.*' That is what we have not and can not have where columns are ordered by the gross. And this is a matter of industrial conditions." The signed column at San Zeno bears the artisan's guarantee of social responsibility – his name tells us whom to blame should the column collapse; the signed column is also the mark of the artisan's ability to retain his name and face in a society where his desire for creative freedom and personality has a chance to be nurtured. In the modern economic order, on the other hand, the names and faces of artists are obliterated by the logic of mass production — to standardize, to repeat, and so to remove the accidents of personality, so much the better to produce art in its form as commodity: not to repress the "unique" personality — Pound was no believer in mute and inglorious Miltons — but to so establish and saturate the conditions of creativity as to eliminate all social spaces that might be hospitable to the personality of idiosyncratic imagination.

The commodity form of art is the death of what Pound thought literature essentially to be, the essence of real literature a nonessence, historical contingency itself, always surprising and unpredictable, "something living, something capable of constant transformation and rebirth." A true literary event — Eliot would codify the point in a famous essay — is both a radically original moment and a memory of the history of original moments and their authors: the past that has been transformed and reborn lingering, haunting the new, so forming the central paradox of literary history, the tradition of the modern. What the commodity form of art threatens to remove from the historical stage for the first time — this belief is the source of all critical urgency in Pound — is the avant-garde author himself, who is no contemporary phenomenon but a perpetual possibility, the creative traces of whom Pound spent a lifetime recording and preserving in his essays and in *The Cantos*. The avant-garde author as the exemplary "individual": not God's gift to society, but a recurring historical phenomenon motivated by various tyrannizing social contexts, and his best paradoxical example may be Pound himself, whose sensibility was born with specific historical density, or so "Patria Mia" would indicate, as an emerging counterstatement to the society and culture of the commodity which he was so concerned to excoriate.

At its highest Poundian pitch, literary modernism was *desire for* authentic individuality in literary style and voice, a necessarily harsh critical impulse directed against the proliferated methods and ideals of mass culture. Literature is "constant transformation," or else. Even yesterday's transformations, when they become hardened – the style of 1880 become a school – are the agents of aesthetic death and the collective loss of memory for readers and writers both. And it was precisely the (Pre-Raphaelite) style of 1880, Pound argued in 1910, that the magazines were beginning to promote as a "contemporary" product. In effect, the commercialization of recent poetic styles is a relentless attack upon the historical sense, with the history of literary invention relegated to the junk heap of antiquarian interest (an outmoded product), rather than what it should be, a living legacy. Pound's attack on American magazines with mass circulation is an attack on the packaging of poetic manners and the making of literary fashion, the circulation of literature a la mode. Because of the mass-cultural circumstances of its birth, Pound's avant-garde sensibility demands escape from the fashionably contemporary, demands historical quest, research, and preservation.

"Patria Mia" forecasts Pound the poet as patron of poetic styles (the troubadors, the seafarer poet) and of forgotten social heroes (Sigismundo Malatesta) whose values contemporary magazine editors and anthologists cannot peddle as "new." Pound's poetry will become a sort of vocal gallery, a hospitable space for the exhibition of often unsung and always original talents; and Pound himself, a tissue of masks. But what he does not become, despite his celebratory reference to what was possible in " 'San Zeno' at Verona," is an escapist longing to recapture some lost golden world. One meaning of Pound's directive to "make it new" is "make it old." In Pound modernism (a word he never used) is the desire for radical originality, not in order to wipe out history, but to recover and join it as a tradition of individual talents now blocked from our contact, from our memory, by the totalitarian present of the commodity.

It is the function of American millionaire businessmen, capitalism's potential Medicis, he wrote in "Patria Mia," to die and leave gifts for the support of artists, so that artists might exempt themselves from "the system of circulation," so that they might – Pound means this literally – be free to experiment. The hope for America, as he saw it in 1910, lay not in a revolution against capital but in a utilization of capital that would release writers from the marketplace, and the temptation to sell out, by setting alongside the logic of mass culture an alternative logic of patronage which would nurture the expression of *virtu,* Pound's name for that quality in authorship and writing most absent in the heavily academicized American poetry of 1910. *Virtu* is the goal of experiment; *virtu* is the literary expression of individuality (in no two writers the same), the basis of an original ("self-reliant") writing and the reason for its persistence; *virtu* is bravery, courage, strength – in a word, the *manliness* that has been obliterated by a feminized culture and whose absence explains why literature in America "is left to the care of ladies' societies, and of 'current events' clubs, and is numbered among the 'cultural influences'" – and Pound's quotation marks (a favorite satiric device) around "current events" and "cultural influences" set the contemporary-culture business in an acidic perspective. *Virtu* is the virtuosity of individual performance, the only virtue Pound would ever recognize, until, in his later writing, more than aesthetic virtuosity, *virtu* becomes the basis of a social model.

What he did not question in 1910 – how much potential virtue would have to be crushed as those American Medicis gathered the financial means to become generous patrons of the virtuous artists – he implicitly questions in his late political writing, where, in his new model for society, not only artists and powerful capitalists are given the space to find their virtuoso selves. Pound's idea of *The Cantos* – a literary curriculum all by itself, a literary National Gallery in one volume – and his idea of the humane state would become strictly homologous: "A thousand candles together blaze with intense brightness. No one candle's light damages another. So is the liberty of the individual in the ideal and Emersonian state" – except for the fact that these sentences were written in Italian, in 1942, under the heading "Fascio" and the phrase is actually "ideal and fascist state," the better place, Pound imagined, for the safekeeping of the American dream and the avant-garde writer.


Less than a month after writing to John Bartlett from England, in November 1913, about his ambition to be a best-selling writer, Frost expressed doubt about his own capacity to bring it off and about the generic suitability of poetry for the task. In a letter to another old American friend, in which he wrote, "At most poetry can pave the way for prose and prose may or may not make money," he admitted not having much stomach for the moneymaking side of writing and that he wasn't, at any rate, all that inclined to prose. In his bad old American days, he told Ernest Silver, he would try prose for two or three days at a time, "having resolved it was the thing for a man with a family to do. But just when I bade fair to produce a novel, right in the middle of chapter three or four I would bring up in another inconsequential poem. . . . It remains to be seen whether I shall take hold and earn a living as a writer."

Frost's novelistic energies in fact came to some consequence as they were rechanneled into poetic narratives, dialogues, and monologues, into those longer poems, outside his lyric mode, which dominate his second volume, *North of Boston,* published in 1914, about a year after he had uttered his true confessions of econo-poetic need to Bartlett and other friends. Frost returned home in 1915 to find himself famous, still poor, and wondering in a letter written in April of that year what he might have earned had he had freshly in hand, in the moment of his newfound poetic notoriety, those longish *North of Boston* poems ready to be sent off to the very magazines that had routinely rejected him before: "The thought that gets me," he writes, "is that at magazine rates there is about a thousand dollars worth of poetry in N.O.B. that I might have had last winter if the people who love me now had loved me then. Never you doubt that I gave them the chance to love me." Just a few days later in another letter, in more expansively embittered mood, he wrote: "These people once my enemies in the editorial offices are trying hard to be my generous friends. Some of them are making hard work of it. Some are making very hard work. . . . Twenty years ago I gave some of these people a chance. I wish I were rich and independent enough to tell them to go to Hell."

Now that he was home, however, and being made such a fuss over "in a country where I had not one [friend] three years ago," he found that he really could get up some stomach for the moneymaking part of writing: "While the excitement lasts you will see that it would be affectation for me to pretend not to be interested in it. It means nothing or next to nothing to my future poetry." He then adds an afterthought that would predict the scornful highbrow modernist reaction to him, while showing how even he, the ordinary man's modern poet, had internalized Pound's avant-garde perspective on the necessary antagonism of mass-cultural values and authentic aesthetic value, the idea of the modern being perhaps unintelligible outside that antagonism of commercial and aesthetic. Frost himself would never forget that his first two volumes were brought out by a small London publisher; Frost also had his thoughts about "patria mia." The new (me too) American excitement over his English success fueled his interest in his own fame, the pursuit of which would shortly become virtually his vocation.

By June 1915 all had changed. He told another correspondent that his "rage has gathered considerable headway," that Ellery Sedgwick, editor of the *Atlantic Monthly*, "has just written me a beautiful letter and sent me fifty-five beautiful dollars for poetry." In August 1915 Frost made the first of his many appearances in the *Atlantic* with a group of short poems that included "The Road Not Taken," likely the most anthologized poem of the important modern American poets. "The Road Not Taken" would soon become the lead-off poem of his first American volume, *Mountain Interval* (1916), and eventually would lend its title to all manner of books and articles, including a biography of Frost, a study of U.S. race relations, at least one work of feminist scholarship, a study of U.S. social conditions, an essay that excoriates American literary theorists for not going the way of the Italian Marxist Antonio Gramsci, a proposal for alternatives to prison for nonviolent felons, a biography of an eighteenth-century Jesuit, a self-help text which occupied the *New York Times* best-seller list for over seven years, and an analysis of a crisis in highway repairs and maintenance in Connecticut. The poem is also a chestnut of high-school teachers of American literature and a frequent citation on greeting cards of rugged American sentiment. All in all, a veritable American adage, a pithy concentration of our proudest wisdom of self-reliance from Emerson to John Wayne: the very idiom of American desire. Ellery Sedgwick apparently knew what he was doing when he welcomed Frost into the pages of the *Atlantic.* Frost was well on his way to selling books "in their thousands," to standing on his legs "as a poet and nothing else," but not, apparently, to being "a poet for all sorts and kinds."

Frost once said about his basic strategy as a poet in search of mass cultural impact that he would "like to be so subtle at this game as to seem to the casual person altogether obvious," a remark that decisively clarifies the split between mass and modernist cultural desire which marked the difference of Frost (and Robinson, Lindsay, Masters, and Sandberg) from the company of the high modernists, Stevens, Pound, and Eliot. For who could ever imagine for Stevens, Pound, and Eliot a "casual" reader who could respond to *The Cantos, Notes toward a Supreme Fiction,* and *The Waste Land* as if they were "altogether obvious"? Frost's desire to reach a mass audience by becoming, among other things, acceptable to mass-circulation magazines like the *Atlantic,* shaped his rhetorical literary relations to his imagined ordinary reader. He could become a poet for all kinds, but only by favoring the ordinary reader, by fashioning an accessible and seductively inviting literary surface that would welcome the casual reader of poetry (as opposed to the intellectually armed scholar of modernism), while burying very deep the sorts of subtleties that might please those accustomed to Pound's aesthetic caviar. And judging by the reaction to him from high modernist quarters, Frost buried his subtleties right out of sight. For by choosing to fashion a transparent instead of a forbidding surface, he succeeded in telling his highbrow critics that his writing was undergirded by no challenging substance. If obscurity of surface in high modernist writing has typically been received in standard accounts of modernism as an index to complexity of social analysis, then the fact that the "easy" Frost *looked* like no modernist poet meant, in modernist context, that he required no effort of engaged reading.

The stylistic difference between Frost and Pound may in some part be a difference in temperament (style is the man), but it is also a historical difference, one conditioned and driven by the difference, say, between the *Atlantic* and the *Little Review,* an engendering sort of difference, moreover, which conditions and drives alternative means of literary reception – a popular as well as an elite academic canon – and, therefore, alternative accounts of the history of modern American poetry. In 1920, the arguments within modernism in the United States were fully engaged and unresolved, with Conrad Aiken taking the side of Pound, Eliot, and the avant-garde, and Louis Untermeyer taking the side of Frost and the native tradition, the low modernists out of Whitman. Frost's side lost. Our recent chief accounts of modernist poetic history find him anomalous, a poet of the twentieth century but not a truly "modern" poet. Yet if modernism out of Pound means an attack on official genteel poetic culture, then the poet who wickedly links the beautiful with money rather than with poetry (as in "fifty-five beautiful dollars") may be making not only a comment that no modern American (male) poet could be out of sympathy with, since no modern American (male) poet could help worrying about securing the means of his and his family's subsistence; he might also be launching a sneak attack on the airy ideals of conventional accounts of poetry (with a capital P) and "the beautiful" which had descended to Frost through Stedman and his Victorian forebears.

"The Road Not Taken" might actually be the best example in all of American poetry of a wolf in sheep's clothing, a hard-to-detect subversion of both the principal American myth — that of autonomous selfhood — and the deeply abiding Fireside poetic form within which, in this poem, Frost chooses to embody his dramatization of cardinal liberal principle and his reflections thereon.

> Two roads diverged in a yellow wood,
> And sorry I could not travel both
> And be one traveler, long I stood
> And looked down one as far as I could
> To where it bent in the undergrowth;
>
> Then took the other, as just as fair,
> And having perhaps the better claim,
> Because it was grassy and wanted wear;
> Though as for that the passing there
> Had worn them really about the same,
>
> And both that morning equally lay
> In leaves no step had trodden black.
> Oh, I kept the first for another day!
> Yet knowing how way leads on to way,
> I doubted if I should ever come back.
>
> I shall be telling this with a sigh
> Somewhere ages and ages hence;
> Two roads diverged in a wood, and I —
> I took the one less traveled by,
> And that has made all the difference.

Self-reliance in "The Road Not Taken" is alluringly embodied as the outcome of a story presumably representative of all stories of selfhood, and whose central episode is that moment of the turning-point decision, the crisis from which a self springs: a critical decision consolingly, for Frost's American readers, grounded in a rational act when a self, and therefore an entire course of life, are autonomously and irreversibly *chosen*. The particular Fireside poetic structure in which Frost incarnates this myth of selfhood is the analogical land-scape poem, perhaps most famously executed by William Cullen Bryant in "To a Waterfowl," a poem that Matthew Arnold praised as the finest lyric of the nineteenth century and that Frost had by heart as a child thanks to his mother's enthusiasm.

The analogical landscape poem draws its force from the culturally ancient and pervasive idea of nature as allegorical book, in its Amer-ican poetic setting a book out of which to draw explicit lessons for the conduct of life (nature as self-help text). In its classic Fireside expression, the details of landscape and all natural events are cagily set up for moral summary as they are marched up to the poem's conclusion, like little imagistic lambs to slaughter, for their payoff in uplifting message. Frost appears to recapitulate the tradition in his sketching of the yellow wood and the two roads and in his channeling of the poem's course of events right up to the portentous colon ("Somewhere ages and ages hence:") beyond which lies the wisdom that we jot down and take home:

> Two roads diverged in a wood, and I –
> I took the one less traveled by,
> And that has made all the difference.

If we couple such tradition-bound thematic structure with Frost's more or less conventional handling of metric, stanzaic form and rhyme scheme, then we have reason enough for Ellery Sedgwick's acceptance of this poem for the *Atlantic:* no "caviar to the crowd" here.

And yet Frost has played a subtle game in an effort to have it both ways. In order to satisfy the *Atlantic* and its readers, he hews closely to the requirements of popular genre writing and its mode of poetic production, the mass circulation magazine. But at the same time he has more than a little undermined what that mode facilitates in the realm of American poetic and political ideals. There must be two roads and they must, of course, be different if the choice of one over the other is to make a rational difference ("And that has made all the difference"). But the key fact, that on the particular morning when the choice was made the two roads looked "about the same," makes it difficult to understand how the choice could be rationally grounded on (the poem's key word) perceptible, objective "difference." The allegorical "way" has been chosen, a self has been forever made, but not because a text has been "read" and the "way" of nonconformity courageously, ruggedly chosen. The fact is, there is no text to be read, because reading requires a differentiation of signs, and on that morning clear signifying differences were obliterated. Frost's delivery of this unpleasant news has long been difficult for his readers to hear because he cunningly throws it away in a syntax of subordination that drifts out of thematic focus. The unpleasant news is hard to hear, in addition, because Fireside form demands, and therefore creates the expectation of, readable textual differences in the book of nature. Frost's heavy investment in traditional structure virtually assures that Fireside literary form will override and cover its mischievous handling in this poem.

For a self to be reliant, decisive, nonconformist, there must *already* be an autonomous self out of which to propel decision. But what propelled choice on that fateful morning? Frost's speaker does not choose out of some rational capacity; he prefers, in fact, not to choose at all. That is why he can admit to what no self-respecting self-reliant self can admit to: that he is "sorry" he "could not travel both/And be one traveler." The good American ending, the last three lines of the poem, is prefaced by two lines of story-telling self-consciousness in which the speaker, speaking in the *present* to a listener (reader) to whom he has just conveyed "this," his story of the *past* – everything preceding the last stanza – in effect tells his auditor that in some unspecified *future* he will tell it otherwise, to some gullible audience, tell it the way they want to hear it, as a fiction of autonomous intention.

The strongly sententious yet ironic last stanza in effect predicts the happy American construction which "The Road Not Taken" has been traditionally understood to endorse – predicts, in other words, what the poem will be sentimentally made into, but from a place in the poem that its *Atlantic Monthly* reading, as it were, will never touch. The power of the last stanza within the Fireside teleology of analogical landscape assures Frost his popular audience, while for those who get his game – some member, say, of a different audience, versed in the avant-garde little magazines and in the treacheries of irony and the impulse of the individual talent trying, as Pound urged, to "make it new" against the literary and social American grain – for *that* reader, this poem tells a different tale: that our life-shaping choices are irrational, that we are fundamentally out of control. This is the fabled "wisdom" of Frost, which he hides in a moralizing statement that asserts the consoling contrary of what he knows.

In the American situation for poetry in 1915, when "The Road Not Taken" was published, Frost's poem is a critical expression (that manages, for a few readers, to have it both ways) issuing from the very source (the mass circulation magazine) that Pound condemned, and in so condemning launched modern poetry. The poem is an instance, famous at that, of what mass-cultural media demanded from American poets and simultaneously what Frost, like Pound, wanted to say against that mode (their editors, after all, were also his enemies as he struggled to be heard through his twenties and thirties), a savage little undoing of our mainline literary and political sentiments. So "The Road Not Taken" is an internalization of that opposition within the mode of poetic production – mass or avant-garde little magazine? – which was, in 1915, becoming the sign of the modern.

Nonetheless, over the years "The Road Not Taken" has attested to the power of convention to withstand those who would subvert it from within. It remains a famous poem, one of the "best loved of the American people," not for its irony, but for the sentiments that make its irony hard to see. Frost wanted to be a poet for all kinds, but mainly he failed. He is the least respected of the moderns. Pound wanted a few, fit readers, and he got them. Thus far, the alternative means of literary publication in American culture prohibit, in either direction, crossover poetic careers because they engender two different and mutually hostile readerships.

# 3

## ROBERT FROST

B Y 1919, LOUIS UNTERMEYER — Robert Frost's most assiduously cultivated literary operative — could declare in
the opening sentence to the first edition of his soon-to-be
influential anthology, *Modern American Poetry,* that "'America's poetic
renascence'" was more than just a bandied and self-congratulatory
phrase of advanced literary culture: "it is a fact." And on the basis of
that fact, or wish (it hardly matters which), Untermeyer and Har-
court Brace made what turned out to be a lucrative wager on the
poetry market through seven editions of the anthology, the last of
which entered the university curriculum and stayed there through
the 1940s and '50s, bearing to more than one generation of faculty
and students the news of the poetry of modernism and at the same
time establishing, well into the '60s, a list of modernist musts: Frost
foremost, together with strong representations of Pound, Eliot,
Stevens, Williams, Hart Crane, and a long list of more briefly
represented — and now mostly forgotten — poets. What Untermeyer
had succeeded in presenting in his later editions was a stylistic
texture of modern American poetry so varied as to defy the force of
canonical directive. If the poetry of modernism could include Frost,
Stevens, Pound, Marianne Moore, and Langston Hughes, then perhaps the phenomenon of modernism embraced a diversity of intentions too heterogeneous to satisfy the tidy needs of definition.

But the first edition of Untermeyer's book offered no such collagelike portrait of the emerging scene of modern American poetry,

77

no Eliot, Stevens, or Williams, only a token of Pound and the avant-gardists. Untermeyer's anthology of 1919 was in fact heavily studded with names that had appeared a few years earlier in the anthology of his chief genteel competitor, Jessie Belle Rittenhouse, the *Little Book of Modern Verse* (1912), which included the name of Rittenhouse herself. The economic interests of Untermeyer and his publisher insured that his declaration of the new be accompanied not by an avant-garde act of rupture but by a conciliating act that veiled his departures from the popular taste that Rittenhouse, then in her second edition, had so well played to. The first edition of Rittenhouse's anthology had sold over one hundred thousand copies, a fact never apparently lost on Untermeyer, who through all of his editions managed to include poems that Rittenhouse would have admired and that, through no stretch of the imagination, would be included under anybody's definition of modernism.

Rittenhouse was a major literary journalist in America in the first two decades of this century, and she published in 1904 what must have been the first book to attempt a characterization of *modern* American poetry (*The Younger American Poets*), though not one writer she took up has survived in recent accounts of American literary history (not even for a sentence). She made it her business to get to know the literary powers of the day in New York and Boston, interviewing many of them for major northeast dailies, became chief poetry reviewer for the *New York Times* and a founder, in 1910, of the Poetry Society of America. In her various writings and anthologies she could say who was in and who (usually by omission) was out, and though recent historians have not ratified any of her choices and do not know her name, she was a force who, both in her female person and her taste, represented the aesthetic grain against which the emerging modernist male poets were working: the principle of "the Feminine in literature," as Eliot put it, which he was none too anxious to give space to in the *Egoist;* the "Aunt Hepsy" that Pound saw as typifying poetry's contemporary audience in the United States; one of those – again Pound – who had turned poetry (for serious people) into "balderdash – a sort of embroidery for dilettantes and women."

Like E. C. Stedman's *An American Anthology* and Francis Palgrave's *Golden Treasury*, Rittenhouse's *Little Book of Modern Verse* sustained an innocent lyric ideal of sweetness, the voice of unadulterated song. Nothing in her anthology contradicted the literary principles announced by Palgrave and Stedman in their respective prefaces, where they characterized lyric by what they excluded. Eliot would say that a real poet can amalgamate his experiences of falling in love and reading Spinoza because a real poet's sensibility is not dissociated; a real poet does not shrink from the impurities of experience. Palgrave, Stedman, and Rittenhouse were champions of the dissociated lyric of exclusion, the homogeneity of the unmixed feeling, and their books sanctioned and perpetuated that lyric ideal through the young manhoods of the modernists-to-be, who would in some large part learn how to write a "modern" poetry by writing against "poetry" as it was sponsored by these major tastemakers and the mass circulation magazines that gave space to genteel lyric, and precious little else.

Stedman summed up genteel American's poetic ideal when – in an I-told-you-so aside – he noted that the Civil War had motivated no "little classics of absolute song." Democratic cultures are not, of course, supposed to venerate heroic ideals and their "big" epic literary vehicle: we have only the little or lyric classic; but even that is imperiled by the forces of social environment, the penetration of lyric interiority by the immediacies of Civil War history. The unhappy result, in the embedded logic of Stedman's lament, is the birth of the impure or "partial" song not quite emptied of worldly interests and pressures – lyric too much with the world.

Joyce Kilmer thought Rittenhouse had "raised anthology-making to a fine art." Frost thought otherwise. He told one correspondent that her title was "silly." He didn't explain what he meant, but he must have meant that she had no right to the word *modern;* and, of course, by the governing aesthetic dicta of genteel anthology making, she didn't. In the world of Palgrave, Stedman, and Rittenhouse, "modern lyric" was a contradiction in terms, not to mention a besmirching of the category of lyric. Lyric practice by male and female writers seemed to Pound and Frost an effeminate business, and cultural authority in the female person of Jessie Belle must have made it seem doubly so.

Aside from needing to make a buck, Untermeyer needed to make a point or two. If he was at veiled war with Rittenhouse and genteel culture, then he was at open polemics with Conrad Aiken over whose version of the new poetry would achieve cultural authority, which new poets would survive. For Untermeyer, the modern moment was peculiarly American, its progenitors his benign versions of Whitman and Dickinson, its vision hopeful and democratic, its formal manner always submissive to its human content: art with positive social function. The decadence of Stevens, the assiduous internationalism of Pound, the tenuous inwardness of Eliot, all represented an unhealthy foreign strain, an elitist art-for-art's-sake plying of the craft for a coterie audience: in fact, undemocratic to the core, Untermeyer believed, because it was an art that only the culturally privileged could make any sense of. *Modern American Poetry* was aimed at a mass audience for economic reasons, but its democratic point of view also demanded a mass audience, and as a perfectly blended capitalist/populist venture, Untermeyer's book stood against the coterie anthologies only recently issued by the New York avant-garde, by Pound, and by Wyndham Lewis (*Others, The Catholic Anthology, Blast*). So, upon the economic success of *Modern American Poetry* hung Untermeyer's version of the future of the new poetry: his desire for a poetry rooted in diverse American cultures, his hopes for the writing, reading, and dissemination of poetry in a democratic society. Upon the economic success of Untermeyer's anthology hung the cultural authority of the party of Van Wyck Brooks's nativist intellectuals, the cultural politics of "America's coming-of-age," of which *Modern American Poetry* was the anthological representative.

Untermeyer went polemically further in his companion critical volume *The New Era in American Poetry* (also published in 1919), in which he characterized the work of Pound, Stevens, and their aesthetic companions published in Walter Arensberg's *Others* as "mere verbal legerdemain," effeminate and morbid. Aiken, Eliot's college mate and longtime correspondent, counterattacked in a review of the book in *The New Republic* with the charge that Untermeyer's celebration in American poetry of "the unflinchingly masculine" (which he glossed with the words "Americanism" and "lustihood") was unwittingly a celebration of the most conservative of poetic and political values. After all, poetry with the right message – the carefully monitored poetry of the ideal state, good for the education of soldiers – had been welcomed by Plato, poetry's most celebrated historical enemy. Aiken argued that Untermeyer's soft socialist politics, grafted onto a happy version of Whitman, blinded him to the force of the true revolutionaries who were "throwing their bombs into the aesthetic arena": not Frost, Sandburg, Masters, Robinson, and Lindsay (those low modernists who dominated the first edition of *Modern American Poetry*), but the formal innovators, the high modernists of "absolute poetry" to whom Untermeyer had given such short shrift.

Untermeyer never managed to, or could, say why the stance of virility or the politics of social democracy required poetic representation, or what difference it could make to virility or democracy that they be imagined in an aesthetic rather than in some other medium. Aiken, who declared himself on the side of literary experimentation as the agency of art for art's sake, never managed to, or could, say what connection, if any, obtained between literary and social experimentation, or why he should be taken seriously when he described the literary avant-gardist as a bomb-throwing radical. Surfacing in this early argument within modernism is one of the most ancient topics in literary theory, that of the relationship of art and the commonweal, here, in the Aiken-Untermeyer clash, given what would become its definitive framing in the critical literature of modernism, where aesthetics and politics are typically forced by rhetorical heat to stand in opposition even as that same rhetoric of modernist polemic causes them suspiciously (because protesting too much) to lean toward one another, as if revolution in poetry and social change could not be imagined outside a relation of strong interdependence.

But if, in Aiken's view, Untermeyer's introduction to *Modern American Poetry* seemed in its immediate polemical context to cherish too chauvinistically the peculiarly American possibilities for poetic renascence, and too eager to court insulation from European traditions; if Untermeyer appeared to be replaying Emerson's call in "The American Scholar" for an American literature free from servility to British aesthetic rule, rooted in the American commonplaces, and therefore worthy of the American social experiment, then on Untermeyer's behalf it ought to be remembered that his distinguishing heritage was not Emersonian New England but German-Jewish immigrant stock, and that his revision of Emerson's ideas on the relations of literary expression to their cultural matrix was worked out at the high tide of our heaviest period of immigration. What Untermeyer needed to see in the new poetry was aesthetic responsiveness to voices that were never heard at the cosmopolitan finishing schools of genteel America, voices that were virtually unrepresented in poetic traditions before Wordsworth because they were unworthy of the memorialization provided by traditional producers of literature, whose typical objects of representation were people like themselves, with privileged routes to the acquisition of literacy. Alongside genteel authors Untermeyer published a black poet, Paul Laurence Dunbar, several Jews, a Philadelphia Irish-American journalist, T. A. Daly, whose specialty was Italian-American dialect, and numerous poets from outside the northeast corner of the United States. In his critical book he devoted an entire chapter to the Italian immigrant socialist admirer of Whitman, Arturo Giovannitti.

American was changing and, as an untraditional literary voice himself, Untermeyer, the revisionist literary historian as anthologist, found himself in the sensitive political position to disseminate his vision of an America in which poetry emerged not from one or two culturally elite centers but from everywhere; a poetry which, in refusing legendary, traditional, and classical poetic materials and their generally economically advantaged authors, in choosing its *materia poetica* from everywhere but the traditional sources, was fashioning itself as a revolutionary literature standing against what literature had been. From the traditional perspective, the new poetry was an antipoetic poetry that even the "conservative *New York Times*," as Untermeyer put it, had to acknowledge had dislodged poetic traditions in this country in favor of a writing that insisted on prosaic everydayness, not only as subject but as its very medium of expression: a poetry which, in following the lead of Howells, Twain, and the new novel, would spell the demise of genteel aesthetic ideals and at the same time signal a larger death, that of genteel America's cultural and political authority.

Although Untermeyer probably tuned into much of this American cultural and social change on his own — he was a keen observer of the literary scene — his sensibility was nevertheless being shrewdly coached by his correspondence with Robert Frost, his favorite poet of the new school, who by the time he returned home from England in 1915 had set himself against the self-conscious avant-garde and was fully engaged in the entrepreneurial process of staging his own image as a different, an American, kind of modernist. The Frostian directives that found their way into both Untermeyer's anthology and the critical volume of 1919 must have sounded to Aiken like Wordsworth's Preface to *Lyrical Ballads* revisited, an effort to finish off a poetic revolution that had gotten sidetracked by Tennysonian aestheticism and the various moods of the 1890s. Untermeyer thought he saw in the new American poetry the discarding of a "stilted" (he meant a rare, rhetorical, *writerly*) vocabulary in favor of what he called a sincere, simple "daily vocabulary" (a vocal language of everyday situation): a radical realism of diction which appears to overcome the very mediation of print itself, so that we can virtually hear the speaker on the printed page; a stylistic sea change whose most powerful effect would lie in the illusion it creates of its un-literariness – an illusion born from its refusal to borrow its verbal modes and tics from official poetic history, from Poetry with a capital letter under the imprimatur of Francis Palgrave. Modern American poetry, Untermeyer thought, would be recognizable by its unliterary (vernacular) borrowing directly from life itself: like Frost and the realists, by "life" he meant the lives of the historically unsung – therein lay the radical, the "modern," and the "American" character of "modern American poetry." But what this account of the new poetry left out (this, perhaps, is the root of Aiken's impatience with Untermeyer's downplaying of the aesthetic dimension) is that such radicality is mainly perceptible only to those with keen aware-ness of the history of English poetry, because only those readers (not the unlettered man celebrated by Untermeyer's Whitmanesque ideal) are in a position to grasp basic shifts in literary history, to grasp, not a change from "literariness" to "life-likeness," but a change from established kinds of literariness, and the social bases that supported such writing, to a new kind of literariness, presum-ably an organic expression of a new kind of social arrangement: literary change, in so many words, as index of social change, glimpse and push in the direction American society might be head-ing – a culturally diverse democracy unheard of in human history. The historically startling idea is that social change might be re-flected in and directed by lyric poetry, of all things, as well as in the grungy bourgeois forms of prose fiction, where accounts of social conflict are to be expected – reflected in a novelized poetry which (Untermeyer's words) "explores the borderland of poetry and prose" and thereby, at that generic crossing, explores fundamental social differences. This activist conception of poetry was perhaps the most deeply buried issue of the relation of aesthetics and politics that lay unexamined between Untermeyer and Aiken.

In his battle with inherited poetic diction, Frost believed that in *North of Boston* he had scored a decisive victory in literary history, because there he had "dropped to an everyday level of diction that even Wordsworth kept above"; there, in *North of Boston,* he had performed "in a language absolutely unliterary" and had barred from his writing all "words and expressions he had merely *seen*" (in books) and had not "*heard* used in running speech." "Words that are the product of another poet's imagination," as he declared in his strongest avant-garde moment, "cannot be passed off again. . . . All this using of poetic diction is wrong." This, he explained, was the essence of his "war on clichés," which he later described as a war on all systems and system-building. But he didn't want to be misunderstood, as he believed Pound had misunderstood him, as "a spontaneous untutored child," because he was not "undesigning." What Frost's design amounted to was an antinomian intention to undo all design (all intention, all structure) in its institutional incarnation and sanction. "What I suspect we hate," he wrote in 1937, "is canons, which are no better than my guidances insisted on as your guidances." Canons are on the side of stabilization and tradition, and would give the rule of the dead over the living, once and for all. But literature, Frost thought, is the very spirit of insubordination, and as such the anticanonical spirit verbally incarnate. If nothing is "momentous," if "nothing is final," then, he concluded, literary canons and the critical generalizations which produce and sustain them are instruments of literary repression wielded by professors in Frost's constant institutional target of literary repression, the university or college.

The logic of Frost's poetics equates literary insubordination with literature itself, and literature with modern literature, not as some specific historical style evolved in the early twentieth century but as something like the very spirit of literature finding its fullest incarnation in an American scene that provided its true (because demo-cratic) political directive: no literature except in radically individu-alized expression. In his arguments on behalf of the vernacular as locality, intoned and intransigent, the basis of a vital and living literary voice, "entangled somehow in the syntax, idiom and mean-ing of a sentence," Frost named the multiheaded enemy of literary insubordination – that is to say, the enemy of *literature* – as the professorial sentence, the dead, grammatical discourse taught at school; the poets of classical tradition, fawned over by professors who teach them as literary models but whose sentences in living speech are not accessible to us; and the reiterated poeticisms of English tradition preserved and sustained by contemporary antholo-gists like Stedman and Rittenhouse: all those enemies of a living (that is, a "contemporary," a genuinely "modern") literature who come at us from the feminized crypt of manliness, the book.

"Words," Frost said in a striking proverbial moment, "exist in the cave of the mouth," their masculine origin, "not in books," their effeminate emasculation. He told his son Carol, in a startling letter of sexual-poetic self-evocation, that Carol had written "No sissy poem such as I get from poetic boys. . . ." And note "poetic boys": the provocatively gendered responses of Frost, Pound, and other male modernists were to a literary style, a cultural feminization, at work in the writing of both sexes. It seems that Carol (who, with a name like that, maybe needed to hear this) had managed to "ram" his writing "full of all sorts of things"; the poem he sent his father had been "written with a man's vigor and goes down into a man's depth." The mark of Frost's own "prowess" lay (this a frequent boast in his letters) in the success he had in breaking through the genteel lyric, as if through a cultural chastity belt, a vernacular desert from which the genteel cultural critics had outlawed the conversational voice. And his prowess lay (as summoner of voices) in his success in "bringing to book" tones never before heard in poetry; in bringing the book closer to its vital literary source in the cave of the mouth.

Frost's struggle against canonical forces was a struggle carried out on behalf of a new lyric diction and therefore new (and low) lyric social materials (below even Wordsworth), for the purpose of reengendering lyric for "masculinity," a word in Frost's and other poetic modernists' lexicons signifying, not a literal opening of the lyric to actual male voices and subjects, but a symbolic shattering of a constrictive lyric decorum that had the effect, in Frost's America, of denigrating poetry as the province of leisured women in their land of cultural irrelevance. (Frost's experiments in fact often featured at their center economically disadvantaged females.) Unlike the old lyric, the modern lyric (like modern America itself) would be (should be) indecorously open ("full of all sorts of things"). The old lyric, which Frost talked about as if it were coextensive with poetry itself and what it had been, "left to its own tendencies" "would exclude everything but love and the moon" from its decorous world. Frost's struggle against the traditional lyric was simultaneously a struggle against both social and literary exclusion. The new lyric would be "modern" because it would implicitly stand as a political rebuke to traditional literature: revolutionary because heterogeneous in form, style, diction, subject, social origin, and social reference. In Untermeyer's and Frost's vision, the new manly lyric would be an expressive medium of the collage of cultures America was fast becoming, the literary resistance to the cultural melting pot, a genuinely American creation.

Frost made his points in letters, not in essays, but those points reappeared in Untermeyer's critical prose, and they functioned as the hidden genius of his anthology. Untermeyer was the conduit of Frost's critical ideas. Concurrent with Frost's socially expansive efforts to rethink and rewrite lyric, Pound and Eliot pursued parallel efforts to open up the lyric to all sorts of things, but in more public ways, in essays of immediate critical impact which eventually gave rise to a codified theory of poetry, the critical reflection of modernism that came to be known as the New Criticism. In one of its most elegant expressions, Robert Penn Warren, in "Pure and Impure Poetry" (1943), provides at once a focus for the issues of the emerging new lyric around 1912 and the ironic costs of the institutional prestige it had achieved by the late 1940s, when Warren, Cleanth Brooks, John Crowe Ransom, and Allen Tate had secured the domination of T. S. Eliot's poetics and criticism.

Like Frost, and in a gesture typical of the drastically narrowed idea of poetic types that had taken hold early in the nineteenth century, Warren – following Poe's pronouncement that a long poem is a contradiction in terms – identifies poetry with the singular intensity of the short lyric and its tendency to exclude everything but feeling anchored in its own self-regard. ("The thing you hate in poetry," Frost said, "is segregated stuff. . . ."; poetry, in other words, "by common consent.") In a key allegorical moment of alliance with the aesthetic ideals that he wanted to revise, Warren says, "Poetry wants to be pure, but poems do not." The impurity that lyric would exclude – and that Warren would put back into poems – turns out to be coextensive with the world of "prose and imperfection," by which Warren means the everyday world represented in realist fiction – "unbeautiful, disagreeable, or neutral materials," "situation, narrative," "realistic details, exact description, realism in general." In Frost's example, even "the axe-handle of a French Canadian woodchopper."

Warren's list of excluded impurities is notable for its aesthetic conservatism. If there are such things as inherently unbeautiful or disagreeable materials, then there must be (as Poe believed) an inherently beautiful object toward which "poetry" might properly yearn. And his list is notable as well for its interesting confusion of realms, with some elements in the list referring to things in the world that "poetry" (to its detriment) doesn't wish to take account of, and other elements referring to the realist literary medium of their representation. The oddity of Warren's effort to liberate poets from the straitjacketing decorum of "poetry" is that it must grant the genteel aesthete's point – that there is a realm of the beautiful which is poetry's proper object – precisely in order to establish the identity of the "poem," whose character would lie in its act of avoiding "poetry." Strong mixtures of subject, diction, tone, and allusion are the trademarks of the tough-minded modernist poem that Warren and other New Critics admired in Eliot, and which they theorized in their essays as signs of highest literary value. But these signs of the new poetics often bear a haunted quality – an uneasy consciousness (ironic, nostalgic, sometimes both at once) of the way things used to be, of what can no longer be written but which is nevertheless evoked in gestures of modernist farewell.

Warren's account of traditional lyric would appear to identify lyric substance with unsituated feelings of love, a subjectivity whose object knows no history. Poe's beautiful dead woman would be something like the logical object and fulfillment of this aesthetic and affective drive, the essence of lyric idealism, not its deviation. Frost calls the traditional lyric object "love and the moon"; Warren's examples of lyric are almost all drawn from the literature of love. So Frost and Warren pursue, because they understand, the issue of lyric purity in its late-nineteenth-century embattled context in which the contemporary genteel lyric was being pushed gleefully into the grave by the polemical defenders of realism. They implicitly define the modernist moment for poetry as the moment of realist pressure upon the lyric. Both castigate a late-nineteenth-century lyric impulse drained of historical specificity, because they are exceptionally sensitive to the generic dominance of a kind of writing (realist fiction) whose central claim to cultural value was precisely its empirical and historical density. The struggle for literary liberation in the early modern moment of American poetry was directed against genteel idealism and its Victorian and Romantic sources, but the seductive pull of that idealism in the embryonic moments of modernist literary culture turned out to be greater, more insidious, and more invasive than might appear at face value in modernist polemic and manifesto.

Frost's effort to destroy what Poe, Tennyson, and Swinburne had wrought (and Palgrave, Stedman, and Rittenhouse had institutionalized) by dramatically adapting the rhythms and aural qualities of the traditional lyric to the cacophonous, speaking rhythms of voices in worldly situations is an effort to come to terms with the novel, as is his theory that everything "written is as good as it is dramatic – even the most unassuming lyric," which must be heard as "spoken by a person in a scene – in character, in a setting." His desire to be known as a poet who had "summoned" (not created) tones and rhythms from actual speech is as good a sign as we have of how far down in prestige traditional notions of a "poetry" had sunk in the rankings of the literary genres by the early twentieth century. If in middle-class societies the novel had displaced the epic of traditional culture, and if classic forms of drama were increasingly being "replaced" (Pound's acidic reflection) by more popular and economically feasible forms of theater, then what role could possibly be imagined for the lyric? Only half jokingly, Wallace Stevens asked Elsie Moll, the woman he was to marry, to keep it a secret that, some ten years after his Harvard experiments in decadence, he was returning to the making of verses, a habit he described as "positively lady-like." In a letter of 2 May 1913, Frost expressed similar male discomfort when he remarked on the ease with which English men, as opposed to their pragmatic American counterparts, could attend to their aesthetic inclinations without sparking a scandal of gender-decorum violated: "I like that about the English – they all have time to dig in the ground for the nonutilitarian flower. I mean the men. It marks the great difference between them and our men." In the same letter, Frost went on to nominate himself the rare exception among American males – a digger of the wildflower, like a man he knew who "was a byword in five townships for the flowers he tended with his own hand" (pansy!). With sardonic joy he linked his cultivation of the poetic with that same nonutilitarian and – this is the American cultural logic – unmanly pursuit ("I have certain useless accomplishments to my credit"). So when, twenty years later, he praised his son for the manliness of his poetic style, and added, "You perhaps don't realize what this means to me," he was reflecting in the precisest terms possible the crisis in the genteel lyric that he, Pound, Eliot, and others had precipitated when they decided (after, in Frost's and Pound's cases, brief flirtations with the novel) to devote their literary energies to producing a new (manly) lyric mode.

This issue of manliness is the historical thread binding Frost and Warren's New Criticism and an index of the difference between the historical situation of the new lyric at its point of emergence and the historical situation of its triumphs of the 1920s and 1930s, when it was difficult to see it as new writing in a struggle against official forms of literariness. In fact, by the early forties, when Warren's essay appeared, the new lyric's open ("impure") character was fast becoming no longer perceptible as a historically specific discourse, because it had been thoroughly institutionalized as the way poems at their best always had been. Brooks's landmark of 1942, *The Well Wrought Urn*, in effect so canonized the modernist lyric by carefully explicating what he offered as examples of poetic discourse from all the literary periods; by projecting the modernist moment backward in time (*Modern Poetry and the Tradition* [1939] is the title of his first critical book) Brooks, in patient elaboration of the argument Eliot had tossed off in a few sentences in the essay "The Metaphysical Poets," thought he had found a poetics good for all time. Warren, for his part, had inveighed against locating the poetic in some specific subject which then becomes the sign of poetic essence here and everywhere and forever, but he ended by celebrating, like his coauthor Brooks, the heterogeneous lyric (contra all canons of decorum, presumably) as itself a poetic essence, the standard of a new ("modernist") literary decorum no less constraining than the old decorum enforced by Palgrave, Stedman, and Rittenhouse; and no less canonical in its repressive effect, as the revolt of the Beats and various poets of the sixties in so many words testifies.

If love is lyric poetry's purest inherent tendency – in Warren's terms, lyric's "soft" subject, and the exclusionary principle par excellence – then the principle of impurity is embodied by Mercutio, the spirit of hard masculine wit, who brings love back from the far empyrean to bawdy earth. Mercutio, in lines Warren cites, by carrying the news of the unrequited phallic urge to Romeo and Juliet, becomes the representation of the principle of impurity who transforms "poetry" into a *complex, ironic,* and (key new critical word) *mature* "poem." In terms closer to the effete literary culture that the American modern poets would have understood because they grew up in it, the genteel yearning for a desexed Keats – a superb blue moth, as Stedman would have him, the genteel representation of the poetic itself, free from the Victorian scandal of the Fanny Brawne letters – this fairylike Keats must be surrounded by an unidealized consciousness that, so far from doing in and doing away with the purity of "poetry," actually acts as its world-toughened shield, the realist protector of airy romantic ideality, "poetry" safely tucked away inside the "poem": Keats made safe for modernist tough guys. No poet dare not make his peace with Mercutio who, if he is not invited inside, will do his bawdy debunking work destructively from outside, relegating "poetry" for the males who take it up to the self-embarrassed sphere of the ladylike (Stevens), the work of sissy boys (Frost), and to societies of leisured ladies who have nothing better to do, having left business and politics to their men, as Pound once roughly put it in allusion to Jessie Belle Rittenhouse.

So the lyric is sanctioned in modernist polemic when what is culturally branded (and denigrated) as essentially female is not done away with but married to the male principle: such marriage is the mark, for Warren, of impure lyric *tout court* and not only of the historically circumscribed modernist lyric, which is lyric's most recent incarnation. In context, however, the issue of poetic manliness in the first decade of the twentieth century in the United States was not just another testament of patriarchal authority asserted (though Warren's essay is open to this last charge). For Frost and other young

poetic modernists, manliness was quite simply the culturally excluded principle in a life devoted to poetry that made it difficult for
the modern American male to enter the literary life with a clean
conscience. In the young Frost's case, the prospect of a literary life in
poetry could raise only the most bitter of issues. His assumption of
the culturally imposed, feminine posture as seeker of the beautiful
not only cut against the authoritative and rapacious male models of
vocation that life in the Gilded Age offered him, as ironic gifts of
social acceptance, it also cut severely against the actual lives of the
females closest to him: his mother and his wife, neither of whom was
blessed with the role of privileged-class woman upon whom ideals of
cultural feminization in America are typically based. Neither Frost's
mother nor his wife could qualify in the technical sense as working-
class, but both were tied to toiling joylessly and without hope of
respite in jobs of no glamour and to lifetime grooves of family
obligation that permitted no life in high cultural activity for themselves; no life, certainly, in the leisured-class work of cultural pro-
mulgation – the taming of the materially driven spirit of men via
the values of religion, poetry, and domestic commitment; no life, in
other words, in the cultural work enshrined in America's sentimental nineteenth-century feminine tradition.

The accolade of manliness that Frost gave his son and his desire to
get rid of poetic diction altogether are the related acts of insubordination and resentment of an economically marginal American college dropout, who enjoyed none of the social privileges of the great
English poets he admired, whose class formation denied him even
the easy pleasures of idealizing the life of his womenfolk. The wom-
en he knew best knew only the hardest of times. For Frost, the
fashioning of a new lyric mode was an opening to all that his social
identity had declared out of bounds. The cultural issue of manliness
had for him immediate, personal impact: it was what structured his
relationship to his family, to himself as a male, and to literary
history. It was not, as it would become for the institutionally power-

ful practice that Warren helped to initiate, a symbolic issue concerning associated sensibilities and the course of English literary history in the seventeenth century.

In his earliest efforts to open lyric by rejecting the heritage of official poetic diction preserved and passed on to his generation of poets by his Anglophilic culture, Frost in effect predicted the shape that his literary career would take. It was to be a career committed to nativist values. The struggle of any young American poet who would be an original, he argued, must be against those custodians of culture who betray the American scene by directing him to write in a banalized, special language found only in books (and English books at that), a language with no sources in the "cave" of the "mouth," a language that "everybody exclaims Poetry! at." The American sounds and rhythms in running speech were to constitute Frost's newfound virgin land, the uncanonized territory that gave him the refuge of aesthetic freedom because he could refuse, as "no one horse American poet" after Keats could refuse, the mimetic idolatry of Keats's yearning, romantic diction. Frost proffered the endlessly echoed word *alien* from "Ode to a Nightingale" as the exemplary piece of ironic evidence of American self-alienation, a denaturing of the American thing by poets who could not help but indenture themselves to Keats and a continuing display of aesthetic servitude to British rule that Emerson and many others had lamented in the 1820s and 1830s, in their call for literary emancipation.

The generally conservative lyric practice of Frost's first volume, *A Boy's Will* (1913), was followed by the dramatic and narrative experiments in the blending of dialogue, storytelling, and a vocality "lower" than Wordsworth's, in his second volume, *North of Boston* (1914), which was in turn followed by his final major transformation into the sententious poet of public fame who came to dominate most of what he wrote after the publication of his third volume, *Mountain*

*Interval* (1916). These neat divisions of Frost's career tell the familiar modern American tale of youthful genius emancipated from convention only to be seduced by money and heavy media attention. But in this case it is a story that partially misrepresents, because it segregates what at Frost's most original was the fusion from early on, in a single literary impulse, of lyrical, narrative, dramatic, and didactic moods. His most radical moment as a new poet is discernible, not in the dramatic and narrative successes of *North of Boston* ("Mending Wall," "The Death of the Hired Man," "A Servant to Servants"), but in the deceptive poems of *A Boy's Will,* where, in a context of tame, historically recognizable lyric practice, which won him (before he traveled to England) some acceptances in mass-circulation magazines, we come across "Mowing," a poem in which he thought he had come so close to getting down everything he wanted to get down, that he despaired of ever matching that effort again:

There was never a sound beside the wood but one,
And that was my long scythe whispering to the ground.
What was it it whispered? I knew not well myself;
Perhaps it was something about the heat of the sun,
Something, perhaps, about the lack of sound –
And that was why it whispered and did not speak.
It was no dream of the gift of idle hours,
Or easy gold at the hand of fay or elf:
Anything more than the truth would have seemed too weak
To the earnest love that laid the swale in rows,
Not without feeble-pointed spikes of flowers
(Pale orchises), and scared a bright green snake.
The fact is the sweetest dream that labor knows.
My long scythe whispered and left the hay to make.

Frost plunges us into a poetry of literary satisfaction wrested from a context of labor that is at once the antagonist of the literary moment and the trigger of its gratification. Labor is the grudging basis of poetry for those who have no traditional means of economic and cultural support for the writing of lyric — those whose lyricism, like Frost's, had better somehow be supported *by and in* the course of the actual tasks of daily work because there is no alternative system of literary support available, those who somehow must be simultaneously poets and laborers. Frost's penchant for titles featuring the present participle promotes the biographically telling fiction that his writing is coincidental with the actual processes of work it describes ("Mowing," "Going for Water," "Mending Wall," "After Apple Picking," "Putting in the Seed"). These poems obliquely focus the biography of a writer who, from his childhood, was required by circumstances to work: between eight and eighteen as newspaper carrier, waiter, gatekeeper at a mill, farmhand, and more than once, as assembly-line worker — first at twelve years old in a shoe factory, the second time at a woolen mill, at age seventeen, for sixty-three hours per week.

Wordsworth often composed in his head, wandering at his leisure in the Lake District, and Stevens did likewise, walking purposively through the districts of Hartford, Connecticut, to his executive desk at the insurance company. Frost's most intriguing poems imply the fiction that he created his poems *as* he worked, that their written forms are unnecessary — the gratuitous recordings of an act, antecedent to writing, an act of labor aesthetically intersected for a laborer who may never actually write, either because he will have no time for it or because he will have no skill to do so. The poetics of Frost's lyric poetry of work implies the statement that this is a kind of writing which claims nothing special for its being written or for the values of writing as such: an antipoetics of work for those who may never have heard of poetics or read a poet; a highly literate poetry, nevertheless, that needed, in sly guilt, to efface itself as literature — as if poetry were a high-falutin' indulgence, yet for some reason necessary — and in such effacement gives us access to life in the here and now; access, in other words, to "modernity."

Unlike in Wordsworth's "The Solitary Reaper," upon which

Frost's "Mowing" mounts a criticism empowered not a little out of resentment, there is no separation in Frost's poem of poetic and laboring voices. Wordsworth, a third-person observer, coolly notes "yon" Highland lass, reaping and singing. His poem's key rhetorical directives ("Behold her . . . Stop here or gently pass!") tell us that his physical distance from the reaper is an aid to the distance required for imaginative reflection. And distance, physical and contemplative, is a figure for the class hierarchy and privilege that define Wordsworth's relation to the working presence named in his title. These social distances produce the very possibility of this poem and also this, its pivotal question: "Will no one tell me what she sings?" Frost, a first-person participant, answers Wordsworth's innocent question with a parodic allusion to it that amounts to a workingman's joke on a comfortable outsider, whose purpose is manipulation of pastoral conventions, not knowledge of labor: "What was it it whispered? I knew not well myself." The reaper is the occasion for Wordsworth's imaginative excursion; Wordsworth is in part recollecting his experience as a literal tourist who doesn't speak the language, but it hardly matters. In fact, his outsiderly perspective (linguistically, economically, and educationally inflected) is all to the good: he is not obligated to communication, only to searching his own inwardness. So, just as fast as he can, and while seeming to honor the mesmeric power of the reaper's song, Wordsworth moves in his second stanza from the site of the reaper's work to faraway romantic places, "Arabian sands," "the farthest Hebrides." Through Frost's lens, Wordsworth's poem is everything that Frost's is not: "a dream of the gift of idle hours." Frost's poem, in this dialogue of literary history, claims that this man who writes *is* working, he *is* the solitary reaper.

Wordsworth's polished displays of rhythm and intricate rhyme pattern, sustained flawlessly from beginning to end, sound monological next to Frost, who moves between the effortless lyric grace of his opening two lines (with anapests, trochees, and iambs fluidly integrated), to the sudden interruption of a rough talking (not sing-

97

ing) voice at line three ("What was it it whispered?") and its playful, prosy surmises (perhaps, perhaps), then on to the flat declarative and epigrammatic moment for which he will become famous in the penultimate line: "The fact is the sweetest dream that labor knows." Never a poet of discontinuities and fragments in the sense made famous, and synonymous with modernist collage, by Pound and Eliot, Frost is yet, in his subtlest vocal experiments, a maker of the quiet vocal collage which, more than anything else in his repertory of strategies, is the mark of his mixed identity as writer-worker, his difference from the traditional poet represented by Wordsworth.

Frost did what Wordsworth never had to do (worked at lower-class jobs) but also what all those represented by Wordsworth's female reaper were not likely to do (write poems of literary sophistication). Frost's virtuoso vocal changes, worked through a heavily Anglo-Saxonate diction, flaunt his difference from Wordsworth, whose nondramatic, smooth song voice, bodied forth in high literacy, highlights the critical social difference between the poet who imagines and the object which is the cause of his imagining. The socially and economically comfortable male poet builds visionary stanzas tranquilly upon his recollection of a female laborer, who becomes a peculiarly modern muse for a socially sympathetic English lyricist, the very same who had gone officially on record, in his famous polemical Preface, as intending to honor ordinary voices, but who is himself no ordinary voice, and whose poem "The Solitary Reaper" unintentionally acknowledges his privileged relation to the base of rural labor that inspired him.

Although the poverty and the sex of the solitary reaper doubly and drastically preclude her access to the ease of literacy that might eventuate in a career like Wordsworth's, and although Frost's male mower performs roughly the solitary reaper's kind of work — therein lie the connections of class across gender — at the same time Frost's male mower can do what Wordsworth's female reaper cannot (this is Frost's pact with Wordsworth): make knowing allusion to literary tradition, in this instance, a Shakespearean song in part about work

("Perhaps it was something about the heat of the sun"), thereby revealing his learned, bookish ways in the very voice of the ordinary worker. This laborer is an American who has had the advantage conferred by democratic commitment to mass education. And his whispering scythe talks not only Shakespeare but also more than a little Andrew Marvell, whose "Damon the Mower" Frost recalls in order deftly to send up – in his critical allusion to "fay or elf" – a patently literary device, an artifice out of touch with the quotidian of farm labor ("The deathless Fairyes take me oft/To lead them in their Danses soft"). No fairies are taking Frost's poet-laborer anywhere.

Closer to literary home, Frost's whispering scythe implies, through a criticism of W. B. Yeats, the dominant living poet in English in the first decade of the twentieth century, Frost's own self-criticism: in denying "dream" and the work of "fay or elf," Frost, in the directness of his vernacular voice, mounts an internal commentary on the ninetyish poetic diction of a number of his own early dreamy lyrics in *A Boy's Will*, while forecasting the colloquial richness and unpretentiousness of *North of Boston*. Frost stakes his claim to difference, not only from Wordsworth's elite position, but also from Yeats and his overt celebration of dream in his early poetry and plays, which Frost knew intimately, having produced the plays of heart's desire while a teacher at Pinkerton Academy in 1910 – difference from the Yeats who had famously declared in flight from the world of fact that the "dream" of the poets "alone is certain good." So "dream" becomes, in Frost's poem, a doubly burdened term of criticism signifying both the leisured idleness of the British poetic classes and an unmanly contemporary aestheticist fashionability, a world-fleeing imagination whose diction Yeats would purify from his writing with the help of Pound's editing, but which Pound himself would have trouble getting out of his own system until after Frost, in his early-century obscurity at the Derry, New Hampshire, farm, had succeeded in doing so, though without the proper critical organs at his disposal to declare his triumph of having made it new.

Boring from within Wordsworth's pastoral territory and Yeats's domain of dream-as-imagination, Frost reduces visionary dream to vision (as in visual) and imagination to a pure act of perception (as in image-making), an act that yields a precious because fleeting knowledge of fact, and fleeting because labor will not permit leisurely lingering in aesthetic pleasure of natural detail strictly irrelevant to the task of labor. It is a knowledge that Frost comes to have not as independent agent – the laboring agent knows little freedom – but as agent of *labor's* action. Labor, not Frost, in Frost's most radical identification of literature with work, "knows" "the fact," which is also and at the same time the ultimate dream of imagination; Frost may know only insofar as he labors. The act of labor as an act of imagination rescues dreaming (Yeats's synonym for poetry) from both Wordsworth and Yeats, in this context impractical "dreamers" in the worst sense of the word.

Frost dreams in riveted attention to the incidental fact unveiled in work: a glimpse of fact for itself alone opened briefly, in a throwaway moment of syntactical subordination, as if it would be a desecration of work to permit those images of flowers (only parenthetically named) and the "bright green snake" to take over center stage and distract the laborer from his real task. This moment of syntactical subordination in "Mowing" is the expressive sign of a culturally subordinated aesthesis, an American guilt of poesis: the image garnered for no profit, stolen from the process of work which opens the possibility of aesthetic experience for a laborer momentarily out of the groove of the job at hand. Work, a ruthless end-directed activity, not in hostile opposition to an activity valuable in itself – as the story of nineteenth-century idealist aesthetics would have it – but work as both constraining and productive context, necessary economic ground of the aesthetic for those, unlike Wordsworth and Yeats, who find work inescapable, whose own labor, not someone else's, is their peculiarly modern muse.

Yet what comes seeping through this effort to write out of a sympathetic antipastoral of work is a social arrangement similar to the object of Frost's criticism of Wordsworth. Social distance and its corollary attitude, the sentimentalizing of common country labor – an attitude virtually demanded by traditional pastoral – make a subversive return in "Mowing" in order partially to trip up Frost's intention and to reveal the duplicity of his would-be realist antipoetics. This literate farmer is more literate than farmer, but uneasily so. This is guilty pastoral, written not out of leisure-class privilege but out of American social constraint by a man who wanted his work to be writing, not those other jobs he did that qualify officially in our culture as work and that he found so dissatisfying. The "earnest love" of this farmer's "long scythe" that "laid the swale" (not just any meadow but a low-lying, moist depression of a meadow), this farmer's productive phallic love throws into even greater subordination the moment of aesthetic vision as an interior moment of pathos, a moment freed from the act of labor (which makes hay while the sun shines) – productive, masturbatory, the indulgent feminine moment; in "Mowing," the literal parenthesis of lyric impression.

The didactic point of Frost's difficult penultimate line becomes clear and sharp against the background of the huge cultural claims for poetic function made by traditional theories of poetry from Aristotle to Wordsworth. The role of poetry for a poet who is constrained by inescapable labor is perhaps a diminished thing in light of the portentousness of those earlier claims. But perhaps poetic function is newly enhanced, after all, in this kind of modern setting of work. Poetry now is a pragmatic personal urgency, an aid to getting by in a social setting which, for Frost (in this he is representative of the modern American writer), doesn't make getting by very easy. Frost's implied comparative and his explicit superlative in "Mowing" condense a complex story of literary and social history: dreams sweet and sweeter, the dreams of Marvell, Wordsworth, and Yeats – the easy poetic gold of idleness – yield to dreams sweetest. Sweetest dream – the best dream of all – is a form of laboring consciousness, somehow and oddly identical with "fact" – what is presumably raw, informational, objectively there. But "fact," in that ordinary sense, is turned by this poet into an extraordinary thing; this constricted laborer just happens (an American happening) to be schooled in Latin etymologies of English ordinariness. *Factum:* a thing done, or produced, a matter revealed by and for a laboring consciousness, for no end beyond the momentary refreshment of its own act. *Factum:* a feat, a kind of performance, a display of prowess, the virtuosity, the poetry of work, but also (how could aesthetic contemplation be otherwise for a practical American male?) a kind of crime, as in an accessory after the fact.

When the poet who worked working-class jobs as a teenager and farmed and taught as an adult took his family to England in September 1912, he was virtually unknown, verging on forty, but willing to gamble his modest resources on one last effort to achieve a literary breakthrough — so that he might farm and teach no more. In short order, he made his way into the London literary scene; published his first two books there to excellent notices; impressed many writers, including William Butler Yeats; and came to the attention of Ezra Pound, tireless and superbly effective entrepreneur of the modern, who touted him, perhaps no more usefully than in a review of *A Boy's Will* in *Poetry,* Harriet Monroe's new but immediately influential little magazine. Two and a half years later, in February 1915, Robert Frost returned home to find himself on the eve of his American fame.

Whatever pleasure Pound's review must have given was more than matched by the political anxiety it caused. Pound said that Frost had been ignored by the "great American editors," who had also ignored, not incidentally, many new-wave poets (for example, Ezra Pound). Better to seek out English publishers, as Frost had, whose sensibilities were not yet fatally shaped by the new symbiosis of conventional taste and mass-market lust, and who had somehow found a way to balance economic necessity with the love of good letters. Frost wrote to his friend John Bartlett that he objected "chiefly to what [Pound said] about the great American editors. Not that I have any love for the two or three he has in mind. But they are better ignored — at any rate they are better not offended. We may want to use them some time."

On the eve of his American fame, Frost knew who he was and knew what he must do. Although he was writing against the grain of prevailing genteel standards, he believed (correctly, it turned out) that he did not require the little magazines to see the light of literary day because his style was not shockingly new — it never called openly for a coterie of specially armed readers. His sharpest effects were easily as subtle as they were unsettling, but his verbal surfaces were accessible, even kindly. Maybe he could bore subversively from within while doing what countless avant-garde writers could not do: make a living from his writing. But until those anglophilic American editors learned of his English triumphs, he would not be acceptable to them, and he would not make a living from his writing. "The thought that gets me," he told Bartlett in another letter, "is that at magazine rates," he meant commercial magazines, "there is about a thousand dollars worth of poetry in [*North of Boston*] that I might have had last winter if the people who love me now had loved me then. Never you doubt that I gave them the chance to love me."

What made the great American editors change their minds? Frost raised that question to Bartlett in the same letter, confessed he didn't have the answer, though he had his suspicions: "Doubtless you saw my countenance displayed in The [Boston] Herald one day. The Transcript will [do] me next. The literary editor of The Chicago Post writes to say that I may look for two columns of loving kindness in The Post in a day or two. It is not just naught — say what you will. One likes best to write poetry and one knew that he did . . . before one got even one reputation. Still one can't pretend not to like to win the game. One can't help thinking a little of Number One. . . . I need money as I suspect you may yourself."

After he came back from England, and with driven application to the end of his life, Frost played to win. With the possible exceptions of Ernest Hemingway and Norman Mailer, no important American writer in the twentieth century promoted himself more successfully to wider celebrity. After Henry Holt brought out the American editions of his first two volumes within weeks of his return, Frost's career took off. From 1916 to 1963, the year of his death, almost no year passed without the conferring upon him of some major honor: here and abroad, more than forty honorary degrees; four Pulitzers and one Bollingen Prize; a slew of gold medals for literary achievement from various colleges, universities, and civic organizations; the prestigious Norton professorship in poetry at Harvard; and, toward the end, like the giants of nineteenth-century American literature whom he admired and whose cultural force he coveted, he acquired political recognition and function as a literary ambassador, first for Dwight D. Eisenhower and then for John F. Kennedy (who was once photographed reading one of Frost's volumes). And any one who saw it will never forget the conferring of his greatest honor, which coincided with his greatest performance before an audience of many millions who watched it on television. With a mean January wind blowing through the fabulous thatched white hair of America's poet, and a harsh sun-glare making it impossible for him to read what he had written for Kennedy's inaugural, he righted himself like a great actor avoiding disaster without missing a beat and recited "The Gift Outright," from memory.

In his last years Frost's poetry sold in numbers that not even the combined sales of his powerful modernist company could match. Joyce, Pound, Eliot, and Stevens have their fame, but it is pretty strictly enclosed in the small pond of other writers, critics, and our sometimes reluctant students. Just a few months after his first book appeared, Frost, writing from England, told Bartlett that he would never be satisfied with the snobby pleasures of avant-garde renown, "success," as he put it, "with the critical few who are supposed to know," because "really to arrive where I can stand on my legs as a poet and nothing else I must get outside that circle to the general reader who buys books in their thousands." To the delight of their publishers and inheritors, Frost and the other famous names of modernism now sell "books in their thousands," but Frost did it while he was alive, and he did it long before he and the others became fixtures in the captive market of the university curriculum in English and American literature.

In the same letter to Bartlett, he said he wanted "to reach out, and would if it were a thing I could do by taking thought." In 1913, Frost was apparently something of an idealist. He wanted to get to a mass audience, but only on his own terms: by thinking, by writing poems, by being appreciated for what he was. His instincts were democratic; he believed that the people could "know," that the "critical few who are supposed to know" probably don't. After he returned to America, he must have come to the realization that in this culture, in this time, to stand on your feet as a poet and *nothing else* is a hope of utopian order. If he wanted to reach those who buy books in their thousands, he would need to do more than toil away in his writer's room. In 1915, he found himself on the eve of his American fame; in his later years, he found himself about as famous as a serious poet can ever hope to be; in between – and now the passive voice must be dropped because it obscures the truth – he spared no effort to bring his fame to its high noon, as he became his fame's shrewdest agent.

Getting one's picture in major dailies in Boston and Chicago wasn't just nothing if one needed money. Frost was never innocent about the power of the press, but until he returned to the United States with two books under his belt and a budding reputation he was in no position to seize the engines of publicity. But then seize them he did: alongside his career in poetry-making, he forged a complementary career in fame by granting in the neighborhood of one hundred interviews, including one to television's Sunday must of the '50s and '60s, "Meet the Press"; by frequenting, and working – really working – writers' conferences, including the prestigious one held at Breadloaf, Vermont, for which Frost played, year in and year out, the role of genius in residence; and, most of all, by mastering the poetry business, the reading circuit for which he performed (that is the word) brilliantly and indefatigably. In a prejet age, he spent on the average of three to four months per year on the road, doing readings and riding on trains to and from engagements all over the country. In other words, he learned quickly that although he couldn't, in the strict sense, stand on his feet as a poet and nothing else, in a looser sense he could do so by selling himself and his poems as the complete product. He learned that his poems sold better as he sold Robert Frost, famous American poet who, far from scorning average people, as Pound and his avant-garde friends were doing, actually spoke to them, or at the least dearly loved to give the impression of doing so.

In 1921 fame brought Frost to the university as writer-in-residence, only the second in America to hold such a position: an industry-inaugurating moment at the University of Michigan, his legacy to serious American writers who couldn't make a living by writing alone. His appointments at Michigan and, later, on and off, at Amherst and Dartmouth, contributed heavily to the livelihood set up by the sales of his books of poems and by his fees on the reading circuit. In a country without patronage, it was the American way: "I've never had to write a word of thanks to anybody I had a cent from," he boasted to the *Paris Review*. "The colleges came between."

According to the myth of artistic authenticity conceived and disseminated relentlessly by writers, artists, and critics since the late eighteenth century, real writers are supposed to be alienated, difficult in person and style, and expected to take a stand as their cultures' most withering critics. They are supposed to be all these things because they come to us (they tell us) bearing alternative values. Frost, instead, put himself on constant public display as the people's poet, the antithesis to all avant-garde ideals of the writer. In an interview published in the *New York Times Book Review* on the occasion of the publication of *New Hampshire,* the volume that won him his first Pulitzer prize, he said that inspiration "lies in the clean and wholesome life of the ordinary man." "Men have told me, and perhaps they are right, that I have no 'straddle.' . . . That means that I cannot spread out far enough to lie in filth and write in the treetops. I can't. Perhaps it is because I am so ordinary." In another interview, he said that a "poet should not include in his writing anything that the average reader will not easily understand." The shocking word is "easily." No doubt that's why Frost chose it – as the signal of his democratic nativism, the mark of a poet who not only didn't write according to the norms of the avant-garde (so full of contempt for the bourgeoisie), but who would so define and proudly advertise himself as ordinary to those who might buy books in the thousands, if only they could be confident that those books would speak to *them,* coming from one of their own. If we try to imagine Pound or Joyce saying the things that Frost said about being wholesome and ordinary, much less performing publicly as Frost did, according to such dictates, we shall come quickly to Frost's difference from high modernist company.

Frost succeeded so well in selling his greatest poem, his self-creation as Mr. Ordinary – kindly, wise, and readable – that, after his death, when Lawrence Thompson's three-volume tell-everything biography appeared, revealing him to be Mr. Ordinary in some unkindly ways, an overreaction set in that was surprising only for its orgy of self-righteousness. (Frost was a "monster," said one reviewer; "a more hateful human being can not have lived," said another.) But his greatest feat of self-creation and promotion lay in his ambidextrous ability to pass himself off as cracker-barrel Rob, all the while dramatizing himself as The Only Genuine Robert Frost in Captivity, in Randall Jarrell's phrase, America's poet, but a poet nevertheless, precisely the figure that modern America had difficulty in recognizing as anything but an outsider in the culture, at best a triviality. Frost told us openly, in countless ways, that he was ordinary and not to be feared. He also told us, in countless covert ways – by standing before us in public, for example, a famous man – that he was different from us, that we should love and venerate him for his difference and fear and envy him a little for having what the ordinary don't have (its absence being the definition of democratic ordinariness): charismatic power.

If the freshness of Frost's manner in a few of his earliest poems lay in his creation of a lyricism indigenous to (and jostling with) the vernacular voice of an ordinary man engaged in ordinary tasks (so it goes in Frostean theater), and whose extraordinary flirtations with literary history are submerged, not flourished in poetic self-consciousness; if the poetry of "Mowing" would thereby sponsor the sprezzatura of an American democrat (and college dropout) who only incidentally happened to be a poet, then we have to say it is a poetry not much in evidence in *A Boy's Will*. Frost's first book was heavily marked by the tone of the fin-de-siècle – the ambience of un-anchored grief, the moodiness of autumnal sorrows (the youth of the poet notwithstanding); here and there by an unaffected plainness of song lyric; and, more than here and there, by a style whose diction and syntax refer us not to the writer who draws his power from the unassuming, but to one too much in love with books of elevated, antique voice, from which he picks up words and phrases whose origin is not living speech but the graveyard of bookish eloquence: "o'er," "e'er," "wend," "vainly," "tremulous," "zephyr," "whither," "thine," "thou," "misty fen," and (the Tennysonian theft) "in airy dalliance." The paradox of "Waiting: Afield at Dusk," a characteristic performance in *A Boy's Will*, is that it was written by someone with the right sort of disruptive aesthetic for his time (his desire to freshen Palgrave's *Golden Treasury:* "the worn book of old-golden song," as he calls it), but whose own voice is still indentured to his memories of earlier poets; who is willing to give away his poem's opening words to *A Midsummer Night's Dream* ("What things for dream there are . . ."), and then its closing lines to an imitation of the Shakespeare of the sonnets: "But on the memory of one absent, most, / For whom these lines when they shall greet her eye."

Set in the context of the main drift of his early practice and the banal lyric norms of the early century, *North of Boston* is radical stuff. With a couple of splendid exceptions ("After Apple-Picking" being one of them), most of the poems in Frost's second book are mid-size narratives, carried mainly by dialogue seemingly gathered without mediation (this is their subtlest art) directly from the lives of the suffering rural poor, whose only psychic leavening occurs in moments of lyric burst that come as if from out of nowhere, their discontinuity with the narrative flow of depressed rural existence being perhaps their ultimate point: as if Frost's sudden jump from storytelling and dialogue into lyricism were the literary sign of lives that could not support and sustain lyric imagination and therefore had to snatch it desperately when its time came, at the least excuse.

What Frost sees in New England's rural poor are images of the poet-laborer he had debuted in "Mowing": figures of himself. *North of Boston* is the objectification, in a series of little dramas and stories, of the central (econo-aesthetic) issue of Frost's early life and poetry. In "The Death of the Hired Man," "The Mountain," "The Black Cottage," "A Servant to Servants," and "The Housekeeper," the rare but shrewdly placed lyric passage often stops domestic working time and redeems for a brief space lives that are by turns lonely and boring and horrifying and dull; relationships that bespeak little relating; tales of the coldness in the heart, stupefying routine, sexual betrayal, and madness. Far from banishing his lyric impulses to the margins, *North of Boston* places them at the psychological center, where they function as release mechanisms for freedom, however constricted, however brief.

The radically realist aesthetic that drives the writing of *North of*

*Boston* is on uncompromising display in "A Servant to Servants" (a monologue) and "The Housekeeper" (mainly a monologue), two plotless narratives that resist summary, come to no epiphany, yield no detachable wisdom. In these poems what is put on display is voice itself, too long pent up. Frost's craft encourages us to imagine life before these poems begin, to imagine it as a time of long, female silence. These poems begin as a sudden breaking of silence, with vocal energy released in a torrent of plain speaking – reflective, anecdotal, lyrical, mercilessly self-descriptive – to a stranger who happens by into the lives of two house-keeping and house-bound women, a stranger who gives audience to these two talking writers, the housekeeper in the poem of that title literally house-bound, who tells us she's so fat that they won't be able to get her through the door: "I've been built in here like a big church organ." These women talk as if the sole point of talking were to produce more talk. What they know, without ever quite knowing it, is that narrative shapeliness and closure, perfectly concatenated beginnings, middles, and ends, only hasten the death of talk and a spirit grimly hanging on; a thousand and one nights, New England country style.

If Frost has a point, it is to say: Behold, these too exist, they suffer, and there is nothing you or I can do about it. This is the way it is *North of Boston,* a title he said was inspired by the real-estate section of the classifieds. The success of his radical realism in *North of Boston* depends for its strongest impact on our hearing his volume as a whole as a rebuke; as a book with a critical agenda, set slyly into literary history and pitched, with great deviousness, to readers of urban sophistication; a sharply sardonic commentary on conventions of sentiment concerning the supposed simplicities and therapies of the pastoral life.

Nothing in either volume, but the change itself from *A Boy's Will* to *North of Boston* suggests a portrait of the writer in the act of finding his true material and medium (Frost's art makes it difficult to make the distinction), now practicing his craft confidently, no longer looking over his shoulder at those who came before. In fact, though, a new kind of self-consciousness stirs embryonically in *North of Boston,* born in literary obscurity and economic need, in imagination of the fame and consequent cultural authority that might come to be his, and we experience this form of self-consciousness as the sound of a voice: this time a sophisticated poet's voice taking pleasure in its own writerly presence, the poet once again looking over his shoulder, now in order to observe, with pleasure, the act of his writing in the act of doing it. In such moments of self-observation he creates the image of the writer he wanted to be and the major subject and style of what he wrote and became after *North of Boston.* The image of Robert Frost, famous American poet, is the source and authentic substance of much that is very good and very bad in the poems of Robert Frost, famous American poet. Frost inaugurates an early but rigorously postmodern phase in the history of American literature, preceded by similar efforts in image-retailing made by Whitman and Twain.

This poet who imagines his emergence into fame can be heard even in *North of Boston,* as if he were always lurking in Frost's heart, in what will become one of his best-known poems, "Mending Wall," which Frost placed as the lead-off, misleading tone-setter of *North of Boston.* Here, desire for the therapy of conversation becomes just another poetic subject. The playful narrator, all self-possession and aplomb, addresses himself to an audience focused on the delightful peregrinations of his voice, not on his dramatic situation; on the narrator as a poet, not on the narrator as a character with a crippling problem, a poet who talks to us about conversation, a topic among other topics, how he'd rather his stolid neighbor wouldn't introduce the conversation-killing proverb into a discussion that he'd like to get rolling. "Mending Wall" is laced with jokes and puns, all shared with us, all at the expense of that Johnny-one-note who is deaf to Frost's deft play. The poem's secret subject is the bond that a writer

would like to forge with his audience; the writer-speaker's true need
is to perform successful literary seduction on his possible public. He
tells us between the lines that we're no blockheads; we've been
honored by his confidence. He assumes, so generously, that we get
his game. This wily rhetorical note – it's the presiding tonality of
"Mending Wall" – is one of the keynotes of Frost's later career, and it
sounds prophetically, in the properly placed lead-off poem of his
third volume, *Mountain Interval*, "The Road Not Taken," whose
deepest subject is the sentimental American fiction of self-making
that the speaker imagines pitching (that is the word) to a gullible
audience sometime in the future. This gullible audience, which will
need to hear it, will also need to be distinguished from those who
get his poem's quietly unnerving point, those honored by his rhetorical embrace as elect readers. But this distinction between audiences
in fact can be made only *by* the elect – here is the brilliant deviousness of Frost's rhetoric; because in making the distinction they prove
themselves *to be* the elect. So do the self-defined elect, with Frost's
subtle prodding, separate themselves from the American masses who
must get him wrong, who must read him sentimentally, and who
must make him famous.

In the persistent, ever-renewed moment of self-creation (its power
will shape his future), the modernist writer typically defines himself
against the standards of mass-market literary expression as the
champion of radical originality and the maker of a literary text that's
a one-of-a-kind phenomenon (in other words, no "kind" at all). This
severe ideal of modernist aesthetic demands constant experimentation, the creation of writing forever refreshed and refreshing (to
writer and reader both, like an injection of radical individualism),
never repeating itself. Frost and T. S. Eliot are the modernists who,
only partially against their wills, made themselves into deluxe commodities, poets whose poems are unreadable unless we grasp their

true subject: the poet in the act of talking, *as a poet,* to audiences not assumed to be hospitable. *Four Quartets* cannot have its strongest impact unless we accept it as the meditation of the world's most famous man of letters, reviewing his journey to date and taking further steps in the private spiritual adventure which, by the time of *Quartets,* was, thanks to Eliot's efforts, a public text. The modernist desire in Frost and Eliot – to preserve an independent selfhood against the coercions of the market, a self made and secured by the creation of a unique style – is subverted by the logic of the market, not because they wrote according to popular formulas, but because they give us their poems as delicious experiences of voyeurism, illusions of direct access to the life and thought of the famous writer, with the poet inside the poem like a rare animal in a zoo. This was the only commodity Frost and Eliot were capable of producing: the modernist phenomenon as product, mass culture's ultimate revenge on those who would scorn it.

But in spite of his contempt for the self-conscious avant-garde and his will to self-commodification, the poetry Frost made from *Mountain Interval* onward is more varied in tone and style than any of the poetries made by the canonical modernists whom he is not supposed to resemble, Ezra Pound perhaps excepted. The later poetry of Frost is riddled with the warmly humorous sayings of cracker-barrel Rob: rambling pontifications on the world that we are to imagine as spoken from deep in the heart of Yankeedom, pleasing takes on country matters, poems concluding so many times with proverb-like turns, epigrams, the wise insights of the bard ("trust my instincts – I'm a bard") – all those vaguely optimistic lines we're supposed to remember, write down, refer to when the going gets tough. This public poetry of uplift connects Frost firmly to those Fireside poets who played cultural minister to America's nineteenth century and whose rhetorical role was inherited and restaged in different ways by Frost and Eliot: a vein of writing particularly rich in Frost after *Mountain Interval;* the kind of writing for which he is best known, best loved, and best depreciated by champions of the high modern.

And this new Fireside poet did not hesitate to reach for the dead metaphor, not in order to refresh it but in order to foreground it: "It's when I'm weary of considerations/And life is too much like a pathless wood." That's from "Birches," a *Mountain Interval* poem about the one-on-a-side-sport called poetry, a celebration of the wholesome, self-reliant background of the country-bred poet, too far from town to learn baseball as a boy, a team sport that the real Robert Frost learned and loved early and late – he was commissioned by *Sports Illustrated* to write on the 1956 All-Star game. But baseball is here put down in favor of birch-riding, a game of invention one plays alone.

The mythical Robert Frost who never played baseball gives us, in "Birches," the oft-quoted "Earth's the right place for love," an unanswerable, moralizing line followed by this answer: the not often quoted, "I don't know where it's likely to go better" (a chuckle-stimulator from the bard, until we think about it twice and feel the total and delightful nastiness of Frost's humor). The mythical Robert Frost in "Hyla Brook" gives us a last (you must remember this) line of ethical nobility, phrased with vernacular elegance: "We love the things we love for what they are." But "Hyla Brook" is an even cagier *Mountain Interval* poem about poetry whose easily detachable last line (*what* "things?") will seem calculated to make happy those readers who desire Fireside comforts. In the concluding, pithy didactic moments of his writing, Frost gains entry to that traditional kind of audience, to the dismay of those who want their modern writers obscure and antididactic. But, in context, the line "We love the things we love for what they are" makes virtually no sense because its referent is a brook that exists only as a series of rapidly turned figures, a dried up non-brook that lives only in imaginative metamorphosis, in the guise of poetic "things," including one, most unvernacular poetic "thing": "Like ghost of sleigh bells in a ghost of snow." So the traditional figure with which Frost opens "Hyla Brook" ("By June our brook's run out of song and speed") is transformed into an unthinglike "thing" hard to see unless we can dance with Frost through styles of figurative remembrance, in high literary and vernacular alternation. The detachable wisdom of the last line of "Hyla Brook" does not come cheaply and is not really detachable from its context. It is a rarified literary joke that depends on an occulted allusion to Tennyson. But Robert Frost, famous American poet, always encouraged us to think him easy and made a living from a readership he schooled to think him easy.

Alongside such self-consciously literary performances in *Mountain Interval* the stark manner of *North of Boston* persists in "An Old Man's Winter Night," a portrait of encroaching physical and mental decrepitude, ruthlessly detailed, in lines in which the horrifying repetition of a simple verb extinguishes the human difference. Here is a poetry of unrelievable depression that makes a mockery of Frost's better-known poems of uplift: "The log that shifted with a jolt/Once in the stove, disturbed him and he shifted." In the even less varnished, "Out, Out, — " whose title is a quotation from Macbeth's despairing last soliloquy, Shakespeare is brought down from heroic altitude to the grinding rural level and its routine tragedies. Frost tells a story about a boy who loses his hand to an electric saw when he's distracted by the call to supper. At the awful moment of severance, Frost turns his usual benign whimsy to the work of gruesome humor: The saw "Leaped out at the boy's hand" as if to demonstrate that "saws knew what supper meant." At the end of the poem, which coincides with the boy's unexpected but not much grieved death, Frost turns harshly self-conscious in order to say something about local-color writing, something about how to end poems that depend for life on local incident, as if to reflect on the sawlike nature of his own art of feeding off unheralded catastrophe (anything for a poem); this from a poet renowned for his warmth and "old saws." Like those relatives of the boy who carry on with their affairs, he, too, must move on, find new matter for poetry: "No more to build on there."

With a few strong exceptions ("The Witch of Coos," "The Subverted Flower"), the vein of harsh narrative writing pretty much peters out, as Frost proceeds through his long years of acclaim. More and more, the poet who had played hard for, and had been granted, cultural centrality takes over and begins to speak. His own cultural authority becomes the grounding assumption of his speaking, the reason why we listen. One of the dominant tones struck in his later career, beginning in his fourth volume, *New Hampshire* (1923), with "Fire and Ice" and continuing through later volumes – in "Spring Pools," "Once By the Pacific," and "Sand Dunes" – is the tone of bardic apocalypticism: the prophetic voice of decisive upheaval telling us that fearful change is at hand, but which upon closer analysis rather unbards itself by being unable to specify the causes of apocalypse. In these poems, fear floats free of its objects, becoming all the more fearful for its vagueness, and more fearful still when we consider that its vocal vehicle is exactly the sort of poet who is supposed to have himself well in hand. How else shall he be capable of consoling us in our hour of crisis? How else shall we know him as a bard, a famous man, an authority, not one of us? For what other reason would we bother to listen? What could be more unsettling than an insecure bard? And it doesn't help, not at all, in fact it hurts, to remember that the last instance of the poetry of reason undone, "The Draft Horse" – Frost doing Kafka – occurs in a volume, Frost's last, called *In the Clearing* (1962).

Often, the later Frost is a poet who writes as if he were running out of energy, looking back to his earlier work in order to mine in cold blood materials that once gave off an existential glow (whether they had actually been lived through is beside the point). The poetry of work, so richly done in "Mowing," becomes in "Two Tramps in Mud-Time" an exercise for the purpose of making the utopian point that it's better when work and play are the same activity (and when you're a famous writer, they are). Sometimes this famous Frost seems to need to measure his prowess against Eliot, as in the awesome "Directive" (*Steeple Bush*, 1947), which gathers up elements in the poetic landscape he had been fashioning since *A Boy's Will*, as if to rewrite, in a single sweeping and triumphant gesture, both *The Waste Land* and *Four Quartets:* as if he were saying he could do it better than Eliot had – more economically, more accessibly – and with a lightness of touch beyond Eliot's ken. "Drink and be whole again beyond confusion," directs the bard in the wicked last line, after having told us that the drinking goblet he's hidden is broken (the goblet, like the Grail, hidden in a native chapel perilous, a ruined farmhouse in an America gone urban). With that gesture, Frost plays a joke on his mythic projection as the speaker of maxims, and on anyone not used to reading him with close slowness of attention, any reader who takes Frost in once only, for the bardic impression, as if Frost were speaking to him from the platform like a media phenom.

And it is that sort of passive auditor of Frost the famous writer, precisely the sort of reader he cultivated in the press and from the platform, who will be unequipped to take in one of the most sustained and varied stretches of virtuosity in American poetry, some eight or nine poems in *A Witness Tree* that share nothing but independent brilliance, as they survey the prime topoi of modernist concern: the linguistic self-sufficiency of a love poem sustained by a single, generative conceit ("The Silken Tent"); the vicious narrative of repressed sexuality ("The Subverted Flower"); myths of origin, political, religious, and aesthetic ("The Gift Outright," "Never Again Would Birds' Song Be the Same"); the epistemological priority of subjective consciousness, and the toying with such heaviness ("All Revelation," "Come In"); and the modern poet's anxious relationship to literary history ("Carpe Diem"), rendered with an ease that bespeaks little, perhaps no, anxiety.

*A Boy's Will* in 1913, *North of Boston* in 1914, *Mountain Interval,* his first American volume, in 1916: an illusion of creative renaissance.

All of the first two and much of the third volume had in fact been written in obscurity, over the twenty-year period before he left for England. Once back home, the obligations of an emerging and seductive fame consumed him. At a time when he could have published virtually anything, anywhere he wanted, he had little to give: from 1917 through 1920, only four of his poems appeared in periodicals; his fourth volume, *New Hampshire,* came out seven years after *Mountain Interval.* In its title poem, which is also its lead-off poem, the man who had been working the circuit hard – fashioning and plying the image of himself, to the point of distraction – transmutes his labors in the disciplines of fame into poetic substance. The famous poet steps forward in full dress.

The center of interest in "New Hampshire" is a speaker who identifies himself as a writer, showing us his mind and manner (and manners) in the act of turning over Subjects of Importance, from a site of speaking, rural New England, presumed to give him a unique point of view. The binding rhetorical contract that Frost makes with his readers in the poem will guarantee that the speaker is special because he is organically connected, the authentic voice of a place whose values are different. And that difference gives the voice authority of judgment because the difference is one of superior values. And we listen because we are not where Frost is, because we are living lives we wish would be shaped by the values that shape him and his place. The contract presumes an insider and an underprivileged outsider. If we listen attentively, Frost promises to ease our deprivation. The local-color aesthetic is at the same time an ethic, and in "New Hampshire," Robert Frost – a new and important force in the literary scene – offers himself as representative and incarnation of it. To read him is to partake of him (like partaking of communion) and all he stands for.

The poem itself is all cunningly controlled ramble, full of pleasant, funny, and very chummy stretches, carried in a voice of colloquial and anecdotal style: "I met a lady from the South who said . . ."; "I met a traveler from Arkansas/Who boasted . . .":

## Robert Frost

I met a Californian who would
Talk California — a state so blessed,
He said, in climate, none had ever died there
A natural death, and Vigilance Committees
Had had to organize the graveyards
And vindicate the state's humanity.

The point of these anecdotes is that everyone, except those who live in New Hampshire, is in the market selling or buying, and that the market is unavoidable — except, of course, in New Hampshire. Poets sell ideas; Californians, their climate. If modernist poets want to define themselves against the market, then New Hampshire, which doesn't have enough of anything to sell, is their unexpected land of heart's desire, not London or Paris (take heed, ye high modernists). The search for the sometimes guilty pleasures of the aesthetic — pleasure for its own sake — which preoccupied Frost early and late, from "Mowing" to "Two Tramps in Mud-Time" (and beyond), is here in "New Hampshire" a theme, a vantage point, a seat of judgment, that which gives structure to the rambling voice.

Having hooked us with the genial comedy of his opening sections, the poet quickly expands his aesthetic criticism of America, sparing neither New Hampshire or himself. He offers us a mythic history of the founding whites of New Hampshire as a tale of primal imperialism. An unnamed reformer, who would reform the world in order to make it hospitable for artists, sounds suspiciously like Frost, taking a page from Pound's text while reflecting upon his recent rise in literary and economic fortune, splashing bitters into his genial style. Where was the attention when I needed it most? We need a world reformed so as to be acceptable to artists, "the minute they set up as artists,/Before, that is, they are themselves accepted. . . ."

The poet who embodies the good way feels compromised. New Hampshire produces nothing in serious quantity and quality to have to worry the producers about disposing of the surplus — except for writing itself. The poet reveals himself a reluctant merchant, more assiduously businesslike than the genuine article:

> Do you know,
> Considering the market, there are more
> Poems produced than any other thing?
> No wonder poets sometimes have to *seem*
> So much more businesslike than businessmen.
> Their wares are so much harder to get rid of.

At the end, having declared himself to be — and having performed as — a "creature of literature" rather than of any region, Frost concludes with these self-ironic lines, which pretty much invalidate the terms of the contract he's made with us:

> I choose to be a plain New Hampshire farmer
> With an income in cash of, say, a thousand
> (From, say, a publisher in New York City) . . .
> At present I am living in Vermont.

The games Frost plays with his readers in "New Hampshire" are unsettling but benign (more or less: perhaps less than more; it's hard to tell). Later poems tell a different story. Who, for example, is Frost imagining as his ideal reader in "Neither Out Far Nor In Deep?" Not those referred to, certainly, by the first two words in the poem, and then again referred to in the third quatrain, not "the people." Not those who all "along the sand" will "look at the sea all day," and whose act of looking in this plain-styled allegory (not a word here that couldn't "easily" be grasped by "the people"), whose ability to know anything, including themselves, is coldly evaluated by Frost's title and by his fourth and final quatrain:

> They cannot look out far.
> They cannot look in deep.
> But when was that ever a bar
> To any watch they keep?

Lines to remember, wisdom spit forth (but for whom?) about "the people." Has anyone ever pronounced "they" with more deadpanned contempt? "We" who are implicitly addressed, "we" truly understand, "we" are not "they." But wasn't it precisely "they," not "we" (the "critical few who are supposed to know") whom this ordinary American, who happened to be a poet, was courting all along, who made him famous?

"Neither Out Far Nor In Deep" occurs in *A Further Range* (1936), a volume blasted by several reviewers, including one of America's best close-reading critics, the high priest of modernist complexity, R. P. Blackmur. The same volume contains "Provide, Provide" (among other strong performances), separated by only a few pages from "Neither Out Far Nor In Deep" (Blackmur noticed neither), this one addressed, seemingly, to "the people," a lacerating analysis of fame's basis and likely course:

> The witch that came (the withered hag)
> To wash the steps with pail and rag
> Was once the beauty Abishag,
>
> The picture pride of Hollywood.
> Too many fall from great and good
> For you to doubt the likelihood.
>
> Die early and avoid the fate.
> Or if predestined to die late
> Make up your mind to die in state.
>
> Make the whole stock exchange your own!
> If need be occupy a throne,
> Where nobody can call *you* crone.
>
> Some have relied on what they knew,
> Others on being simply true.
> What worked for them might work for you.

No memory of having starred
Atones for later disregard
Or keeps the end from being hard.

Better to go down dignified
With boughten friendship at your side
Than none at all. Provide, provide!

The entire tone and manner is that of the public poet speaking to his democratic culture. The diction is appropriately drawn from the accessible middle level, with the exception of "boughten," a regionalist trace of the authentic life, meaning "store-bought" as opposed to "homemade," the real thing as opposed to the commodified version; no major problem if the subject is ice cream or bread, but with "boughten friendship" we step into an ugly world. The bardic voice speaks, but now in mock-directives ("Die early and avoid the fate," "Make the whole stock exchange your own"), counseling the value of money and power; how they command fear; how fear commands, at a minimum, a sham of decency from others (better that than the authenticity of their meanness). Genuine knowledge? Sincerity? Devices only in the Hollywood of everyday life. Try them, they might "work."

But who, really, is Frost talking to? Who is this "you"? He appears to be addressing the audience he had been reaching (for twenty years at this point) through the press and from the platform: "For you to doubt the likelihood" is a bardic reminder to the masses. "What worked for them might work for you" is cynical and contemptuous counsel offered to the same. The penultimate stanza, however, whose triplet rhyme condenses the entire poem, makes no sense in *that* rhetorical scheme:

No memory of having starred
Atones for later disregard
Or keeps the end from being hard.

Who among the ordinary, the unassuming, the obscure from fame, has any memory of having starred, of having lost it, of having to find a way to make up for later disregard? From a rhetorical point of view, the poem becomes incoherent here, but the incoherence is interesting and, I believe, calculated: an expressive sign. We know who has this problem: Hollywood's poet, talking contemptuously to and at himself, looking down the road at a possible fate that he would not be able to say he hadn't chosen, were it to turn out to be his — because he had made the decision to commit himself to fame's course, within the cruel range of choices our culture offers to its serious writers, whose wares are so hard to unload. America's serious writers are all like the biblical Abishag, who, though young and beautiful, could not warm King David: she could not arouse him, and her trying only degraded her.

# 4

## WALLACE STEVENS

I N BETWEEN HIS TIME at Harvard University (1897–1900), when he published frequently in undergraduate magazines, and his move to Hartford, Connecticut, in 1916, when he was beginning to appear with regularity in the newly emerging little magazines of avant-garde writing, Wallace Stevens led a double life in New York City, with the lion's share of his waking hours spent trying (and failing) to earn a wage good enough to enable him to resume the comfortable upper-middle-class style he had been accustomed to in Reading, Pennsylvania, where he grew up, and in Cambridge, where he was supported by his father's faithful checks. In the late hours of evening during his New York years he read and occasionally wrote verses. On weekends he became the part-time exemplar of Teddy Roosevelt's ideal of the "strenuous life," taking marathon walks in the country of twenty to thirty miles.

In the period between Harvard and his appearances in the little magazines fell his courtship of Elsie Moll. It went on for about five years, because Stevens was not about to be married until he felt himself economically secure as his father had defined economic security for him. Part of his courting of Elsie Moll involved sharing with her his passion for poetry. In a letter written to her about a year and a half before the appearance of "Sunday Morning," his famous early poem, and with a deceptively light tone, Stevens touched upon an issue central to the course of modernism in the United States:

I sit at home o'nights. But I read very little. I have, in fact, been trying to get together a little collection of verses again; and although they are simple to read, when they're done, it's a deuce of a job (for me) to do them. Keep all this a great secret. There is something absurd about all this writing of verses; but the truth is, it elates and satisfies me to do it. It is an all-round exercise quite superior to ordinary reading. So that, you see, my habits are positively lady-like.

Stevens's designation of verse writing as "positively lady-like" ("lady-like" feminizes in the direction of the leisured class: he is not talking about working women) will make no sense to the reader whose understanding of the history of poetry tends to be limited to the major figures. The most powerful poetic presences of Stevens's young manhood were Keats and Tennyson on the English side and the Fireside poets (males all) on ours. Moreover, when he wrote to Elsie of his ladylike activity, Whitman had at last won acceptance. The curious thing about Stevens's letter is that without even a gesture of argument the heavy fact of male literary authority is simply set aside. The facts do not count in his case, he implies, because something other than the leisured (classically schooled) male privilege of English literary history is at work in his life. Verse writing is for me, Stevens suggests, a thing for ladies. American males have to be practical.

But there were other poetic forces in Stevens's young manhood, and their gender complicates his male literary inheritance and begins to make some sense of the sexual and literary self-deprecation that he voiced to Elsie. Those poets who have not survived in the canon of American poetry — those ever-mournful, ever-self-renouncing, and, in the culture of Stevens, ever-present women (especially in newspapers) — define the poetic female as a special kind of American cultural agency, maybe even the agency of culture itself. So commonplace was this figure of the woman poet that Mark

Twain could count on his readers to recognize her in his collective send-up in the Emmeline Grangerford episode of *Huckleberry Finn*. ("She warn't particular, she could write about anything you choose to give her to write about, just so it was sadful. Every time a man died, or a woman died, or a child died, she would be on hand with her 'tribute' before he was cold. She called them tributes. The neighbors said it was the doctor first, then Emmeline, then the undertaker.") Emmeline Grangerford was a type of the poet that Stevens could not admire and yet (at some level) could not help but assume as a figure of himself, so pervasive was her cultural presence when he was beginning to think of a life as a poet.

So, in spite of the effort, which marks many of his letters to Elsie, to fend off issues of gender, vocation, and money with flippancy of tone, Stevens registers and unmasks, against his desire, what proved to be the unmasterable situation that he would prefer to submerge in "the gaiety of language," which is supposed to, but cannot, redeem his social *malheur*. His "absurd" habit of verse writing embodies this unavoidable contradiction of his culture: as it brings forth feelings of pleasure ("it elates and satisfies me to do it"), while engaging him in the sort of exertion synonymous with work ("a deuce of a job"), it triggers at the very moment of pleasure the negative judgment of his superego, because this job can bring no economic support, cannot earn the characterization "work" – hence is really no job at all. His "absurd" habit of verse writing forces upon him a feeling at odds with his maleness – the feeling of the sexual other within, in the mask of poetic culture: the lady poet. So when we ask, just who is this "me" made happy by verse writing, the implicit cultural logic of his letter to Elsie makes us answer that Stevens's "me" is in some fundamental sense a ladylike, economically unproductive "she."

Fifteen years earlier, Garrett Stevens, successful lawyer, small businessman, and poet himself (the first Wallace Stevens, as it were), had sent his son, then at Harvard, this letter. It haunted Wallace for the rest of his life:

## Wallace Stevens

Our young folk would of course prefer to be born like English noblemen with Entailed estates, income guaranteed and in choosing a profession they would simply say – "How shall I amuse myself" – but young America understands that the question is – *"Starting with nothing, how shall I sustain myself and perhaps a wife and family – and send my boys to College and live* comfortably in my old age." Young fellows must all come to that question, for unless they inherit money, marry money, find money, steal money or somebody presents it to them, they must *earn it* and earning it save it up for the time of need. How best can he earn a sufficiency! What talent does he possess which carefully nurtured will produce something which people want and therefore will pay for. This is the whole problem! and to Know Thyself!

A few years after he received this letter, while toiling unhappily in the competitive world of New York journalism, Stevens in fact requested guaranteed income from his father so that he might pursue another kind of career in writing, one which could not sustain himself, much less a wife, family, a college education for his sons, and a comfortable old age. His father refused. The son of Garrett Stevens had begun to understand, but apparently had not yet learned to live with, the primary lesson in American history that was to be his burden, as it was the burden of most of young America's males. His father was passing on the wisdom of Poor Richard and Horatio Alger that to be born an American is typically to be born without a sustaining economic past: to start with nothing, even if your father (like Garrett Stevens) has supported himself, a wife, and has sent his boys (not his daughters) to college, because such a father in achieving such accomplishments was likely to have exhausted most of what he had earned. What little he might leave would never be enough for his son to support himself, his wife, and so on. To be born an American is to be born into a situation where literary patronage virtually does not exist and where your father cannot be your patron. I have done it, Garrett Stevens was saying to his son, now prove your manhood by imitating me to the letter.

Stevens's move to New York in 1900 forced him to bear witness to the thinness of his middle-class insulation. Shortly after getting there, he entered into his journal a reflection on a Harvard graduate he had never met, but of whom he had heard much, one Philip Henry Savage. This journal entry echoes the Poor Richard letter his father had sent to him at Harvard, and it touches a new theme. This would-be ruggedly independent new American man would some-how, if he could, join his aesthetic sense, already heavily cultivated as a teenager and at Harvard, to what he was beginning to see as the unavoidable economic plot of his existence:

> Savage was like every other able-bodied man – he wanted to stand alone. Self-dependence is the greatest thing in the world for a young man & Savage knew it. I cannot talk about the subject, however, because I know too little about it. But for one thing, Savage went into the shoe business & still kept an eye on sunsets and red-winged blackbirds – the summum bonum.

Very soon, Stevens would know much more about the subject. His New York years (1900–16) quickly became an effort to achieve Savage's sort of balance between necessity and pleasure, work and art, because that sort of contradictory balance ("the summum bonum") was the very thing that his up-bringing as the son of Garrett Stevens taught him to desire. But the story of his New York years was mainly one of Stevens's failure to achieve the summum bonum, or of his success, if weekend aestheticism must suffice. The means of self-dependence were pursued Monday through Friday; things for themselves pursued and savored on Saturdays and Sun-days: "I doubt if there is any keener delight in the world than, after being penned up for a week, to get into the woods . . . every pound of flesh vibrates with new strength, every nerve seems to be drinking at some refreshing spring."

One way of mitigating this solution of the "weekend" – a therapeutic as well as a temporal concept in bourgeois life – and of joining his vocation with his avocation, or so it seemed to Stevens, lay in his first choice of career in journalism, a field he tried, with the assistance of his Harvard teacher Barrett Wendell, as soon as he got to New York. The guiding principle behind his choice seems to have been: Write all the time, write sometimes because you want to, and write when you must, for a living, but write. He quickly learned, however, that the monetary rewards of journalism were erratic, the writing assignments mainly a grind, and his future as a journalist just too chancy. All of which was brought sharply into focus for him in the depressing spectacle of the funeral of a fellow journalist, who also wrote fiction that he respected. Stevens found the affair "wretched"; hardly anyone went to the church. Those in attendance were obviously lower-class. A few literary types showed up, but in appearance it was impossible to distinguish them from the nonliterary and merely poor. Stephen Crane's funeral gave him a glimpse of a possible writerly future. He entered law school.

Three years later, in August 1904, about a month after being admitted to the New York bar, he brooded in his journal on the perilous comforts of middle-class life as he had known it. Theodore Dreiser couldn't have done it better. It is a meditative moment that marks the birth of Wallace Stevens as self-conscious economic man for whom the American dream was no longer an abstraction; Wallace Stevens – real-life brother of some of the most compelling figures in modern American fiction: Carrie Meeber and G. W. Hurstwood in *Sister Carrie*, Thomas Sutpen in *Absalom, Absalom!*, Jay Gatsby. What made Stevens different and maybe more typical – neither Dreiser nor Faulkner nor Fitzgerald would tell his story – was his sense that he had been expelled from Eden, that his particular form of the American dream involved the recapturing of a lost social and economic status that he had never earned but which he had nevertheless enjoyed, the resumption of a life that had fashioned the mode of his desire and had given him a taste of the good life. Suddenly he felt a shocking solidarity with the poor, who had hitherto only repulsed him in their filth and poverty (the sight of Italian immigrants had once made it impossible for him to finish a snack of clams on the half shell); he was coming to know a new sort of closeness with those who had hitherto made him feel faintly disgusted when they sat too near him on commuter trains.

At the age of twenty-five Stevens came to the existential knowledge of economic difference and the peculiar privilege of middle-class life in America. The Italian immigrants he saw in Greenwich Village, like the bums in the Bowery he observed on his walks through the city, might dream the dream of upward mobility: they could sink no lower economically. The fabulously wealthy of his time, legends even then – the Carnegies, Mellons, Rockefellers, the class Fitzgerald called, simply, "the very rich" – could pass out dimes in the streets if they liked (and they did). *Their* children, whatever spiritual descents they might experience, could look with impunity upon the poor: they would never be one of them. But Stevens, and those like him, knew better than to dream the dream of upward mobility. Passage into the realm of the Rockefellers was not realistic; a repetition of one's father's economic status was more likely, and it was clearly preferable over that other possibility which is the special privilege of the middle class: the possibility of economic descent. The dream of the middle class in America is the nightmare of downward mobility: Stevens's version of the nightmare concluded with an effort to resist it, with what in his writing is an almost never expressed impulse, the utopian urge toward classless society: "There was a time when I walked downtown in the morning almost oblivious of the thousands and thousands of people I passed; now I look at them with extraordinary interest as companions in the same fight that I am about to join."

For this middle-class professional, endowed with capitalist values through his father, in part against his literary desires, the inescapable question pressed upon him first by family and then by his New York experience was: How can I turn some part of myself (my "talent") into a commodity that people will want and "therefore pay for"? The choice of profession need not "amuse," it need not give pleasure, but (as Father said) it must pay. To Know Thyself, according to Garrett Stevens, is to know yourself as economic man, fit for the hurly-burly of the marketplace where the big boys slug it out. To Know Thyself for Garrett Stevens's son meant that in finding his productive talent he would prove his masculinity in general and prove it in particular as equal to his father's. But knowing himself also meant knowing that he derived pleasure from his verse-writing talent, and to know himself that way as a young man meant to know himself as the potential subverter of his official role as a young American male. Only leisured women and leisured men could do what he wanted to do. Modernist poetics in the United States began with the great problem of the bourgeois world: the antagonism between duty and happiness. Modernist poetics in the United States is sexually and economically framed (in both senses) from the beginning.

Garrett Stevens was by most standards an unsuccessful poet, and in the end his failure in business was so disastrous – he went bankrupt – that his son had no choice but to stand on his own. His son's life and career as poet and superb man of business were therefore at once an imitation and stunning transcendence of the father. A brilliant success in two areas (he rose to the vice presidency of a major insurance company), Stevens's bifurcated career was the perfect realization of the contradictory values of his society.

> Complacencies of the peignoir,
> And late coffee and oranges in a sunny chair
> And the green freedom of a cockatoo
> Upon a rug. . . .

In a figure with which he will enter into troubled dialogue to the end of his career, the "she" of the opening lines of "Sunday Morning" is represented as a comfortable woman of class, whose expensive and leisured femaleness Stevens insists upon: By their peignoirs ye shall know them. "Sunday Morning," in its atmospherics and in its ideas, appears to be a conventional poem, very much of its intellectual period: a late-nineteenth-century set piece on behalf of the religion of art that happened to be written in New York City in 1914 and published in 1915, in Harriet Monroe's *Poetry*.

"All New York, as I have seen it, is for sale – and I think the parts I have seen are the parts that make New York what it is." Stevens wrote that in a depressed mood shortly after moving from Cambridge. He found everyday life in New York an exhibition of consumer capitalism, a frustrating spectacle, surreal and narcissistic, with "Everybody . . . looking at everybody else – a foolish crowd walking on mirrors." In this setting, all commodities become promises of romance, whispers of fulfillment quite beyond the explicit use of commodities: vehicles of an imagined entrance into an existence (with ourselves as heroes and heroines) definitively more pleasurable than one's own, and available for a price. The world of New York, a "field of tireless and antagonistic interests," is the ultimate marketplace: Stevens called it "fascinating but horribly unreal" – he meant "unfortunately real" because so destructively tempting. Nature is sometimes exempted from this economy of desire, but only because (he notes sardonically) winds and clouds are not "generated in Yorkville" or "manufactured in Harlem."

"Sunday Morning" came at the end of almost fourteen years of mostly unhappy New York life. We cannot locate the elegant interior and woman of "Sunday Morning" there, but we can place Stevens in New York, in shabby elegance, inside a room of his own. The interior decoration in Stevens's apartment bore pictures of what he thought "most real" and (in the heart of the city) out of reach.

The carpet on the floor of my room is grey set off with pink roses. In the bathroom is a rug with the figure of a peacock woven into it – blue and scarlet, and black, and green, and gold. And on the paper on my wall are designs of fleur-de-lis and forget-me-not. Flowers and birds enough of rags and paper – but no more. In this Eden, made spicy with the smoke of my pipe which hangs heavy in the ceiling, in this Paradise ringing with the bells of streetcars and the bustle of fellow boarders heard through the thin partitions, in this Elysium of Elysiums I now shall lay me down.

The contentment and control Stevens communicates in this journal entry about his protected little apartment veils his feeling of being out of place in a world he can't help but encounter daily on the streets of New York. The world of aesthetic enjoyment, often identified in his journals with experiences of art exhibits and nature – not nature in a vacuum, but nature as a motivated negation of New York: what he walked away from on weekends – this aesthetic world of the weekend is not enough in itself to alleviate the dissatisfaction he felt throughout the workweek. His radical desire was for the aesthetic Monday through Friday, and he got it at night in the privacy of his apartment, in the middle of the city, where decor and furnishings appeared to be freed from the "field of tireless and antagonistic interests." Commodities like rugs and wallpaper, so cherished, are the image of heaven – Stevens called it Eden – and their delights are even more keenly felt thanks to the thinness of partitions that do not block out the sounds of the city.

In Stevens's early letters and journals we are taken into the social kitchen of his poetics, where Ezra Pound's modernist shibboleth "Make it New" becomes "Make it Private": the aesthetic as a lyric process of moving toward the interior, from the real space of the streets of New York to the private space of his room, and then into the psychic space of consciousness (now perilously sealed to the outside); lyric aesthesis, the formation of sensuous impression, as the repression of the seedier side of New York – a process that first transforms the bums in Washington Square into "crows in rainy weather" before taking the final leap into subjective freedom – the atmosphere of an impressionist painting, color abstracted from all objects:

> The other morning as I came home I walked up to Washington Square to take a look at the trees. . . . I was surprised to find the large number of people who were sleeping on the grass and on the benches. One or two of them with collars turned up & hands in their pockets shuffled off through the sulphurous air like crows in rainy weather. The rest lay about in various states of collapse. There must have been a good many aching bones when the sun rose. The light was thin and bluishly misty; by the time I was in my room it had become more intense & was like a veil of thin gold.

In light of the vocational anxieties Stevens experienced in New York, the journal passage on the rug with the peacock woven into it and the opening lines of "Sunday Morning," placed side by side, unveil a decisive scene for modern American poetry: the author imagining himself as sexual as well as economic transvestite: a liberating impulse that he feels (the impulse, as he wrote in his journal, to be "all dream") but that his male obligations tell him he must not choose. The apocalyptic seventh section of "Sunday Morning" returns us to the world, now phallically renewed:

> Supple and turbulent, a ring of men
> Shall chant in orgy on a summer morn
> Their boisterous devotion to the sun,
> Not as a god, but as a god might be,
> Naked among them, like a savage source.
> Their chant shall be a chant of paradise,
> Out of their blood, returning to the sky;
> And in their chant shall enter, voice by voice,
> The windy lake wherein their lord delights,
> The trees, like serafin, and echoing hills,
> That choir among themselves long afterward.

# Wallace Stevens

As a vision of the future this passage is absurd, but Stevens's absurdity is important because it joins mainline American literary visions of male utopias, realms of delicious irresponsibility: certain raft passages in *Huckleberry Finn,* the "Squeeze of the Hand" chapter in *Moby-Dick,* Rip Van Winkle's fantasy in the Catskills of men at play, many things in Whitman and, more recently, the Brooks Range conclusion of Norman Mailer's *Why Are We in Vietnam?* What Stevens imagines for the social future is a place without women; men who work, but whose work cannot be distinguished from homoerotic pleasure; men who work nakedly – and in their nakedness bear no signs, as the peignoired woman bears signs, of social difference. Their nakedness and their arrangement in a ring speak the classless language of fraternity (brothers, but no sisters) and equality. And they chant: collectively they create a fundamental poetry – a devotion to a "lordly" nature that is spun out in the sentimentality of choiring angels, a metaphor wrested from traditional Christianity and transvalued with outrageous deliberation into the music of pagan naturalism. The contradictions of Stevens's early life and poetry – work, poetry, and nature itself, the conventional realm of female authority – are fused in an image of masculine power: Father Nature.

In his Harvard journal Stevens makes this incisive remark, whose immediate target might appear to be popular women poets like Frances Osgood and Lydia Sigourney, but whose true object is genteel culture in America: "Poetry and Manhood: those who say poetry is now the peculiar province of women say so because ideas about poetry are effeminate. Homer, Dante, Shakespeare, Milton, Keats, Browning, much of Tennyson – they are your man-poets. Silly verse is always the work of silly men." Yet the power of those silly men to affect the cultural conscience of their time might be measured precisely there, with Stevens saying, in so many words, that he knew better, and yet while knowing better nevertheless played out his literary youth as if he feared that he just might be one of those silly men who would be denied poetic manhood.

135

As a student at Harvard, Stevens learned to distrust (in a thickening fin-de-siècle atmosphere) overtly moralizing art. He recoiled from Bryant and the Fireside group because, as he put it, the "New England school of poets were too hard thinkers. For them there was no pathos in the rose except as it went to point a moral or adorn a tale. I like my philosophy smothered in beauty and not the opposite." Philosophy smothered in beauty is nevertheless philosophy, not the opposite of philosophy. Aestheticist theory – "the sensuous for the sake of sensuousness" – Stevens found to be "the most arrant as it is the most inexcusable rubbish." "Art," he argued, "must fit with other things; it must be part of the system of the world. And if it finds a place in that system it will likewise find a ministry and relations that are its proper adjuncts."

Stevens's poetics is therefore not unfriendly to his American predecessor Fireside poets, who would have recoiled from his exotic lushness. He was trying to be a poet who would succeed in donning their mantle of cultural ministry – the cultural power that the Fireside poets had assumed for themselves and wielded throughout the American nineteenth century. It was a mantle of authority that neither the economic nor the aesthetic culture of Stevens's young manhood could have granted. The cultural discourse that Stevens was heir to encouraged him to fantasize the potential social authority of literature as phallic authority, and to desire that poetry should be well endowed with social power inside a social formation that cannot itself permit such endowment. However strained, Stevens's music in "Sunday Morning" – it would be replayed in Picasso, Lawrence, and Eliot – speaks the barbarous desire for natural force, not as escape from culture but for manly literary power within.

In 1941, in a lecture Stevens gave at Princeton, called "The Noble Rider and the Sound of Words," when he was well beyond what his earliest reviewers took to be – not without the poet's partial assent –

the self-conscious and insouciant aesthetic experimentation of his early period, in a surprisingly blunt passage on the meaning of one of his key words, he defined the genteel social base from which his avant-garde sensibility had improbably emerged and the social change – so traumatic to genteel culture – to which the styles of his first book, *Harmonium* (1923), were caustic, exuberantly comedic, verbally prodigal, and elegiac responses. The key word is "reality"; it fairly peppers his essays, letters, and poems as some ultimate ontological portent, and it is constantly coordinated with two other major obsessive terms, "imagination," Stevens's inherited word of high romantic desire, and "transparency," this latter bearing his American intellectual and social past.

In a striking passage from Emerson's "Nature" (1836), notorious even in its own day – that of the transparent eyeball – the eye pure and unmediated itself becomes a medium. In moments of transparency, Emerson says, "standing on the bare ground," his head "bathed by the blithe air and uplifted into infinite space," he becomes "part or parcel of God." Stevens's terms are antitranscendental and naturalistic, atheistic and aestheticist; but with Emerson he tends to believe that these moments of vitality cannot happen in the streets of our cities, and that when they do happen, our fundamental social relations, even those obviously hinged on power, are made meaningless. Emerson again: "The name of the nearest friend sounds then foreign and accidental: to be brothers, to be acquaintances, master or servant, is then a trifle and a disturbance." Such moments of the "real" are urgent and final because they are presumably uncapturable by history's various forms of social gravity. In these moments we are most ourselves, wonderfully alone, cut loose from tradition and community.

That most surprising passage on the "real" in Stevens's Princeton lecture makes reference, however, not to nature but to history and society as twin forces of gravity, powers of determination almost irresistible and which the poet's imagination does not cherish. The social real, which rarely makes center-stage appearances in Stevens, is revealed in his Princeton lecture as the repressed monster, the unsuccessfully negated condition of his being – this "real," Stevens's most haunted word, is given, in the lecture, the most precise historical boundaries. There is the "reality," he says, that is "taken for granted"; it is "latent and, on the whole, ignored." This reality "is the comfortable American state of life in the eighties, the nineties, and the first ten years of the present century," a period that pretty much coincides with the first thirty years of his life, a period – though he doesn't say so in his essay – in which he lived unreflectively in comfort given and protected by his mother and father, and when he could with impunity take life for granted, until he left Harvard and went to New York to live on his own, cut loose for good (but not without regret) from his father's economic support. At which time "reality" changed for him personally (and painfully) and personal change triggered new social vision. "The Victorians had been disposed of," he says, "and the intellectual and social minorities began to take their place and to convert our state of life to something that might not be final."

At the actual moment when Stevens came to know this social change in an existentially pressing way – some thirty-five years before he composed the Princeton lecture – he had seen himself suddenly cast out among New York's unprivileged, exiled from comfort, and forced to worry (somehow unfairly) about economic survival, even though he was graced with an educated sensibility, a predilection for reading, writing, and the things (elegant paintings, gourmet food, oriental rugs) that the working-class types he feared might be his new mirrors could never claim for their own interests or talents. At the actual moment when he was learning that the state of existence, and innocence, that his father had maintained for him was not final, that there was a life outside "the comfortable American state" being lived by millions who did not share "our state of life" – who could take little for granted – at the actual moment when he was learning that he might have to become one of them, at this moment of class-consciousness, his ethnic consciousness was rudely awakened by what he saw on his frequent walks through Greenwich Village and the lower East Side, the radical demographic change whose impact would upset blue-eyed America for good, the flooding mass of new immigrants.

This new reality, at once economically and ethnically disturbing, Stevens calls in the Princeton lecture "tense" and describes as "instinct with the fatal or with what might be the fatal." In this new reality, a "possible poet" must set aside his romantic imagination of sympathy and in its place put an imagination capable of "resisting or evading," but without illusion, because tomorrow's reality might be even deadlier for those like himself whose existence had been put in jeopardy by these new Americans. By "possible poet" he means a poet like himself, who might have gone to Princeton or Harvard in the days when only the blue eyes went to those schools: working-class and immigrant poets of the early twentieth century in fact wrote sympathetically of the new Americans; evading them was not part of their aesthetic or social agendas. Stevens's Princeton audience would not likely have questioned the clubby rhetoric of "our state of life"; his Princeton audience would not have found his rhetoric xenophobic: "The minorities began to convince us," he says, "that the Victorians had left nothing behind." Stevens's "possible poet" must hear this futile injunction: resist if you can, but probably you can't, this distasteful new world; try to remember the world you loved and that has been replaced, and that through the lens of your nostalgia begins to "look like a volume of Ackerman's colored plates or one of Topfer's books of sketches In Switzerland" – remote and irretrievable for those who had lost it, who had found it so comfortable, and who used to take it for granted as the way things would always be.

In the distinctions of the genius of the American race it is to be considered that it is not indiscriminate masses of Europe that are shipped hitherward, but the Atlantic is a sieve through which only or chiefly the liberal, adventurous, sensitive,

*America-loving* part of each city, clan, family are brought. It is
the light complexion, the blue eyes of Europe that come: the
black eyes, the black drop, the Europe of Europe is left.
                                    — Emerson in his journal, 1851

The social and cultural change Stevens lamented late in his career in
his Princeton lecture he also lamented very early when still a Harvard dandy and publishing in the *Advocate* a poem he called "Ballade
of the Pink Parasol," which mirrors an aestheticist vogue for Villon
("where are the snows of yester-year?" in Rossetti's translation) with
questions that mourn half-playfully, with decided triviality, the
passing not of natural but of social time: "where is the old-time
wig?" "the lofty hat?" "the old calash, the light sedan?" "the coat of
yellow and tan"?

> . . . these baubles are far away,
> In the ruin of palace and hall,
> Made dark by the shadows of yesterday —
> But where is the pink parasol?

The lament is mostly light-toned, a little gaudy in rhetoric in
Stevens's early manner, and half-ironic (the half-irony being the
master timbre of his voice, early and late), and yet — this, too, a
mark of the early manner — it is a genuine lament, only *half*-ironic
and surprisingly poignant in that unlikeliest of refrains, "where is
the pink parasol?" The parasol: the apt, quintessential figure for a
departed aristocratic context, a shield against the sun which keeps
white ladies' complexions free of those darker tones that used to tell
the tale of class difference.

   In his Princeton lecture, the problem is not the absence of an
aristocracy, which Stevens, like other American writers, could not
have known, but the "expansion" of the middle class in the twentieth century, with its little bit of learning, thanks to mass education, with its "ideas," thanks to "liberal thinkers," and with "its
realistic satisfactions," by which he means its mass-produced way of

life. The realistic satisfactions of the middle class involve, not only its appetite for realist fiction and art, but also its vast apartment-house complexes and its kind of food (no doubt from the A&P, Stevens noted). "We no longer live in homes but in housing projects. . . . We are intimate with people we have never seen and, unhappily, they are intimate with us." In other words, by "realistic satisfactions" Stevens intends something like "commodity culture." His taste for gourmet food, the search thereof being one of the reasons for his frequent New York excursions from Hartford, and a recurrent theme in his letters; his pursuit of avant-garde paintings from France and the precious hand-crafted artifact from far-flung places on the globe; his desire for the unique thing to be cherished for itself, are all indications of a sensibility in revolt against the middle class and its satisfactions and the mass culture of capitalism that ministered to those satisfactions.

Stevens's avant-garde sensibility was doubly engendered: on the one hand by the demographic change propelled by the massive influx of the new minorities (the black eyes), and on the other by the power of mass culture to dominate everyday life at the material level to such an extent that it was difficult for those like Stevens, who wanted to, to avoid its affective impact. The distinctive, the one-of-a-kind, where are they gone if not with the old-time wigs and pink parasols to their proper places in museums? Living in a world of repetitions (whether in groceries, popular genre fiction, or apartments: "the ennui of apartments," as he phrased it in *Notes toward a Supreme Fiction*) had the effect of withering Stevens's aesthetic sensibility, which inclined him to want precisely that rare thing which his commodity culture by intention does not produce. In a late metapoem, he wrote that the motive for metaphor is the exhilaration of change that verbal figuration introduces into consciousness: verbal surprises are experiential surprises. It is also the motive for money. Stevens's supreme fantasy was an aesthete's utopia and an interior decorator's dream: to have so much cash that he could completely renovate his home every autumn. For those who have it, monetary wealth, like verbal wealth, also produces experiential change, the new, the exhilaration that gives life to the life that wanes and dulls.

So the search for originality in poetic and life styles is a search for the pleasure of the original, a pleasure sought in reaction to a culture of numbing sameness. Everyday life in the culture of the commodity represented nothing less than a phenomenological police state from which his lyric muse, his Ariel, would rescue him, or so he hoped. He would go to a watercolor show and see "the same old grind of waves and moonlight and trees and sunlight and so on." He would walk up Sixth Avenue after dinner looking in the store windows and see "millinery, postal-cards, shoes and so on." Back in those leaner days in New York, he took "shabby tea" (Stevens knew his teas), ate corned beef, dry biscuits, and chopped pineapple. From this, the prison house of "and so on" – "and so on" is a verbal tic in his letters which registers his feelings of perceptual and emotional death, the boredom of *la vie quotidienne*, the social texture which threatens his sensibility and drives it in an aestheticist direction – from this social nightmare he is pressed (of course) into his nature walks. But once there, with a sensibility already hammered by repetition, the sentimental pleasures of pastoral landscape are not to be found. There is no nature except what is shaped by a social experience that makes nature over into just another boring arena of "and so on": "the truth is . . . that it is chiefly the surprise of blossoms I like," meaning *not* the blossoms themselves. "After I have seen them for a week (this is great scandal) I am ready for the leaves that come after them," meaning *not* the leaves themselves but the change from blossoms; he takes some complacent pleasure in his unconventional view, but not before trying to cover up another truth: that he had gone to the country precisely to find what his conventional expectation had longed for, a change of scene.

Nature walks, like those on Sixth Avenue, are a bore, because walks in the woods and walks on Sixth Avenue are alarmingly similar – and a walk through conventional literature will give no relief.

What is wanted is the "quick" and the "unaccountable," the true means of escape from all manner of police (economic, literary, and natural) and their prison houses of replication. What is wanted is a radical deviancy of experience that only literature in its most committed avant-garde form can provide: a radical deviancy whose home must be "literary" because Stevens, with his social experience, could not imagine (hope) that it could be "social" or "natural."

Stevens's rejoinders to the various kinds of police may take the form in *Harmonium* of "The Snow Man," a moving, plain-dictioned search for an impossibly pure plainness of vision: a desire for unmediated vision, a seeing for the first time, put in the appropriate form of the infinitive ("to regard," "to behold"), verbal form of desire itself; or it may take the form, in "Disillusionment of Ten O'Clock," of a sympathetic satire on middle-class life, sadly colorless (literally so), undecorated by distinctive sartorial imagination, and therefore (an aesthete's logic) utterly without joy; or it may take the form of the life-affirming directive for a funeral, "The Emperor of Ice Cream," a poem which bares the driving fear of Stevens's aestheticist urge for sensuous experience and for gaiety of language and dress: death itself; or it may take the form of playfully analytic metapoems, like "Anecdote of the Jar" and "Metaphors of a Magnifico," which imply the story of the epistemological and ethical necessity of the image (they are inseparable), of the need for the perceptual clarity and individuality of the image freed of all habitual thought, even reason itself: "On the image of what we see," he wrote in *Notes toward a Supreme Fiction*, "to catch from that/Irrational moment its unreasoning"; or it may take the form of bawdy critiques of middle-class Christian piety in "A High-Toned Old Christian Woman," "The Plot Against the Giant," and the poem about Saint Ursula and the virgins — all outrageous sexualizations of Christianity.

The forms and styles of counterstatement in *Harmonium*, though not literally numberless, give the impression of a writer capable of endless inventive reactions, willing to try anything to ward off the torpor of repetition that his culture imposed. And should that effort take the form of too much seriousness, waxing pompous, then he will turn on himself: "Hi! the creator too is blind." But all of these maneuvers, in the end, are haunted by what Santayana said of Emerson, a writer who, though he could not retail the genteel tradition, had really nothing to put in its place, a writer of interiority, finally, and of inner play, attempting to digest vacancy. Stevens knew the individualistic pleasures of merely circulating in his interior world, but he also knew that the life of the mind of a modern poet, who assiduously courts the unrealistic literary satisfactions of avant-garde alienation may be the life of a skeleton, or so he feared in the late poem "As You Leave the Room" (1954).

In (for him) a remarkably direct apostrophe to his lyric muse, "O Florida, Venereal Soil," he left us a record of his response to what Emerson had called "the black eyes and the black drop" (*drop* in this context is horticultural, meaning "fallen fruit"; *black drop:* "rotten fallen fruit"). What drove Stevens inward, in his characteristic lyric direction as a disbeliever in "reality" who desires to free himself from the social impediments of his lyricism, he tells us, with no punches pulled, is the "dreadful sundry of this world," the social minorities he would allude to in his Princeton lecture some twenty years later:

> The Cuban, Polodowsky
> The Mexican women,
> The negro undertaker
> Killing the time between corpses
> Fishing for crayfish

Unusual for its bluntness of revulsion from non-Anglo America, this apostrophe to Florida, site of his winter vacations, is as typical of Stevens's literary posture as anything he would write, early or late, with its lush diction and sensuous atmosphere marking it as a poem of his early career, and with its cerebral, metapoetic quality pointing to where Stevens would later go as a writer for whom lyricism was essentially problematic, less a poetic mode than an object of ago-

nized reflection and quest: a writer whose lyricism consists in the
desire for a lyrical purity of feeling untouched and untouchable by
social context, a writer whose place is at the painful brink of a
consummation impossible to consummate.

Florida is "venereal," under the sign of Venus: stock lyric subject
and inspiration. Florida – site of potential erotic relation of poet and
landscape – is the muse of modernist aesthesis: sensuous experience
of "things for themselves," approached in a lover's mood, with no
ulterior motive, and preserved in crystalline freshness by what T. E.
Hulme and Ezra Pound were polemicizing as the "image." But
Florida's social "black drop" breaks into the poem, as if from outside, with disjunctive effect, as some hostile force, as the disease of
love, "venereal" in the other sense, an effect of invasion Stevens
achieves by giving these "dreadful sundry" no proper grammatical
habitat. They come in the form of a sentence fragment and an aside,
a parenthetical moment indecorously forced upon him, a diversion
of the poem's proper lyric course, rendering him incapable of the
kind of consciousness that can attend to a thing for itself: as if lyric
aesthesis, the object of Stevens's love, had met its ultimate match in
Florida's minorities, spoilers of his holiday mood, as if the mere
presence of the minorities makes lyric (holiday of the spirit) impossible, as if they heralded, these venereal mediums, the death of poetry.

The minorities will become sources of "character" in the realist
fiction that Stevens alluded to so condescendingly in his Princeton
lecture ("the realist satisfactions" of the middle class); they will offer
the realists new subjects of vernacular speech; they will give blue-
eyed America strange new cultures. In short, the minorities will
provide a motive for Stevens's avant-garde imagination, because
with their realist needs they will propel an ever-expanding market
for realism. In Stevens's youth, lyric was the prized and imperiled
(prized because imperiled) genre of genteel literary America, then
under pressure from realist fiction, genre of the vernacular. Lyric
utterance – a writing that would be historically free and socially
uncontaminated – in Stevens and the genteel tradition of which he

is reluctant and culminating heir, stands in specific combat with the minorities and their culturally rooted vernacular. With erotic urgency Stevens writes:

> Swiftly in the nights
> In the porches of Key West,
> Behind the bougainvilleas,
> After the guitar is asleep,
> Lasciviously as the wind,
> You come tormenting,
> Insatiable . . .

Underneath the romantic conventions newly pressured by his social scene speaks the poet who is driven by a longing that cannot be satisfied by his lyric muse's splendid social indifference ("You might sit, / A scholar of darkness, / Sequestered over the sea"). Stevens, a tormented lyricist, sporting an erotics of diction no genteel poet could abide, could not hide the causes of his unhappiness. He desired either full aesthesis or full banishment of his lyric muse ("Conceal yourself or disclose / Fewest things to the lover"), was granted neither, and in this tension made in *Harmonium* a modern lyric poetry out of genteel crisis, a sexy lyricism resonant with trouble, that could not successfully suppress the lost social ground of its emergence and its despair of social relation in America.

Probably no subject is more conventionally dear to the aesthete than death, since death is the antithetical instigator of various aestheticist pursuits of pleasure. In *Harmonium*, Stevens tapped the convention with dazzling virtuosity in the improvisational poetry of "Thirteen Ways of Looking at a Blackbird," where various styles of perspective and experiment are trailed, and scarily organized, by the blackbird, at first appearance a mere literary prop, but by the poem's end a menacing and insidiously omnipresent final fact. Social death in the Princeton lecture (the new social reality is "instinct with the fatal") and existential death in the blackbird poem blend, in the

Florida poem, in a single, punning image: "The negro under-taker/Killing the time between corpses."

The myth that Stevens promoted about himself in letters to friendly critics seeking help with his difficult poetry is that he actually grew up as he grew older, and that the proof of his maturity lies in his later long poems, where he at last achieved the requisite (churchly) tone of high seriousness and important human reference. That myth of personal growth is important because it is strongly echoed in a wider cultural dimension in the self-reflexive song of canonical modernism, in the full terror that modernists feel for what they fear is their own social irrelevance. Beginning with aestheticist principles, modernists ask – with an art that presumably turns its back on the world, turns inward to sensation and impression, as Pater urged – how can we put art back in, give it connection, power, or, in Stevens's words, "a ministry in the world"? Georg Lukács's storied excoriation of the subjective and plotless qualities of high-modernist literature is perfectly just, as far as it goes. What it leaves out is one of the most interesting things about high modernists: their discomfort with what they suspect is their own self-trivializing ahistoricism.

Reviewers of Stevens's first volume said over and over again that he was a precious aesthete – that he had nothing to say and, worse, that his poems were, on principle, mindless: maybe gemlike, but also without point. These negative assessments bothered Stevens, but not for the usual reasons. The fact is he had heard it all before. His reviewers had only uttered publicly what he was telling his friends in letters during the months when he was deciding on the contents of *Harmonium,* reading over all he had written in the previous decade, thinking about what to keep in and what to leave out. He was saying, in those self-conscious days, that his poems were "horrid cocoons from which later abortive insects had sprung," that

they were "witherlings," "debilitated." At best, "preliminary minutiae"; at worst, "garbage" from which no "crisp salad" could be
picked. Stevens, at forty-four, would not be one of those writers who
could gather sustenance by reading over his old works. He was one
of those modernists who suffered from a severe originality neurosis
whose sources were equally literary, social, and economic, and whose
obsessive force was determined by equally decisive experiences of the
literary avant-garde and the monied edge of consumer capitalism.

As his master category of value, originality simply made nonsense
of the conventional modernist opposition of aesthetics and economics, because it not only prized the new as the different, the rare, and
the strange, but could and did find triggering releases of pleasure
equally in original poems and in exotic fruits bought at a specialty
market for gourmet shoppers. Stevens was one of those writers who
find their old things just old – and psychically unprofitable to
reencounter. And given the significant social role he had imagined
and would imagine for poetry from his Harvard years on to the end
of his life, his judgment upon what he had actually managed to
produce from his late twenties through his early forties must have
been difficult to take. But even as he condemned himself, he was
allowing himself the hopeful fiction of organic growth. He might be
looking at abortions, but he could imagine and believe in the possibility of full-term birth and teleological perfection, both for himself
and for his poetic project – a distinction which became harder and
harder to make as he absorbed the failure of his marriage to Elsie
Moll.

Stevens's beginning as an aesthete, if only a beginning, in the
delights of pure perception and linguistic riot was yet the right sort
of beginning. The aesthetic was an isolated moment, withdrawn
from the social mess and forever free from didactic and political
translation. As he grew older and more critical of the modernism he
partly endorsed, he began to believe that if the autonomous aesthetic
moment was to become the urgent and compelling moment he
always felt it inherently to be, then it would somehow have to carry

its purity beyond itself, back into the social mess, to his rhetorical target: those culturally and economically privileged readers who, like himself, needed to transform the basic joyless conditions of their existence. "It Must Give Pleasure" is the title of the final section of *Notes toward a Supreme Fiction. It* must give pleasure because little else does. He declared, in a characteristic moment in the essays he wrote in the later years of his career, that poetry helps us to live our lives, and lucky for us that it does — we get so little help from any place else. He once told his wife that the nine-to-five working-day Wallace was nothing — the sources of his authentic selfhood were at home, quite literally: the site of his marriage and (for this aesthetic burgher) the site of poetic activity. But when love and marriage parted, his writing became the final source of selfhood: his last resort. The fate of his poetic project turned out to be indistinguishable from the fate of pleasure.

The idea of the long poem became attractive to Stevens in the prepublication period of *Harmonium* because it promised to resolve the painful and difficult-to-disentangle questions of his literary stature and his marriage, neither of which he could separate from his economic role as a male, from the social disease of econo-machismo. The long poem, not the small pleasures of minority — those little things of Thomas Campion and Verlaine he had once praised — could be the signature at once of his maleness and of his cultural relevance, a figure of his emerging cultural prowess at a time when he began to have doubts about his sexual prowess.

"Witherlings," that coinage for his early poems was just right. The long poem, which would speak discursively as well as be, could never be so figured. Real men, Stevens once wrote, like Gainsborough, paint landscapes and portraits, not decorations on fans; real men, if they write poetry, go for the long poem of public (epic) import, not the small lyric of bourgeois delight. The poet who in his thirties felt himself marginalized by his social context as a ladylike dabbler in after-hours verse-writing would become, in his imaginative life at least (or is it most?), a Latin lover courting what has to seem for the male modernist a forbidden woman, the epic muse who not only inspired but also had been possessed by a special sort of man, the sort embodied in Homer, Virgil, Dante, Milton. With those types she was obviously well-bedded; could she be persuaded to try somebody new and so apparently ill endowed for the task of epic loving? Could ladylike Stevens become one of those he had once called "your man-poets"? He wasn't sure, and he expressed his doubts with a humor that is always the sign (if we can trust Robert Frost's surmise about this) of virtually unbearable and unshareable inner seriousness: "I find this prolonged attention to a single subject has the same result that prolonged attention to a senora has according to the authorities. All manner of favors drop from it. Only it requires a skill in the varying of the serenade that occasionally makes one feel like a Guatemalan when one particularly wants to feel like an Italian."

In the time between the publication of *Harmonium* (1923) and his second volume, *Ideas of Order* (1935), in the period between 1923 and 1930 or so, Stevens wrote hardly anything. His literary sterility during those years cannot be explained by the largely indifferent and hostile reception of *Harmonium;* bad reviews did not silence him, because he was their virtual author. In "The Comedian as the Letter C," his first attempt at a long poem, Stevens was a previewer of *Harmonium*'s reception, harsher than any of his actual reviewers. The "Comedian" is a tough and hilarious reflection on a poet, like himself, who seemed to him to deserve the deflating mockery of epithets like "lutanist of fleas" and "Socrates of snails," as well as sexually caustic allegorization as a skinny sailor trying to conduct the sublimely frightening music of a sea-storm with a pathetically inadequate little baton: as if poetic and sexual inadequacy were somehow each other's proper sign.

Self-disappointment and the need to think through self-revision are better but not sufficient explanations of Stevens's literary silence: if he was experimenting with new longer forms and new ambition, he was doing it in his head, or in drafts which no one will ever see.

He certainly wasn't trying out his new self in the little magazine scene, whose editors constantly requested his work and would have published pretty much anything he might have given them. By 1923 he was a respected avant-garde writer whose attractiveness was enhanced by his privacy and mysteriousness. He turned down many requests for poems; he had nothing to give. And while he was imagining but doing very little about earning his poetic manhood, he was living out and doing a great deal about earning the sort of manhood that his middle-class superego had taught him to desire or pay the price in guilt.

In this post-*Harmonium* period Stevens seems to have made his greatest effort – in which he succeeded – to rise to the corporate top of his business world: the right sort of thing to do for a man with family responsibilities, who was the sole source of the family's income, who wanted his own home, and who liked oriental rugs. Poetry was power and freedom over circumstances – Stevens, like most writers since the late eighteenth century, needed to believe that – and the more financially unstable the modern writer, the more he has tended to believe that proposition of aesthetic idealism, the promise that there will be refuge even in the filthy prison house of capitalism. Stevens undefensively knew and admitted and even celebrated another, more commonly held proposition: that money is power and freedom, too. Cultural capital, money of the mind, is good, even if it is the opium of the intellectuals: it is a *kind* of money. But money itself, whatever it is, certainly is not a *kind* of money. The logic, which Stevens never resisted, is that money is a kind of poetry. In 1935, the middle of the Great Depression, when he was earning $25,000 a year (roughly the equivalent of $200,000 a year in our terms), when, in other words, he had made it financially – after 1935 his poetic production simply mushroomed – he wrote this to a business associate:

> Our house has been a great delight to us, but it is still quite incomplete inside. . . . It has cost a great deal of money to get

it where it is and, while it is pleasant to buy all these things, and no one likes to do it more than I do, still it is equally pleasant to feel that you are not the creature of circumstances, but are (at least to a certain degree) the master of the situation, which can only be if you have the savings banks sagging with your money and the presidents of the insurance companies stopping their cars to ask the privilege of taking you to the office. For my part, I never really lived until I had a home, say, with a package of books from Paris or London.

Unlike most writers in the romantic and modernist tradition, Stevens knew that feelings of power and freedom in imagination were precisely the effects produced by a capitalist economic context in those writers and intellectuals who hate capitalist economic contexts; he seemed to know that aesthetic purity was economically encased; that imaginative power was good, to be sure, but that economic power was a more basic good because it enables the aesthetic goods (books from Paris and London) that he required. Can poetic power, however acquired and whatever its origin, turn on its economic base, become a liberating and constructive force in its own right? Stevens constantly chewed over the idea, and though he rejected the notion that literary force is also political force – the artist has no social role, he said more than once in his letters of the thirties and in his essays – it may be that the deep unity of his later career was in part shaped by his encounter with radical thought in the thirties. Stevens emerged from that encounter thinking that Stanley Burnshaw's Marxist critique of his work was probing; he emerged believing in the social responsibility of his poetry, everything he says to the contrary notwithstanding. How much more responsible (and guilty) can you get than, on the one hand, writing the rarefied lyric that Stevens wrote, and, on the other, asserting that poets help people live their lives?

What Burnshaw's critique of *Ideas of Order* did was clarify for Stevens his own class position and at the same time that of his ideal and, as it would seem to him, inevitable audience. Stevens found Burnshaw's review "most interesting" because it "placed" him in a "new setting," the "middle ground" of the middle class, the socio-economic space of those who are both potential allies and potential enemies of class struggle. Burnshaw's statement of this contradiction of the middle class is matched and one-upped by Stevens in a letter written shortly after he read Burnshaw in *The New Masses:* "I hope I am headed left, but there are lefts and lefts, and certainly I am not headed for the ghastly left of *Masses.* The rich man and the comfortable man of imagination are not nearly so rich nor nearly so comfortable as he believes them to be. And, what is more, his poor men are not nearly so poor." In the United States, Stevens suggests, the middle ground is vaster than Burnshaw thinks, and the high and low grounds are narrower and not as melodramatically in opposition as the Manichean metaphors of Communist-party rhetoric would make them out to be. As the poet of the middle ground, of those not subject to revolutionary hunger, whose basic sustenance was more or less assured (the "more or less" assuring also a conservative anxiety, a willingness to rock the boat ever so gently), it was Stevens's "role to help people" – people: the middle class is easily universalized in American discourse – "to help people live their lives. [The poet] has had immensely to do with giving life whatever savor it possesses." To supply savor is to supply aesthetic, not biological, necessity: what Marx in *The German Ideology* called the "new needs" (or felt lacks) of women and men after their life-sustaining necessities have been met and they begin to produce not only their sustenance but also the means of reproducing their sustenance. At the point at which leisure becomes real, "we" – those for whom leisure is real – need a civilized poet.

Even in 1938, when he had behind him *Ideas of Order, The Man with the Blue Guitar,* and the difficult period (1923–30) following the publication of *Harmonium,* when it seemed he might be finished; even in 1938, when he was beginning to experience a personal literary renaissance and an onset of personal affluence dramatically highlighted by the collective disaster of the Great Depression, at fifty-nine years old, Wallace Stevens continued to speak, as he would speak to the end of his life, in the contradictions and with the denigrating self-consciousness that had shaped his early sense of himself. He was a writer who had to be responsible to his role as married, middle-class male citizen – his father's son:

> The few things that I have already done have merely been preliminary. I cannot believe that I have done anything of real importance. The truth is, of course, that I never may, because there are so many things that take up my time and to which I am bound to give my best. Thinking about poetry is, with me, an affair of weekends and holidays, a matter of walking to and from the office. This makes it difficult to progress rapidly and certainly. Besides, I very much like the idea of something ahead; I don't care to make exhaustive effort to reach it, to see what it is. It is like the long time that I am going to live somewhere where I don't live now.

The new note in this rehearsal of his old and definitive conflict comes in toward the end, and it brings uneasy resolution. He feels desire for nothing in particular, desire without an object exterior to itself, the sheer feeling of desire as the ground of pleasure. Not quite: he needs to posit an object of hope beyond longing that will bring longing to an end, but he doesn't care to make an "exhaustive effort to reach it" because he doesn't really care "to see what it is." The object that he won't go all out to reach is ostensibly the poetry that he might write, those poems that will not be preliminary, that will not be a bourgeois affair of weekends, holidays, and those few hours just before and after work, walking to and from the office. One way of phrasing the odd theme of Stevens's later life and poems, the odd and necessary game he plays with himself, is to say that it is constituted by a double desire: to *want* to write poems of real significance and, at the same time, not to want to *write* them.

The tone of this entire passage from a letter written in 1938 is shaped by its last sentence: "It is like the long time that I am going to live somewhere where I don't live now." The pain in that remark should be called structural, because the "It" that is like "living somewhere else," the writing he would do had he sufficient world and time, would be embedded in a social context that would be "its" enabling, "its" nourishing ground. *Would:* the entire passage is marked by an implicit subjunctive mood and is itself an example of the kind of writing that it tries to characterize – writing that is preliminary to the realization it imagines but does not quite want: preliminariness being the condition that Stevens wants to transcend and yet is necessary to sustain if fulfillment, the problematic object of his hope, is to be deferred.

What, more specifically, can be said about the imagined social context of an imagined writing that would bring utter fulfillment? It is a place ("where I don't live now") that would not subject him to demands that now rob him of time and force him to give his best (make him feel "bound") to others. But if the imagined context is a place to live without constraints, it is also and most quintessentially *time* itself in the sense of a delicious process of living his life in such a way that fulfillment will be "long." Not the ecstatic arrest of desire's movement once it gets what it wants – culmination, and then what nobody wants, the aftermath of anticlimax – but ongoing ecstasy ("the long time that I am going to live somewhere where I don't live now"). The pathos communicated in the passage derives from Stevens's desire not to be resigned and his implicit admission that he must be resigned to a life of quiet despair because his life and writing feel contained and dominated. The title of one of James T. Farrell's novels (via A. E. Housman) is almost perfect here: *A World I Never Made.*

Not that Stevens wouldn't have wanted to unmake and then

remake his world. But no one will accuse him of being a revolutionary writer — even to say the words *Wallace Stevens* and *revolution* in the
same breath seems ridiculous, extremely so, yet what shall we call
the urge that is being expressed in that key sentence ("It is like the
long time that I am going to live somewhere where I don't live
now"), and specifically in the analogy that says in so many words
that writing the way you really want to write is like living in the
way you really want to live, and you are doing neither, nor will you
ever do either as long as the course of your everyday life continues to
run as it always has. Underlying the analogy is the proposition that
writing is the expression of a material ground at once personal and
social. The particular mix of feeling in this passage, desire and
fatality, might have been a kind of subjective political nitroglycerin.
But it never went off. Stevens was never able to believe that the
social ground of his life and writing was itself unstable, that the
personal subjects it contained and restrained (like himself) might in
their discontent make it unstable, explode its structure by refusing
the very thing that keeps in place social structures which produce
unhappiness: the acceptance of social structure as unalterable fact,
like a thing of nature; by refusing, therefore, resignation to the
structure.

Stevens's writing tends to wander unhappily between criticism
and utopia. If his desire is without clear utopian object, so is his
dissatisfaction without sharply viewed critical object. Resignation to
unhappiness is a massive repression in Stevens, from his young
manhood to his last years, of the personal choice that affirmed
commitment to the system of his unhappiness. *Repression,* an easy
word to use in literary circles, does no justice to the devious rhetoric
of repression which manipulates its subjects by giving them a discourse for saying "happy" when they mean unhappy:

> If Beethoven could look back on what he accomplished and say
> that it was a collection of crumbs compared to what he had
> hoped to accomplish, where should I ever find a figure of

speech adequate to size up the little that I have done compared to that which I had once hoped to do. Of course, I have had a happy and well-kept life. But I have not even begun to touch the spheres within spheres that might have been possible if, instead of devoting the principal amount of my time to making a living, I had devoted it to thought and poetry. Certainly it is as true as it ever was that whatever means most to one should receive all of one's time and that has not been true in my case. But, then, if I had been more determined about it, I might now be looking back not with a mere sense of regret but at some actual devastation. To be cheerful about it, I am now in the happy position of being able to say that I don't know what would have happened if I had more time. This is very much better than to have had all the time in the world and have found oneself inadequate.

If "repression," better than "resignation," captures the psychological quality of this letter of 1950, then "rhetoric of repression" is better than either, because "rhetoric" suggests that Stevens is caught up in a situation in which he is both target and speaking subject, the self-subverting speaker of a kind of newspeak in which regret over not doing what you most want to do – and what, really, is "mere regret"? – and willed superficiality (*choosing* not to go to your depths, your "spheres within spheres") all somehow add up to a "happy and well-kept life." But we have to say that not even "rhetoric of repression" can do justice to the lucid and self-stinging consciousness that says "well-kept" and "To be cheerful about it," to the man who is not cheerful, knows he is not, and knows precisely the costs of his life and can somehow bear those costs because he believes ("of course") that he has chosen them. And perhaps that is the supremest of all of Stevens's American fictions: the sustaining feeling that the life he so often felt he suffered, he chose; that necessity is, in fact, freedom.

When Stevens said in the letter of 1938 that he would like to do something of "real importance," he was alluding both to his negative feelings about *Harmonium* (a book mainly of little things) and to the desire that he felt, in the months when he was preparing *Harmonium* for press, to write the long poem, a desire in great part propelled by his assessment of his early work. The course of his intention as a poet can be traced in two letters written forty-two years apart; the change is from self-deprecating lyricist and a poetry of decorative frivolity, to philosophical consciousness of his age and a poetry of necessary knowledge; the change can be charted in the recurrence of a single word. Consider this passage from a letter to Elsie written in 1911:

> I swear, my dear Bo-Bo, that it's a great pleasure to be so poetical. —But it follows that, the intellect having been replaced by the emotions, one cannot think of anything at all. —At any rate, my trifling poesies are like the trifling designs one sees on fans. I was much shocked, accordingly, to read of a remark made by Gainsborough, the great painter of portraits and landscapes. He said scornfully of someone, "Why, the man is a painter of fans!" —Well, to be sure, a painter of fans is a very unimportant person by the side of the Gainsboroughs.

Compare that with this response to Renato Poggioli, who needed some clarification about certain stanzas of *The Man with the Blue Guitar*, a poem Poggioli was translating for an Italian edition: "I desire my poem to mean as much, as deeply, as a missal. While I am writing what appear to be trifles, I intend these trifles to be a missal for brooding-sight: for an understanding of the world." This comment was intended to serve Poggioli as an explication of *Blue Guitar*, stanza 24:

> A poem like a missal found
> In the mud, a missal for that young man

## Wallace Stevens

That scholar hungriest for that book,
The very book, or, less, a page

Or, at the least, a phrase, that phrase,
A hawk of life, that latined phrase:

To know; a missal for brooding sight.
To meet that hawk's eye and to flinch

Not at the eye but at the joy of it.
I play. But this is what I think.

The change in the career of a "trifle" appears radical: from effeminate "trifling poesies" to missal; from a trivial thing in the hand of a comfortable lady to the book of books in the hand of a fevered young man; from decorative nonsense to world-penetrating knowledge – the original trifle somehow become sacred text. How more dramatically could Stevens have elevated his conception of poetic function? Yet note that he really insists on the importance of trifling things ("I intend these trifles," these poems, these playful stanzas of *Blue Guitar*, "*to be* a missal"), as if the aborted purposes of his "horrid cocoons" (his metaphor for his earlier poems) might somehow still be redeemed, the miscarried insects reimplanted in the nourishing environment of a longer meditative form, so that their potential might finally emerge. The passage from *Blue Guitar* catches Stevens in his later manner: it enacts, not the sensuous immediacies of perception, nor erotic linguistic festivity, but the immediacy of a kind of thought indistinguishable from desire: pleasure now reimagined as something almost final, almost ultimately good, the fruit of fulfillment yet to be enjoyed; the pleasurable object of desire semiobscure, barely but forever out of reach. The effect of later Stevens, especially in the long poems, is of someone discoursing on some tremendous urgency, the thing most needed – poetry, the poem, the supreme fiction – without ever being able to make it clear what the thing is, though getting close, and without ever experiencing the fulfillment that the thing might bring, though getting tantalizingly close. If poetry is the object of Stevens's desire ("I desire my poem to mean as much. . . . I intend these trifles to be . . ."), then the central fact about Stevens in his later manner is that he was not writing "poems," according to the implicit definition of the poem we find in *Harmonium,* a book in which he delivered and did not just hope for poetic payload. What he is writing is a kind of pre-poetry, a tentative approach to the poem, an enactment of desire, not as a state of mind, with all the inert implications of the phrase "state of mind," but as movement, and not movement in a straight line, as if he could see the end of the journey, but a zigzag sort of motion: desire as improvisational action, a jazz poetry that gives us a sense of starting, stopping, changing direction, revising the phrase, refining the language, drafting the poem and keeping the process of drafting all *there* as the final thing because the finished thing can not be had ("The very book, or, less, a page/Or, at the least, a phrase, that phrase, . . . that latined phrase").

Riveting later Stevens draws his reader into the improvisational music of desire, a writing about itself in the sense that the "itself" is longing as language eking itself out, each phrase a kind of blind adventure going nowhere, an infinite and exquisite foreplay. So what precedes foreplay? His version of the bourgeois quotidian, "the effect of order and regularity, the effect of moving in a groove . . . railroading to an office and then railroading back." Above all, the police, who "are as thick as trees and as reasonable. But you must obey them. —Now, Ariel, rescue me from police and all that kind of thing": as if the police were not only who they are but also a *kind* of thing, a metaphor of the social world for which only "books make up. They shatter the groove." But only in books. And what follows foreplay, anyway? Necessarily the end of desire, the police and all that sort of thing: reasonableness, the groove, no play.

In *Blue Guitar* 24 Stevens shapes a doubled image: at the base, the figure of the young man in a maximum agony of desire – ecstatic need matched by ecstatic book. The figure of the young man, the scholar finding the book, discarded like detritus in the mud, not writing the book; a figure at all points repeated by the figure of the poet writing of the young scholar, the poet leaning in late with mounting anticipation, looking for the poem, not writing it in the sense of planning it out or intending to write it by realizing a pre-given structure ("perish all sonnets"), but having it come upon him, out of nowhere – a surprise, like the poem that Stevens wanted to fly in through the window. This second image, of Stevens himself brooding over the scholar of brooding sight, rhythmically replays the scholar's hungriest hunger (his wanting to know) in a lurching rhetoric not only improvisational but repetitively so (that book, the very book; a phrase, that phrase, that latined phrase), a rhetoric verging on stutter – an excitement that would extinguish all language – then modulated without warning into the metaphor of the hawk of life – improvisation resolved into major chord.

That hugest banality of literary modernism – that poetry is a substitute for religion – is openly affirmed only to be radically reduced, shaved almost to nothing (from book to page to phrase): a missal for the purpose of brooding upon the mouse in the grass. At that very point of minimalist pathos comes an abrupt shift to maximalist grandeur (who could have predicted this escape from the literary police of repetition?), a shift embodied in the infinitive form of the verb which, in Stevens, is often the linguistic shape of desire in itself, a mode of transcendence, the sacred text of longing without end: to know without a subject of knowing; to know without an object of knowing, purely to know; not conjugated, not in time.

Turning from the "joy" of such purity of consciousness, away from the hawklike eye that broods over living detail, you "flinch," not at the eye, the vehicle of aesthesis, but at the joy of aesthesis. To have joy is not to have the joy of anticipation. "I play. But this is what I think." Those flat declaratives of the last line, made even flatter by the heavy caesura which separates them, speak with a staged yawn of the poet's withdrawal from joy and of his imagining of joy that he knows will go stale, because all joy eventually does.

Where does this poetry of the desire for poetry finally go? Nowhere at all, as it mustn't. To write a long poem out of such intention, without plot or historical subject or philosophical system, is to write the epic of bourgeois interiority, wherein the life of the spirit is hard to distinguish from the special sort of desire stimulated in the time and place of first-world consumer capitalism: when the life of the spirit is subjected to endless need for the new which alone can break us out of the grooves of boredom. What we want is to be thrilled: "What I want more than anything else in music, painting, and poetry, in life and in belief is the thrill that I experienced once in all the things that no longer thrill me at all. I am like a man in a grocery store that is sick and tired of raisins and oyster crackers and who nevertheless is overwhelmed by appetite." Stevens gourmandized with epicurean delight – he frequented gourmet grocery stores in search of the most expensive, the most exotic, the most sumptuous; he saw, he bought, he ate. His later poetry is a masochistic form of gourmandizing, deliberately teased out and emptied of satisfaction, a sustaining of overwhelming appetite. At the poetic, if not at the economic, level of existence, he found a way to supply the spirit by resisting consumption: a life of indulgence, a poetics of asceticism tempted.

Stevens on the grocery store is Stevens expressing desire in old age – that's what it feels like to be old and still to desire. Grocery stores of the sort that he frequented are not timeless objects of experience: "To enjoy the fine things of life you have to go to 438 1/2 East 78th St., two floors up in the rear, not three floors, and pay $6.00 a pound for Viennese chocolates. One of the men in the office here got talking to me about tea the other day. I asked him what kind of tea he used. Oh, he said, anything that the A&P happens to have." What Stevens felt about supermarkets he also felt about department stores, labor unions, social classes, apartment houses, and any and all forms of life and literary expression that partook in the slightest of generic regularity. Genres, schools of writing and music ("There is no music because the only music tolerated is modern music. There is no painting because the only painting permitted is painting derived from Picasso or Matisse"), mimesis, literary modes, standardized and disciplined production of all kinds – in a word, the generalization of everyday life and the generalization of literary life, for Stevens, all added up to one thing: the potential destruction of an original life of one's own and of an original literature of one's own, the twin goals he announced in a letter long before he wrote his meditation on old age and desire. For Stevens to imagine himself satiated on raisins and oyster crackers, in a grocery store where only raisins and oyster crackers are available, is for Stevens to imagine himself without thrills, locked in the ennui of old age – but old and without thrills in a specific way, in a gourmet consumer's version of hell: not just anyplace, but here and now, for a man who thought that buying a pair of pajamas at Brooks Brothers was a partaking of the "bread of life" "better than any souffle." His late poetry of deferred desire is not the escape of gourmandizing, it is its perfection.

To write the long poem, then, is to string together a collocation of moments and to create a book of moments which hangs together by the force of desire for moments – the moving into the moment, the moving out. Such a long poem, so-called, is only delusively different in scope from his earlier works. Stevens did not advance in scope, ambition, or high seriousness. Of course, like his critics, who take their cue from him, he liked to think he had. He wanted to call his collected poems "The Whole of Harmonium," a wonderfully resolved, teleological construction of the life of a writer who had once toyed with calling *Harmonium* "The Grand Poem: Preliminary Minutiae." He even considered, in his later years, the idea that his sort of poetry could be theorized, become an object for study; he spoke with friends of the possibility of an endowed chair at Princeton in the theory of poetry. But Stevens knew that the one thing you cannot do with surprises that fly in through the window is to theorize them. He knew that improvisation formalized is something else.

What Stevens seeks, early and late, is a mode of consciousness which (after Emerson) he calls, in the introductory poem to *Notes toward a Supreme Fiction* (1942), "vivid transparence" (with punning insistence on the latinate resonance of "vivid") – vision washed clean of all that has been said, a freeing from history:

> How clean the sun when seen in its idea,
> Washed in the remotest cleanliness of a heaven
> That has expelled us and our images. . . .

This supreme, because unmediated, consciousness would effect original relation to things, face-to-face, abstracted from all tradition. Vivid transparence would yield access to what Stevens called, in urgent redundancy, "living changingness," the medium of escape from granite monotony, the culturally enforced repetitions of what has been thought and said. The pleasure achieved would be "peace," a moment attendant upon a "crystallization of freshness": vivid, living changingness aesthetically trapped, as in a crystal, known in and for its uniqueness, then quickly lost in its freshness, having been hardened in verbal form. Vivid transparence is both medium and substance of authentic literariness: avant-garde of perception and perpetual ground of the new, perpetually imperiled by the forms of cultural habit, an imperative constantly to reimagine.

In several poems of 1938, most strikingly in "The Latest Freed Man," Stevens fully entered into his late phase. The aesthete, who had his metapoetic moments of reflection in *Harmonium,* becomes in these poems insistently the meta-aesthete poised at the edge of escape from all life-deadening structures of perception, whose language tries to render not the moment of the sensuous image in itself but its psychic preconditions. The moment is dawn, when the "latest freed man" (the irony of the phrase is wicked), trying to be "Like a man without a doctrine" — trying "To be without description of to be," "For a moment on rising, at the edge of the bed" — becomes movingly inarticulate, his excited dumbness the sign of his original access to presence without doctrine and beyond speech.

The latest freed man's desire to be without a past, merely to be, his desire for original relation, unmediated by tradition, is the revolutionary desire for an American origin announced in the opening sentences of Emerson's "Nature" essay of 1836: the hope of rupture with Europe in the cultural as well as the political realm, revolutionary hope become a way of being in the world, down to, and perhaps most essentially including, revolutionary freshness of perception. Freshness of perception is phenomenological rupture in the wake of political rupture; it is the medium of a revolutionary everyday life. The transparent eyeball passage in Emerson is father to the moment of vivid transparency in Stevens. Between Emerson and Stevens falls, not the struggle of fathers and sons, but a thorough commodification of everyday life. The appetite for American newness, in Emerson transcendental, antihistorical, nature-oriented — become like the roses outside your window, he urges, they are wholly themselves, they make no reference to past or future roses, they are above time — that sort of desire for freshness of natural encounter, always driven in Emerson by social pressure (which is why he urges it), is translated by later Stevens into hope for the freshness of an original relation to the commodity. Consumption in Stevens, literary or gastronomical, is always to be understood under the sign of the gastronomical: his gourmand's idea of fruit becomes the gastronomical equivalent of his avant-garde pleasure in producing exotic literary fare for our savor, so that he might help us to live our lives. In Stevens, capitalism and avant-garde poetics are not opposites but symbiotic complements, the basis of an integrated life, a unified sensibility quite unlike anything dreamt of in the utopian imagination.

"When I get up at 6 o'clock in the morning," he wrote to his friend Henry Church, "(A time when you are first closing your novel, pulling the chain on the lamp at your bedside), the thing" — the idea of a supreme fiction — "crawls all over me; it is in my hair when I shave and I think of it in the bathtub. Then I come down here to the office and, except for an occasional letter like this, have to put it to one side. After all, I like Rhine wine, blue grapes, good cheese, endive and lots of books, etc., etc., etc., as much as I like supreme fiction." Dawn, the time of the supreme fiction, is also the time when, having consumed the night away in fiction, Henry Church — who is really rich, who buys what he wants, reads when he wants, all night if he likes — can go to sleep. Henry Church doesn't have to report to the office. He doesn't work, he doesn't have to wish for a life "somewhere where I don't live now." Dawn, for Stevens, is an intersected moment: the awakening to the desire for supreme fiction and the transition period when supreme fictions must be deferred as soon as they are contemplated, not in order to forget them but in order to do what he must do in order to lay up their representations, the substitutes for supreme fiction that money can buy: good cheese, blue grapes, lots of books, and etcetera — especially, perhaps, etcetera: the endless substitutes that money can buy, the specialty market of supreme fictions he loves almost as much as the imaginative thing for which commodities like Rhine wine substitute.

Work, after all, is the site of his writing to Henry Church; work not only enables the purchase of substitutive satisfactions, it enables reflection on the difference between real and substitute supreme fictions, and on why he has to be concerned with that difference, why he must work, and on what the difference between being Wallace Stevens and being Henry Church actually consists of. Work might have shed light on his difference from Henry Church (an aristocratic émigré) as a class difference — work might have been the site of an embryonic class-consciousness — but I see no evidence that Stevens ever got to that point; although perhaps mentioning to

Henry Church that *he* can put out the lights when others, like Stevens, are turning them on is a gentler form of class-consciousness, with all hostility either utterly absent or civilly repressed. *Notes toward a Supreme Fiction* is appropriately dedicated to Church; in another time, another place, he would have been the patron of Wallace Stevens. In this time, this place – the poem was published in 1942 – the dedication to Church functions doubly: first, it refers to a person living everyday life as Stevens dreamed of living it, as an aesthetic totality; second, it signals the difference between a European leisured aristocrat (a traditional recipient of poetic dedication) and an American (an untraditional writer of poems) whose economic status and literary ambition created difficulties that Church would never experience. The dedication of *Notes* to Church is an idealization, a little self-ironic, a little (how could it not be?) hostile.

Sometime in the mid-1920s, Stevens augmented his two careers as surety-bonds expert and avant-garde lyricist with a third career in collecting: an activity he called his vocation of "spiritual epicure." Collecting was not just another project in an already heavily projected life, but a mediation of his first two careers, the fusion of the aesthetic and the economic Stevens – a fusion made possible by his economic prowess, though this was a fact against which he wanted to defend himself (forget, really) and did defend himself in some of the stranger passages of his correspondence.

A full theme in his letters after about 1922, collecting was already in evidence in his Harvard days, in his journal-keeping activity, where moments of metareflection, even as early as 1899, at twenty years old, seem in the trajectory of the self-conscious, "mature" writer he would become: "Diaries are very futile. It is quite impossible for me to express any of the beauty I feel to half the degree I feel it, and yet it is a great pleasure to seize an impression and lock it up in words: you feel as if you had it safe forever." The psychic plot of his poetics, at best nascent here, and never easy to discern in his life as a writer, is fully overt in his life as a collector. Stevens's vocation of collecting involves seizing an object and making it safe for his consumption by withdrawing it from the social network in which it was embedded and which, embedded or withdrawn, it covertly signifies, just as his quintessential lyricizing act of poetic composition requires the disinvolvement of impressions from their material grounds, a making interior. Collecting was poetry made easy of access because Stevens commanded the necessary monetary wherewithal and the proper contacts with people in the right places: money and contacts, the insurance of aesthetic satisfaction and the guarantee, like poetic discourse, of transcendence (making "safe forever").

Evidence from his early journals encourages us to think that Stevens's beginning as a collector coincided with his beginning as a writer: writing would be a form of collecting, the recording of impressions and reflections a kind of hunting, the quarrying and capturing of trophies by an aesthetic imperialist. Here is an entry for 14 October 1900: "In the morning I called on Frank – Lieutenant Mohr. His den was filled with Filipino weapons, hats, etc – a great variety of Oriental odds and ends. Frank is a first-class fellow + may come to N. Y. His trip took him around the world." There are four other entries for the same day, all of them in the self-conscious style of youthful antiliterary literary play – comparisons of *Paradise Lost,* a heavenly thing, to the shaft of sunlight in which he sat as Milton was read to him by a friend ("The sun was better than the poetry"); a rueful comparison of modern man to the "old fellows," whose thought was so much more "vigorous" (but not that rueful: the young fellow who says "old fellows" isn't feeling all that much anxiety over the masters of the past); drunken apostrophes to starlight and moonlight, "a treasure house" of impressions profaned by the language he must use to invoke them ("Bah – mere words"); and last, a telling little literary game played at the expense of unknowing bartenders and Keats: "Livy and I thought it rather good fun to ask them about Mike Angelo, Butch Petrarch, Sammy Dante. We asked one fellow whether he had heard that John Keats had been run over, by a trolley car at Stony Creek in the morning. He said that he had not — he did not know Keats — but that he had heard of the family." These various entries for 14 October 1900 figure varieties of aesthetic experience and the effect of their sheer listing is reductive: they are radically equivalent. All become stored objects — in forms of notation, forms of pleasure — and the Filipino "odds and ends" are a political instance of the phenomenology of odds and ends, not a unique instance. Journal writing for Stevens was not only a form of collecting, a severing of odds and ends from wholes: it was the Ur-form of the poetic and a crucial step on the way to the lyrical discourse of an interiority that would be free.

It is beside the point to make a point of the snobby game, played by spoiled kids, at the bartender's expense. It is not beside the point to remember U.S. foreign policy at the end of the nineteenth century, our incursion into the Philippines and Cuba, our need to "open the door" to China, and the relationship of this noncolonial imperialism to the needs of an economy whose production, especially in the 1890s, outstripped its domestic market's ability to consume. It is not beside the point to retrieve that memory, because by doing so we mark the political moment of Stevens's journal entry — it simply could not have been written five years earlier.

There is not a ripple of discomfort, embarrassment, guilt, contradiction, nor any telltale verbal anomaly of any sort, in the passage on Filipino "odds and ends." Third-world handicrafts, the contexts of their production, the medium of Stevens's access to that line of handicraft, the specific human costs in producing them in the first place and getting them into the United States in the second — in other words, the complex political signification of third-world objects at the point of their entry, or possibility of their entry, into first-world aesthetic reflection and writing — none of this touches the discernible intention or tone of the entry: it is politically thoughtless. The very status of the entry as itself an "odd and end" among other "odds and ends" depends on such thoughtlessness. There is a political *context* to the entry on Filipino odds and ends, but no repressed reservoir of political *content;* we are not dealing, at this point in Stevens's life as a writer, with the phenomenon of repression. In other words, there is no trace of awareness that he is involved as a writer in an *action of severing* parts from the whole, an act that would be, at the same time, a banishing of the repressed social whole to a place we can call the unconscious. The entry in question is not, for him, a haunted house, though it might be for us.

But if Stevens at twenty was politically thoughtless in the sense that he had no political thought, then Stevens at forty-three was willfully, because needfully, so. In 1922 Harriet Monroe, editor of *Poetry* and frequent publisher of Stevens's writing, introduced him to her sister, Lucy Monroe Calhoun, the widow of William Calhoun, who had been U.S. ambassador to China. Through Harriet, Stevens arranged to have various items sent to him from Peking. The variety of these items and others sent to him by a friend in Paris, like the variety of entries in his journal for 14 October 1900, is belied by similarity of function. Jasmine tea from China is like candy sent from la place de l'Opéra is like a book of Parisian photographs, the likeness of these items generated by their ability to give their recipient the pleasure of release from the office: " a desk that sees so much trouble," as he puts it, in crisp allusion to the economic and legal issues that it was his job to manage profitably on behalf of the company, "is blessed by such reversions to innocence."

The aesthetic leavening of everyday life at the office is good, but even better was the leavening of something else. At the time when he made his contact with Lucy Calhoun, Stevens was collecting something else, his own poems for his first volume, and finding them bad. The carved wooden figure of an old god, a small jade screen, two black crystal lions, a small jade figure, but especially the old god in wood, he tells Harriet Monroe, have a consoling effect. This old god says to Stevens "not to mind one's bad poems," nor to mind his status as an after-hours writer, but, in effect, to bide his time and let his objets d'art supply, for the time being, the poetry that was not being written. This blessed reversion to innocence at forty-three was at once the blessing or forgetting where he worked and what he'd written and the hope that he could begin again. It was a much-needed blessing in a period when life at the office and life as a husband and father seemed to be all the life there might be.

Stevens went to extraordinary lengths to will the innocence of his efforts as a collector and to conceal from himself the intentional character of his hobby; here the term "repression" seems appropriate to the activity that desperately wills its political purity. He wonders, in a letter written in 1935, again to Harriet Monroe, whether her sister might wish to do some shopping for him. He doesn't have sufficient cash; he needs to pay off some income tax first, and "another substantial item," which he doesn't specify. But soon, he writes, "I shall have some money I can call my own" – free money with which to "buy, say, a pound of Mandarin tea, a wooden carving, a piece of porcelain or one piece of tinqueire, one small landscape painting, and so on and so on": as if the series might be extended indefinitely; as if the things desired, however desirable in themselves, were not, in themselves, so desirable; as if the things in the series – and what is the guiding principle of a series that includes Mandarin tea and a landscape painting? – stood in for something else, were representations of a special sort, effigy-like, containing the innocence that he needed to revert to: pleasure bought and brought home. But he would not send the money directly to Mrs. Calhoun; there would be no direct economic contact between himself and the agent of his pleasures. He insists upon this: Harriet would be sent the money, and *she* would pass it on to Mrs. Calhoun.

The point of Stevens's self-conscious exercise in self-delusion was to so mediate the process of procurement of pleasure that he could experience the arrival in Hartford of oriental handicrafts as the purest gratuity. And poetic composition had to have the same feeling: writing not as intention but as surprise, expression as a gift of spontaneity from some unknown benefactor. What he once said of his writing – "I almost always dislike anything that I do that doesn't fly in the window" – describes the phenomenology of his collecting habits as well. The stuff that might be sent him, he explained to Harriet Monroe, like a "small landscape by a scholarly painter," would do him "good" (that's the word: good), but only if "picked up by chance." He would lose the good, he implies, if he asked for something "specifically." Feel free, he tells Leonard Van Geyzel, his man in Ceylon, "to send whatever you like"; "You are not to trouble about telling me how the money was spent" on these (same phrase from the journal thirty-seven years earlier) "odds and ends." In this exercise in motivated innocence there is both intention and an end in view: the procurement of that which is not procurable in the "general market." Original, non-mass-produced – that is the value, and its subject (tea, wooden carvings, poems) is virtually irrelevant. Writing and collecting become twin expressions of Stevens's intention to live outside intention, because all intention is contaminated by an ethos to commodify for a general market which it, the capitalist ethos, brings into being: never mind that he pays his income tax first; never mind the conditions of "opening up" the Orient to his innocent consumption.

A few months later Stevens wrote to Van Geyzel, again, to thank him for the goods (in both senses), which had arrived just in time for the Christmas holidays, and to express hope that when summer came around this "sort" of thing could be done again, "interesting odds and ends" could be found perhaps in some other place – "say, Java or Hong Kong or Siam." "Say" works a lot like "and so on and so on" – "say," because these places are not so much what they are, specific places, but metaphorical names, examples of an exotic geography whose social and political conditions have been bracketed and that Stevens would like to possess: "I selected as my own," he says to Van Geyzel of the things sent for Christmas, "the Buddha which is so simple and explicit that I like to have it in my room." Of course, Van Geyzel cannot visit all those places on Stevens's behalf, but perhaps he knows people who could be enlisted, "people of taste . . . who are really interested in doing this sort of thing as part of the interest of living." Above all, no tourist's junk, and "feel free to incur any reasonable expense." If, in 1900, Stevens seemed genuinely not to know, then in 1937, when telling Van Geyzel to feel free within limits, he does know. The finely fashioned Buddha in his room is therapy for what is being done to his nerves by Hitler and Mussolini – and even Buddha, in these times, he admits, is "hard to get around to."

Very late in his life, in a poem called "The World as Meditation," Stevens returned to the figure of the poet not as virile youth (a figure of the persistent anxiety he felt for his masculinity) but as a woman, Homer's Penelope as himself, without a trace of the self-consciousness that had accompanied his earlier, ladylike poses as the versifier of the trivial. The world as field of heroic action belongs to Ulysses; the world as meditation is Penelope's creation. Penelope's poetry is her special kind of writing, her active passivity; she is his final representation of desire as a capacity for reception rather than an agitated seeking of desirable objects, a traditional female image with which Stevens identifies completely in the last printed poem in his *Collected Poems,* without the safe distancing effect that the character of Penelope provides in "The World as Meditation." It was what, as writer and collector of objets d'art, he had wanted all along; the position, poetical and sexual, that he courted all along; his way of saying "no" to the life he felt forced to lead.

If Ulysses is the male principle expressed as the epic genre of action, then Penelope is the female principle expressed as the lyric genre of contemplation. Ulysses is quickly and tellingly reduced as the "interminable adventurer": a comedic sort of epithet which has a very different, undercutting kind of effect in the context of the heroic style that is being recollected. This is not Homer's man

skilled in all the ways of contending; this Ulysses is closer to Bill
Bailey, whom Pearl of the same surname importunes, in a low
musical genre of domestic relations, "Won't you come home?" Penelope is drawn into the poem's center of consciousness: Stevens's
*Odyssey* is not the famous middle books of adventure but wholly its
beginning, from the perspective of Penelope, who imagines maximum distance, absence, and uncertain return – a radical reduction
of *The Odyssey* to domestic anecdote (Will he ever return?). Ulysses is
an exterior figure, quite literally, outside the room which is the
universe of her waiting; just as the sun, with whom Ulysses is
strategically confused, is outside. The division of the genders (and
genres) is starkly projected in the antithetical figures of male energy
and female enclosure, public and private spheres, "fire" and "cre-
tonnes":

> Someone is moving
> On the horizon and lifting himself up above it.
> A form of fire approaches the cretonnes of Penelope,
> Whose mere savage presence awakens the world in which
> she dwells.

The "savage presence" in this poem of his last years retrieves through
self-quotation the self-conscious, primitive moment of forced phallic
music from "Sunday Morning" 7. This "savage presence" implicitly
grants, without anxiety, what Stevens anxiously desired in his youth
to grant himself, as poet and economic actor: autonomy of the male
principle figured as the energy of a system, the sun itself (in appropriate pre-Copernican vision) like a self-sufficient hero "lifting himself above" the horizon. (Stevens's father might have liked that
phrase: it came so close to his kind of cliché, like lifting yourself up
by your own bootstraps.) Stevens grants to Ulysses what males have
typically claimed for themselves but what he does not wish to claim
for himself now, and in the same act grants to canonical Homer an
authority of epic mastery for which he no longer yearns through the
disguises of sexual self-irony and self-styled minority.

It is the sun (or the thought of Ulysses) which stirs Penelope's consciousness from sleep to vision; she depends upon it (him), it (he) motivates her meditation. The sun lifts itself over the horizon, Ulysses approaches (perhaps), Penelope both dwells in and creates a dwelling place. Her power, located literally within the domestic dwelling place, is the power of lyric meditation, whose actual domestic site is a figure for a site and dwelling that she makes and that is impervious to male presence: it needs no real Ulysses to fill her desire, for there, in the dwelling she makes, she is the composer of selves, the single artificer of the world in which she dwells, the principle of high formalist imagination so revered by modernist writers, now (unlike its earlier canonical evocation in "The Idea of Order at Key West") unequivocally rendered and accepted as a female principle, the autonomous goddess of radical creativity whose function is much more than formal. She composes selves – his as well as hers – and she places them in a shelter beyond violation. She creates them – in that sense she composes them. She consoles them – in that sense also does she compose them – gives them poise in the face of unassuaged grief. She gives deeply founded stability – not a "shelter," but a "sheltering"; not a place but a process of mind, in never-ending meditation, whose security is inviolable; perfection of lyric internalization, Penelope's poetry:

> She has composed, so long, a self with which to welcome
>     him,
> Companion to his self for her, which she imagined,
> Two in a deep-founded sheltering. . . .

Penelope's meditative process is "so long" because its object is absent – and though in the end, in Homer's story, Ulysses is brought home, in Stevens's version he is kept away; in Stevens's version there is no plot, no culmination of touch. Erotic fulfillment is imagined ("His arms would be her necklace/And her belt"), and imagined as an alternative to the worldly booty he might bring but which she doesn't want ("She wanted no fetchings" because "His arms" would be "the final fortune of their desire"). Note: not "*her* desire," which might seem logical, but "*their* desire," which is correct because the world as meditation is wholly hers: Ulysses has no say in it; there, she is the arbiter of all desire, what she wants is what he wants. In Stevens's lyricizing of Homer's narrative, in his draining of plot and time, Penelope is placed in the suspension of an interminable imagining because knowledge of the end is denied her: no narrative climax, no sexual climax.

The trajectory of the long poem Stevens compared to the trajectory of love: prolonged attention to a single subject is like prolonged attention to a forbidden woman, and success in the longer forms is like success in love – if one can write/love like an Italian. Both trajectories were denied to Stevens, and he likewise denies them to Penelope. Lyric longing is no more a choice than erotic longing; they were historically fated impositions, and so he imposes them on Penelope, who "accommodates" her circumstances, what she does not choose, with a tenacity and force that answer Ulysses' savage presence and absence with her own "barbarous strength" that "would never fail." Stevens's Penelope is a revision of Whitman's agonized voyeur ("Song of Myself," section 11), whose desire to be male, painfully described in her fantasy of assuming the classic male sexual posture, only underscores what she really is: a proper and properly repressed lady. Stevens's Penelope refuses all male posture, but she is no "lady" – her sexual and poetic identity is "within her"; it is not imposed by a male superego, it's primitive. Savage to savage. Penelope's meditation sustains her life; Stevens is of no mind to designate it "trifling poesy," as he had once designated his early work.

But Penelope, though the poem's center of meditation, is not the poem's voice: this Stevens reserves for himself, as a kind of frame meditator and would-be storyteller, reduced to brooding over one moment of *The Odyssey.* With all narrative action denied him, the long poem that he attempted repeatedly in the thirties and forties now frankly beyond his possibilities, Stevens here pens his farewell to the Homeric text which he can in no way rewrite in the epic spirit but can appropriate in his kind of lyric mode, converting Ulysses' world as a field of action, male arena, into Penelope's world as interior moment of reflection: the world not as object of meditation but the world *as* meditation – victory over the canonical principle of epic bought at the heavy cost of idealization. Poetry at the interior, lovers at the interior, both set by the frame meditator into a natural context large and inhuman ("an inhuman meditation, larger than her own"), which he insists is itself a creative process of meditation, yet so figured as to render the inhuman domestic, a process of Penelope's mind: the grand natural cycles a reflection of household work, mending and washing ("The trees are mended. / That winter is washed away"), as if Penelope herself were what she never was, a dutiful bourgeois wife. And then, having adopted Penelope's metaphors as his own, Stevens reduces his lovers to greeting-card sentiment: "friend and dear friend." Here, at last, is a Homer for the little things, the small tasks and pleasures of the sort of house that Stevens knew so well because he lived in it. Stevens, who was never confident of his ability to stand with "your man-poets," here, in this poem of 1952, has made over the canonical of canonical poets into an image of himself as writer: the frame meditator becomes Penelope.

If Penelope's isolation is terrible, that is because her lyric idealization fails to compensate perfectly for her exclusion from her husband's world. Hers is an incantatory poetry, dependent on its absent male object of focus: "She would talk a little to herself as she combed her hair / Repeating his name with its patient syllables" (Ulysses, Ulysses). Ulysses is at home in the Greek universe, taken care of by such as Aeolus, even recognized by his dog after all those years. Penelope does not belong: "No winds like dogs watched over her at night." What she has, in the end, is what Stevens had as a young man in New York, his room; what she has is what is left over when all "fetchings" have been refused: purified lyric longing, painful perfection of interiority, her room. And what a miracle of creation "fetchings" is, even for this poet who performed them as second nature. *Fetch:* to reach by sailing, especially against the wind or tide; to go or come after and bring or take back. *Fetching:* attractive, pleasing. Thus *fetchings:* attractive or pleasing things, which bring a price, as in the price a commodity will fetch, brought back over water, defined as commodities by the act of fetching that brought them home, valued as fetchings in the homeland of the actor who fetches: an etymology of imperialism. She wanted none of that.

The poet has been in love, illicitly, for a very long time. He can't remember when he wasn't. The end is now near, and only his beloved will speak, because in this affair the beloved alone speaks. For this last time, what will be said is all that it is possible to say. In other words, we inhabit the world of Stevens's last phase, the poems collected in *The Rock* and presided over by "Final Soliloquy of the Interior Paramour," logically, though not chronologically, the final speaking of Penelope, Stevens's own imaginative capacity, as if she were a person distinct from yet uncannily intimate with the writer himself, looking back, summing up, but centrally speaking in praise, with intense poignant plainness, of ground value, what persists to the end, what will suffice, even at the end.

"Final Soliloquy" (1950) affirms the nourishing value of an affair whose vital boundary is in the mind, meditative consummation without foundation. What sustains is love's enactment of itself, the actual writings, even though no particular enactment can secure the future of love unless it should provoke – and, in Stevens's case, it always does – desire for future consummation. One rendezvous leads to another, because the one just previous was sufficiently satisfying to spur further journeys in desire. The tone is urgent – this much is what must be said (it says), this much, at least (it says), must be acknowledged.

Quickly, urgency shades subtly into desperation. Final loss will need to be faced; it cannot be far away, Stevens is in his seventies. But the great good is still available. This amorous intensity cannot diminish, it can only die. And though this great good is minimal – like a "single shawl/Wrapped tightly round us," in our poverty, in the cold – by the agency of this love, this good, Stevens feels completed, "collected" from his fragments into a wholeness of self, whose sole mode of existence is writerly consummation. So good is this good that the poet will say of it much more than he has the right to say. He will say "knowledge," he will say "miraculous influence," he will say "The world imagined is the ultimate good," and he will say "God and the imagination are one." Need, not reason, propels such mounting phrases, from the very base of poverty, our single shawl against the cold, to impossible richness: "a warmth/A light, a power, the miraculous influence."

Yet the poet has never been more sober, he knows that his poverty will not be escaped; but he knows, too, that the rendezvous is good enough, if no miracle. So he imagines without support, not imagining *something,* but as if "to imagine" were an intransitive verb. The process itself without object, *that* is enough, this sublimest narcissism, this happiness that cannot be taken from him, except by his death.

# 5

## EZRA POUND

MONG MODERNISTS of the English-speaking world, not even Joyce achieved the infamy and authority of Ezra Pound, who inaugurated his career with an act of expatriation in 1908 after being fired earlier that year from his teaching post at Wabash College in Crawfordsville, Indiana. One bitter winter night (so it goes in Pound's telling), Pound gave his bed to a homeless male impersonator, so that he might "bring warmth to her frozen body," while he slept on the floor, fully clothed, wrapped in his topcoat. The president of Wabash and Pound's landlady had a different point of view.

About two years later, in the summer of 1910, Pound returned home in an unsuccessful effort to acquire another teaching post, this time at his alma mater, the University of Pennsylvania. That winter he spent considerable time in New York City pondering the literary scene and gathering the impressions and notes for "Patria Mia," his single most important piece of literary and social criticism, which he would publish in 1913 in the *New Age* when he was twenty-eight. Early in 1911 he left America for good, returning to London until 1920, a period during which he became the leading international instigator of a new poetry and poetics; the unofficial agent and publicist for Frost, Eliot, Joyce, H.D., and Wyndham Lewis (among others); and the foreign editor and correspondent of arguably the two most important of the little magazines of the period, *Poetry* (Chicago) and *The Little Review.*

# Ezra Pound

In late 1920, Pound left London for Paris, marking his departure with the satiric autobiographical and cultural retrospective he called "Hugh Selwyn Mauberly." While in Paris he served as editor-in-chief of *The Waste Land,* a poem whose famous modernist form we owe to Pound's excellent, merciless advice. He left Paris in 1924 for Italy, where he lived until 1945, when he was arrested and brought back to the United States to face charges of treason for his wartime Rome Radio broadcasts on behalf of fascism. Thanks to a judgment of madness, he escaped execution and was incarcerated at St. Elizabeth's Hospital in Washington, D.C., for thirteen years. Meanwhile, his *Pisan Cantos,* composed while he was detained under harsh conditions in Pisa at a makeshift military prison, were published in 1948 and awarded the first Bollingen Prize for poetry, an act which touched off one of the fiercest storms of cultural controversy in this century, only recently surpassed in rhetorical heat and existential consequences, as it was replayed in a different religious context, by the scandal of Salman Rushdie's *Satanic Verses.* Can a traitor and an open anti-Semite write worthy poetry even as he expresses traitorous and anti-Semitic sentiments? Or, as the maximum Ayatollah might have put it, who would not have raised the question because he had the answer: a traitor and an open anti-Muslim cannot . . . , and so on. In 1958, thanks to the efforts of numerous writers, Pound was released from St. Elizabeth's, whereupon he returned to Italy to live out his final years, mainly in silence. He died in Venice, 1 November 1972: the high modernist who lived the longest.

The Rome Radio broadcasts, whatever else they were, were an act of criticism – and as such, a shocking (when not totally incomprehensible) expression of the central, career-defining act of expatriation with which Pound began his official literary life in 1908. "Patria Mia," the essay engendered on native ground in the winter of 1910–11, was the archetype of the kind of indictment of American culture that Pound pursued indefatigably. And, for Pound, the critical act was indistinguishable from the teaching act. *How to Read,* the

*ABC of Economics, Jefferson and/or Mussolini, America, Roosevelt, and the Causes of the Present War* – all were exemplary sorts of cultural interventions whose titles tell us how basic (and how grandiose) his ambitions were. His efforts in anthology-making in *Des Imagistes* (1914), the *Catholic Anthology* (1915) – which gave Eliot his first international press – the *Active Anthology* (1933), whose title says it all, and *Confucius to Cummings* (1964) were the efforts of an incorrigible educator for whom the lack of a conventional teaching post was never any hindrance. Seeing to it that the right sorts of writers were published, properly reviewed, and remunerated; getting out the right sorts of collections, in timely fashion, as representations of the right sort of literary way; working cunningly for the magazines – seeing to it that their editors published according to his, not their, wishes; himself publishing a mind-boggling number of critical pieces (over three hundred in one year alone) – all of this is saliently glossed by his primal act of criticism, the choice to live outside his country but not (as he noted in "Patria Mia") outside his American identity, a consummation he would not have wanted, even if it were possible.

All appearances to the contrary notwithstanding, Pound was from the beginning an American writer. His driving energy was critical, totally devoted to the goal of an "American *risorgimento*" (a phrase he liked) which he eventually concluded would never come to pass without fundamental economic renovation. As the poet of *The Cantos*, the project that occupied him from 1920 on – a work that grew to more than twice the length of *Paradise Lost* – Pound's critical energy assumed the form of a poetry whose intention was the retrieval and resuscitation of all that had been lost to the modern world; a poetry whose goal was to provoke literary and social change by providing its essential curriculum.

With the generalizing wit of the satiric diagnostician, Pound gave some telling names to the literary culture he found in force as a

young man, none more quintessential than that of "Tennyson,"
whose poetic tone exemplified a Victorian rage for expurgation and
exclusion. What made Tennyson the god of expurgative desire,
a sensibility willfully and desperately dissociated, was the fact
that there never was nor ever could be, Pound wickedly predicted,
"an edition of 'Purified Tennyson.'" The problem was not Tennyson himself, whose actual life suggested saltier possibilities. The
problem was cultural, "that lady-like attitude toward the printed
page . . . that ineffable something which kept Tennyson out of his
works." Pound was not identifying what he thought of as the badness of his literary culture with women, as if the origin of Tennysonian badness were a contagious female psyche. Pound's liber-
tarianism was in fact radical: "Our presumption," he meant the
American presumption, "is that those things are right which give
the greatest freedom, the greatest opportunity for individual development to the individual, of whatever age or sex or condition." His
support for H.D. and Marianne Moore, among other women writers, was unswerving. Sappho's lyrics were one of his consistently
touted corrective models of the ladylike attitude whose literary victims were male and female alike.

The feminization of Pound's culture was an ideological phenomenon based on the presumed economic uselessness of an economically
privileged female whose leisure was assured by her father's or husband's economic prowess. For a man, like Pound, desiring a literary
life in the mainly unremunerative genres of lyric poetry, for a man
unwilling or unable to play the commercial game run by genteel
editors, the situation seemed hopeless. A male life spent on lyric was
an absurdity.

In this feminized setting, Pound's most unmerciful criticism of
American literature was reserved for a "certain [male] versifier," who
seemed to him especially worthless in a society that values more than
anything else the adventurous spirit whose ability to make things
happen, literally to "make it new," captured his admiration in spite
of everything he had to say against capitalist culture. The entrepre-

neurial spirit, Pound thought, constitutes America's most interesting cultural force, because its heroes of nineteenth-century capital make the country "a different place each decade." These innovators of capital who scorn all stasis, not the American poets, are the American models of the avant-garde sensibility, exemplars of identity for those (like Pound) who would make it verbally new and who believe that "no good poetry is ever written in a manner twenty years old." In a country whose actual poetic models were Tennyson, the genteel version of Keats, and the versifiers regularly appearing in the commercial magazines, the entrepreneurs of capital represented to Pound forces whose power to effect palpable social change in America made genteel poetry, in its flight from the world that capital dominated, seem simply irrelevant.

The entrepreneur ensures that the country will not look the same in two successive decades; no genuine poet writes in a manner twenty years old: by Pound's logic the successful entrepreneur and the genuine poet are twin images of creative force, makers of social and literary change, and proof of the possible harmony and even interchangeability of culture and power. Pound's criticism of genteel culture is not, moreover, directed to a phenomenon confined to late-nineteenth-century America. Like Santayana's, his is a criticism of what he thought culture had always been here, a decorative touch, an ability to quote the oracles of wisdom — Emerson and Mrs. Eddy — and he thought us incapable of distinguishing between the two. A year or so before Santayana delivered his famous indictment of American culture in his lecture at Berkeley, Pound was also arguing that the genteel tradition in America was synonymous with culture in America.

Nowhere more dramatically does Pound make clear his hope for a unified social and literary practice than in an anecdote he relates in "Patria Mia." In the winter of 1910–11 he found himself in New York, spending too much time in the company of a "certain versifier," and in his boredom thought he might do the man some good by taking him to see what he called — in destructive comparison —

two "full men," who had "fought in battles and sailed before the mast and lived on everything from $2.50 per week, precarious, to $7,500 per annum" – *and* they commanded literature between Rabelais and Shakespeare, *and* they wielded "a racy, painted speech that would do no shame to an Elizabethan." In the course of the evening this versifier, believing himself in the company "of the representatives of hated commercialism" (Pound's phrasing notes in acid the knee-jerk genteel response to capitalism), suddenly became (the simile is deliberately, savagely inappropriate) "bold as a lion" and decided to grace the hardened spirits of his hosts with a poetry reading – "a bad poem – of someone else's . . . from a current magazine."

Pound and his friends sat it out in devastating silence. The conclusion of his anecdote sweeps up his linked concerns in a single breath: "that is 'art in America,' that is why 'the American' cannot be expected to take it seriously, and why it is left to the care of ladies' societies, and of 'current events' clubs, and is numbered among the 'cultural influences.'" If that is literature and culture in America, says this twenty-five-year-old American briefly home from Europe, then so much the worse for literature and culture in America. An original literature would take poetry away from a trivializing contemporaneity (literature as a "current event") and the newly founded Poetry Society of America, where it had been safely tucked away in cultural impotence under the direction of Jesse Belle Rittenhouse. A new literature would belong to "full men" like Pound's two business friends, who were the type of the socially vital poet, men skilled, like Ulysses, in all the ways of contending.

His insistent, career-long attacks on "rhetoric and frilled paper decoration"; his desire to get poetry closer to "the thing" (as if poetry had wandered far away into the stratosphere of abstraction, far from thingness or *dinglicheit,* as the New Critic John Crowe Ransom would say in echo years later); his embarrassment as a male lyricist feeling out of place in a lyric territory that he believed his culture had feminized so much the better to trivialize it (poetry, he agreed with Stevens and Frost, had become a "sort of embroidery for dilettantes and women"): these are some of the reactive gestures that became standard in the early modernist period in America and that link Ezra Pound to any number of his contemporaries, not so much in aesthetic solidarity on behalf of a new poetics as in cultural negation. Pound's better publicized efforts – first by himself, much later by the academic Pound industry – to reimagine lyric look at first remarkably like Robert Frost's. He also set himself the project of escaping the demand put upon him by official literary culture that he glean his diction from the lyric masters collected by Francis Palgrave. But if with Frost he shared a target of cultural critique, then against Frost's democratic antipoetics of vernacular voice, which worked toward a novelized lyric of character in the American tradition of local-color realism, Pound worked toward the formal voice of traditional literary culture – a voice he called "curial" with no American shame, at a time when James Whitcomb Riley may have been the most popular poet in America.

So in his critical project he set himself against the poetry in dialect mode descended from Wordsworth ("so intent on the ordinary or plain word that he never thought of hunting for *le mot juste.*"); set himself against the aestheticist poetics of the dreamy line, with all its archaisms and inversions, which he criticized in the early Yeats but which he himself had trouble avoiding; set himself against the tradition of masculinity out of Whitman, the school of self-conscious red-bloods like Richard Hovey and Bliss Carman founded upon "the insight that possession of the phallus differentiates human kind from the lower animals" – an insight that Pound himself seemed to enjoy waving with some frequency from early on; and finally set himself against "the school of normal production" (a phrase of considerable resonance for his analysis of the lyric marketplace of capital), the school that fills the pages of the commercial magazines with "nice domestic sentiments inoffensively versified." Pound's dictum that poetry be at least as well written as Flaubert's prose would stand, in this context, as a counterstatement against contemporary poetry as he knew it. It urges not narrative in poetry but a turn toward the elegant ideals of economy, precision, and hardness – a turn toward Flaubert and Ford Madox Ford as stylistic models for lyric poetry and a rejection altogether of the contemporary poetry scene wherein such models for writing, he was convinced, were not to be found.

With these evocations of the Roman Catholic curia, Flaubert, and various European masters as models of elevated vocal authority in poetry, Pound launched, in his early career, a voyage toward an avant-garde whose essential nourishment would be drawn, not from alliance with some presumably (American) revolutionary and contemporary moment, but from the past. With the epigrammatic flair of the avant-gardist looking for attention, he wrote that line, "No good poetry is ever written in a manner twenty years old." But this avant-gardist had gone to graduate school in comparative literature and philology: "yet a man feeling the divorce of life and his art," he says in the next breath, "may naturally try to resurrect a forgotten mode if he finds in that mode some leaven, or if he thinks he sees in it some element lacking in contemporary art. . . . " Pound's aesthetic preferences would be polemically international and antiquarian, the politics of those preferences apparently authoritarian, though even here, at the outset of his career, his admiration for the novels of Henry James muddles these political waters and sets up his most interesting contradiction.

As the "author of book after book against oppression, against all the sordid petty personal crushing oppression of modern life," James represented for Pound the greatest hatred of tyranny imaginable. And the historical wonder of James lay in the fact that he embodied his critical intentions in the novel, modern form of forms, "not in the diagrams of Greek tragedy, not labelled 'epos' or 'Aeschylus.'" Pound's explanation of the implicit politics of James's fiction is as

fully in the American grain as his literary preference for the curial
voice is not. In one of the most American of his many American
moments, the man from rural, small-town Idaho, of modest cultural
patrimony, writes with the democratic ease of camaraderie this ringing endorsement of James, high-toned American of immense cultural advantage: "What he fights is 'influence,' the impinging of family
pressure, the impinging of one personality on another; all of them in
the highest degree damn'd, loathsome and detestable." When
Pound lamented, in the most deeply felt metaphor for his politics, a
loss of respect for "the peripheries of the individual," he feared for
his literary life. His analysis of the hostile economic context of his
desire to write against the formulas demanded by commercial magazines in the U.S.A. culminated in his strongest poetry of criticism
outside *The Cantos:* the small literary history, semiautobiography,
and social critique he called "Hugh Selwyn Mauberly." This poetic
sequence fuses his complex impulses: a politics of and for the radical
individual, an admiration for Flaubertian realist experiments in fiction, a veneration for older poetic modes out of step with the times,
and a criticism of the one certifiable poetic avant-garde of his youth
– the aestheticism of the 1890s, the turn inward which he thought
disabled writers like Lionel Johnson and Ernest Dowson in the face
of the social evil that culminated in World War I.

Henry James's fictional representations of individuals insidiously
destroyed by invisible impingements of social arrangement is reflected politically in the anti-imperialism Pound shared with his
generation of American modernists who grew up in the shadow of
the American incursion into Cuba and the Philippines. Encounter
with the anti-imperialist movement at the turn of the century was
the trigger of political initiation and commitment for any number of
modern American writers, their chief form of protest against invasion of the individual's boundaries and a protest, as well, on behalf
of the integrity of discrete cultures now newly imperiled by the
expansionist desires of American power and capital. It was an anti-
imperialism whose moral, epistemological, and political themes

were eloquently played for the emerging modernists in William James's writerly activism at the turn of the century.

Pound's distrust of the political horror of abstraction was every bit as deep-seated as that of William James, who had excoriated with the term "abstract" our imperial impositions of value, our intrusions into organic systems of culture, far from our shores. Like James, Pound believed that the world we live in "exists diffused and distributed, in the form of an infinitely numerous lot of eaches," a collection of stories expressed from a collection of discrete localities of value that cannot be unified into a single narrative. And, like James, Pound believed that the diversity of the world's cultures needed to be cherished because, far from being an irreducible and impervious fact of human ontology, cultural diversity was at the mercy of abstractionist modes of writing and thinking; a criminal form of behavior that William James accused Theodore Roosevelt's party of indulging as foreign policy, and that Pound accused the popular poets of the day of indulging as a cultural policy whose human costs were equally unacceptable. And both James and Pound used the word *criminal* to describe the effects of "abstraction."

If the James brothers together fathered American modernism's vision of individuals and diverse cultures under siege, then what Pound did in his early literary essays was to focus that vision on the imperiled literary individual, the would-be author who would survive economic assault on his desire to protect his writing's artistic individuality from the imperial processes of abstraction that American culture imposed upon writing. "The point toward which I strive," Pound wrote in 1910, "is that at no time was there such machinery for the circulation of printed expression – and all this favors a sham." In his social criticism in prose, in "Mauberly," in many of the *Cantos,* he goes after the machinery itself, the material conditions of cultural production; all those, he imagines, who stand to profit from it; and, most harrowingly, its death-ray effects on language, the sustenance and fabric of a healthy (i.e., individualist) culture. Pound explored the possibility of a corrective: a refusal of the literary culture ruled over by "Mr. Nixon," satiric representative of the culture of capital he invented in "Mauberly," who counsels young writers to butter up reviewers and never to kick against the pricks.

In March of 1913, Pound published, in Harriet Monroe's *Poetry*, what quickly became the classic manifesto for a new ("imagist") poetics. The theory of the image he announced there ("an intellectual and emotional complex in an instant of time") was fresh in its immediate historical context because it demanded a *complex* for the lyric – a heterogeneous texture that fused the traditional image (the sensory object) with intellect as well as feeling – a lyric texture in opposition to the conventional lyric *simplex* implicitly demanded and promoted by Palgrave, among other anthologists with whom Pound was at war, whose lyric exhibits and critical commentary thereon would banish everything but abstracted feeling from the lyric mode. But Pound's "image" as "complex" nevertheless remained at its core fully lyric, even visionary in function: "It is the presentation of such a complex instantaneously which gives the sense of sudden liberation; that sense of freedom from time and space limits." This new lyric, with its stress on the poet's psychic integration, would be the verbal index of a thoroughly associated sensibility, a poet recalling Coleridge's romantic ideal who brings the entire personality ("the whole soul of man") into an articulated expressive act, with all faculties in perfect coordination; a poet something like Pound's entrepreneurial friends (a "full man") or like his Renaissance soldier-patron of the arts, Sigismondo Malatesta ("an entire man"), who dominated several early cantos, or like Bertran de Born, war-mongering troubadour, who appears in the early poetry. The reception of the new lyric of the image would release the reader from the constraints of circumstance, so that he could feel transported in an experience of "sudden growth," what Pound had called several years earlier, in *The Spirit of Romance,* "delightful psychic experience," by which he meant an experience akin to what is recorded in ancient myth: the feeling of walking "sheer into nonsense." Like the image, myth was the trigger of that sort of feeling, the occasion of a subjective moment of liberation from common sense. The "image" is lyric, it tells no story. Its existence lies wholly in an eternal present (the "instant"), with no past or future encumbrances attached.

The manifesto on the image was not new for Pound in 1913: he had been at work earlier on a similar conception (he then called it the "luminous detail") and he would continue to press his idea of the image through its revised incarnations in the Chinese ideogram (thanks to Ernest Fenollosa), the theory of the vortex, and into the practice of many of *The Cantos.* The heterogeneity of the new image implies a lyric practice reimagined in the ambience of Ford Madox Ford's fiction and the polemical theorizing of T. E. Hulme on behalf of what Hulme had called a "classical" poetics, a series of characterizations for a new poetry that recalls Pound's technical directives for the new image: "dry hardness," the "accurate, precise, and definite description" that comes only after a "terrific struggle" to bend the generic character of language to the unique perceptual possibility (the radical individuality that defines human difference), so much the better to produce a "visual concrete language" that prevents the reader from "gliding through" to "an abstract process," a language of images which "are not mere decoration, but the very essence of an intuitive language."

But despite the thoroughly up-to-date and revolutionary character of Pound's novelistic insistence on "exact treatment" – a worldliness of lyric, an early urge to write a poem that would include history – in fact his theory of the image looks back to the Paterian 1890s. The image is for release, for an inward turning away from the world, for dream in the manner of the earliest, world-weary Yeats ("dreams alone can truly be," is the major Yeatsean echo from Pound's first volume, *A Lume Spento*), and for brief but vitalizing contact with visionary splendor. In his metapoetic declaration of principle in the opening poem of *A Lume Spento* (1908), Pound prays (from on high) that his songs will be granted the power to light up with divine fire the lives of "grey folk":

As bright white drops upon a leaden sea
Grant so my songs to this grey folk may be:
As drops that dream and gleam and falling catch the sun,
Evan'scent mirrors every opal one
Of such his splendor as their compass is. . . .

In post-symbolist fashion in the wake of Poe, Pound offered the lyric as the normative literary form, the subjective center of all forms. "Even the Divina Commedia," he wrote, "must not be considered an epic. . . . It is . . . the tremendous lyric of the subjective Dante. . . . "

Even so, at the outset of his career, in his early twenties, Pound had wedded his apparently disengaged lyric disposition to social obligation, to the presumed benefit of those he called "grey folk," and to this end (until his end) he pursued the role of the lyric "instant" in society on the assumption that the poet has something so special to contribute that society could not possibly function healthily without him. In the lyric fragments for Canto 117, he wrote: "For the blue flash and the moments/benedetta." In that same fragment of a canto, he wrote, in one of his purest lines of desire: "To have heard the farfalla gasping/as toward a bridge over worlds." In 117, the last of the cantos printed in the collected *Cantos of Ezra Pound,* in this image of the butterfly in transcendent movement, appropriately rendered in a sentence fragment, Pound, last of the living legendary modernist poets, was enacting the very attitude that he and his friend T. E. Hulme had worked so hard to debunk on behalf of the imagist practice that would replace it. As Hulme put it, "the whole of the romantic attitude seems to crystallize in verse round metaphors of flight." One of the genteel enemy, E. C. Stedman, had portrayed Keats, in the quintessential genteel image of the

poet's (dis)relation to the world of capital, as a "superb blue moth."
Not only did Pound never escape from the romantic literary culture
he became famous for criticizing; that culture would constitute one
of the most important ingredients of his poetics of obligation. Shelley had called the poet the unacknowledged legislator of the world;
Pound wanted him acknowledged, not for the laws that poetry
would embody, but for the freedom from law imposed, from the
loathsome oppression that follows when the individual's boundaries
are not respected.

But more even than its definition of the image, Pound's manifesto
of 1913 was powerful for the negative directives that cast light on
what he meant by the image and on the conventional lyric practice
the new writing would displace. Several of his directives (like those
of Hulme) amount to a single warning against everything that the
image was not – "ornamental" discourse in the service of "abstraction." The image, like the "luminous detail" Pound had theorized
before it, and like the ideogram and vortex that came after, was the
exemplary figure of concentration and totality, the essential texture
of a new poetry that would necessarily appear difficult in the context
of the diluted practice where "abstraction" reigned. By "abstraction"
Pound meant not only too much generality but also the act of
dislodging an element from an integrated complex. This prescription for a concentrated complexity – a poetic whole "rammed full,"
as Frost put it, with "all sorts of things," or a "rag-bag," as Pound
described the form of *The Cantos* in a suppressed version of his first
Canto – though followed faithfully in the practice of the short lyrics
of Pound and Eliot, and though it would appear to be a prescription
for the modern genre of poetic genres, the intellectually demanding
short poem, was also the driving structural imagination behind the
writing of the modernist long poem – *Mauberley, The Cantos, The
Waste Land, The Bridge* and *Paterson* – and nowhere is this made more
evident than in the radical editorial compression that Pound urged,
and that Eliot accepted, for a transformation of the bloated manuscript version of *The Waste Land* into the classic modernist collage of

sharp discontinuity that we know. *The Waste Land:* a poem to be read
not as a narrative (temporal) unfolding but a spatial form, an intellectual and emotional complex grasped in an instant of time; an
"image" that included everything that Palgrave and the genteel
taste-makers wanted excluded: dramatic materials, grungy mimesis
of everyday life, vast networks of scholarly allusiveness — all of that
together with purest lyric impulse, all the more poignantly because
so briefly evoked.

As the verbal equivalent of the poet's undissociated self, Pound's
"image" — a way of seeing as much as a new thing seen — is an
honorific figure of perceptual concreteness in opposition to the
method of "abstraction"; a figure for a truthful discourse in opposition to "rhetoric"; a figure of intellectual as opposed to sentimental
control; of aesthetic necessity and social relevance as opposed to
aesthetic "ornament" and social uselessness. "Ornament," "sentiment," "abstraction," and "rhetoric" are the various terms Pound
makes synonymous and which he employs, early and late, to describe the literary practice he deplored: the hated conventional textures of American poetry, the soft post-symbolist practice in vogue
in England since the nineties, the immoral relation to the world that
he believed those textures mediate for readers. Pound's criticism of
those literary textures is at once aesthetic, epistemological, and
political. The luminosity of the detail; the natural adequacy that he
claimed for the image and the ideogram — an ornamental and abstract discourse is the earliest instance of what he meant in Canto 45
by *contra naturam;* the "radiance" of the vortex (a dynamic conception
of the image, not a static complex but a "node from which, and
through which, and into which, ideas are constantly rushing"): all
are urgent theories for a new poetry that would not look like the
poetry represented by Pound's cunning exhibit of the old in his
manifesto of 1913 — "dim lands of peace" — a phrase that embodies
the thematic abstraction it refers to, and whose major effect is to
double the obscurity of the abstraction ("peace") with an adjective
stressing the obscurity (dimming) of vision.

Pound often glosses the proper relation of particulars to generals with references to Aristotle and scholastic philosophy ("generalities," as he put it in Canto 74, must be "born from a sufficient phalanx of particulars"). But his connection with Hulme must have reminded him of what he more typically believed: that there is no proper relation of particular to general, that the particular is not the cognitive base of the general but the desired entirety of knowledge, all else being dangerous illusion. The issue for Pound was never how to adjudicate the argument between realists (like Aristotle) and nominalists (like Hulme) as if he had some stake in the discipline of philosophy. The issue was pragmatic: a function of his needs in actual historical situation. Aristotle and Hulme were names-as-weapons in a contemporary cultural war that he was fighting independently of the epistemological status of their claims. The image, the vortex, and the ideogram are three names for poetic media of particularity that would ensure an aesthetic renovation of abstract writing; an epistemological renovation of that same sort of airiness; and – in the renovated relation of reader to world promoted by a writing sufficiently phalanxed with particularity – a political renovation, a renewed respect for the peripheries of the particular individual, who for Pound is the subatomic foundation of locality, his value of all values ("Humanity is a collection of individuals, not a whole divided into segments or units").

As image, or ideogram, or vortex, the poem would function like an "inspired mathematics" – a special kind of notation for the subjective life of feeling, a "new word" beyond the existing categories of formulated language. Pound's mixing of symbolist dicta via Mallarmé with scientific ideals of exactitude, routinely caricatured by the symbolists and aesthetes whom he only partially admired, his evocation of a poetic language become as precise as mathematical equation, bespeaks the fruitful contradiction in his critical thought to wed the culturally trivialized urge of the poets with a socially honored activity (the language of science). In another rhetorical rescue mission, he would charge the lyric impulse, feminized in

capitalist culture, with the masculine dimension of social involvement; his aim was to join the feminine with pragmatic energy, not
to do away with the lyric feminine but to make it "harder," give it
"shock and stroke." "The poet is a centaur"; his entrepreneurial
friends commanded Shakespeare *and* capital. The poet is doubly
sexed.

Pound's theory of the image came rather quickly to seem to him
inadequate. The image was static, too lyrically disengaged and inward in its emphasis to match his ideal of the poet as a man supremely engaged and worldly. Hence his revisions of the image in
the theories of ideogram and vortex that stressed the image in action, the image as including its situation, particulars in provocative
juxtaposition. The ideogram is the image which knows not the
distinction between noun and verb. The vortex is the image conceived as the whole poem; the vortex-poem a composition of juxta-
posed planes, after the mode of analytic cubism, a spatial construction of elements in superposition, not a *representation* of particularity
but a *phalanx* of particularity – the military etymology is important:
a cultural weapon, something like a body of infantry in close array,
an idea in action, working in the social arena. Far from being an
ornament for ladies and alienated aesthetes, such a poem would be
the proper expressive complement of Pound's idea of the poet – his
culture forced him to think it "masculine" – the proof that poetry
and power were not the antithetical properties of the half-humans
called women and men in the culture in which he grew up.

But the issue of poetic function is no issue at all so long as "the
practice of literary composition" is carried out in secluded domestic
space, "like knitting, crotcheting, etc." For such practice can never
"transgress the definition of liberty we find in the declaration of the
*Droits de l'Homme*" as "the right to do anything which harms not
others. All of which," Pound concludes, "is rather negative and
unsatisfactory." Aesthetic or any other sort of practice so sustained,
in privacy, can do others neither harm nor good: it is trivial. But
literary composition carried on in public will bear directly on the

freedom of others. It may constitute a transgression of someone else's liberty, the worst sort of criminality in Pound's universe. The poet, like the corrupt doctor who makes false reports, may become "responsible for future oppressions." Hence Pound's insistence on clarity, in his prescription for the image – "exact treatment of the thing" – for any "thing" ("whether subjective or objective") may be falsified, at which point the classical ideals of poetics – teaching, moving, and delighting – become their demonic counterparts: we "obscure" so much better to "mislead," and we "mislead" in order to "bamboozle." At the base of such rhetorical criminality is not so much a criminality of persons as a criminality of the literary medium and the institutions that sustain it; a criminality of a discourse gone "slushy and inexact," out of touch with "things," where the "application of word to thing" has gone "rotten." The social relevance of Pound's ideal poet would lie in his power to keep the medium clean, precise, and exact, because the "individual cannot think and communicate his thought," and "the governor and legislator cannot act effectively or frame his laws without words and the solidity and validity of those words is in the care of the damned and despised *literati*."

The politics of Pound's image is close to the politics of Pound's Henry James, with this difference: Pound's imagist (his vorticist, his ideogrammist) would not be charged with writing a poetry against the penetration by the usual social influences of the individual's peripheries. In his commitment to an individuating clarity and exactitude of presentation, the poet would underwrite the health of language by defusing its transgressive power – that power whereby, via the means of an insidious because obscuring abstractness, one individual crosses cunningly, under linguistic cover, into the space of another, so much the better to control him. Language, poetic or ordinary, is above all, for Pound, a medium of communication and exchange, and that is why it is his constant target and obsession. To let it go abstract – this perilous mediator of all identity, this medium of influence, manipulation, bamboozling, and control – is to set the conditions for a reasonable paranoia. Pound's belief that it lies within the power of the writer to keep language healthy and therefore culture safe for the individual is an index of his high social hope; in his Hell Cantos (14–16) he shows us in detail just what his hope must work against, just how powerful the betrayers of language are.

So Pound's various equations for the poet – Odysseus, Malatesta, de Born, the associated sensibility, the full Renaissance man in his American capitalist incarnation; his figures of poetic function, early and late: luminosity, clarity, and radiance; his attacks on aesthetic ornamentation; his insistence on getting accurate representation of "the thing" – he found the decorative verse of his time worthless because it was a language apropos of no*thing* – these clustered motifs in his poetics make sense in the ambience of his social intentions and against the immediate literary backdrop of his thought. Pound increasingly emphasized the image as an irreducible aesthetic monad. More and more, he would think of the image *as* the poem, not part of the poem, an organic whole whose function is defined from Coleridge and Shelley to Pound as a unique unveiling, a moment of radiance in which the film of familiarity is stripped from the world around us. Such mainline romantic theory about aesthetic autonomy, and the value of "the poem itself," feeds the modernist avantgarde but is differentiated and politically turned by Pound's insistence that we see "the poem itself," not as a medium of pure contemplation and imagination, standing in aloof alienation from what Yeats, in constant contempt, called the world of the journalist and the money changer, but precisely as a way of engaging that world. Pound's attacks on the aesthetic of the ornament were not made on behalf of an isolated aesthetic autonomy but on behalf of the necessity of the aesthetic within the human economy: an avant-gardism with a rhetorical, a Victorian and Fireside conscience.

As a rhetoric against the trivializing feminization of literature in capitalist context, Pound's antiornamentalism is not really what it seems to be – a mystical theory of a naturally necessary language – but a coded plea for a writing of relevance. Just as his ideal poet refuses to stand off in a domestic space as a figure of contemplative removal, so in the ideogrammic and vorticist stages of his thought Pound's luminous image is a figure of epistemic action: it is no longer a moment in which readers are propelled into a subjective realm, in the mode of *A Lume Spento,* in order to find their liberation from the gray world of capital, but a heightened moment of new consciousness through which that world's human "things" are revealed in definitive profile. It is as if Pound believed that abstraction, a form of consciousness motivated and fed by a form of abstract writing, once renovated, would spell the end of imperialism, the politics of abstraction; as if the respect of human difference in actual social relations were a necessary consequence of its representation in a writing properly phalanxed with particularity. The unity of Pound's ad hoc theorizing is the unity of a mind seeking to reestablish in a hostile context the old honorable role of the poet as the good cultural doctor, a rearguing, because his environment demanded it by demeaning that role, of the premises of a classic apology: "It is curious that one should be asked," he says, "to rewrite Sidney's *Defense of Poesie* in the year of grace 1913." Pound's career shows us just how curious, necessary, and fated to failure.

As a social and literary critic, Pound is a celebrant of the intensely peculiar, the apparently primordial, autonomous force which he believed stood under and propelled everything that is expressed: what rescues Homer or Dante, Chaucer or Shakespeare – his chief examples – from what would otherwise have been their certain aesthetic and political fate as rank imitators, the lackeys of someone else's mind. Pound's word for this substance of substances was *virtu.* In his populist American logic, *individuality,* therefore *virtue,* and therefore (the aesthetic turn on his politics) *virtuosity,* were threatened at their virile heart by the culture of capitalism and its commodity-based economy. The virtuous artist was Pound's persis-

tent emblem of the free individual and his representation of a generous ideal of culture that he would see translated into the social
sphere at large. "Having discovered his own virtue," Pound wrote,
"the artist will be more likely to discern and allow for a peculiar *virtu*
in others." This, Pound's live-and-let-live company of literary
worthies, is his measure of actual social decency at any given time
and the basis of his political criticism of what he thought American
capitalism had done to our fundamental political ideals.

When Pound told his story of *virtu,* a story he retold obsessively,
he was talking the ahistorical psychology of genius; when he talked
the dilemma of the artist in modern America, he told another story:
that of the vulnerability of genius to social pressures, the curious
inability of the primordial and the autonomous to stay primordial
and autonomous. This second story is the backbone of Pound's career
– the backbone, in other words, of high modernism. The necessity
of reimagining the social sphere is initially a literary necessity, social
change pursued in order to ensure the life of the artist. Later, and
more grandly, in Pound's theorizing of the 1930s, in an odd utopian
echo of a famous passage in Marx, social change is pursued in order
to ensure that every man may fish in the morning for his sustenance
and pursue criticism and poetry in the afternoons; social change on
behalf of the artist in us all; society totally reimagined from the
aesthetic point of view.

But if it is precisely as a celebrant of a linked literary and political
*virtu* that Pound achieved his own *virtu* as a critical voice – he
became the polemical engine of high modernism – then the oddity
of Pound the poet is that he was haunted for his entire career by the
suspicion that he was not original, that he was a poet of no *virtu*
whatsoever. Out of this haunting by the spirits of literary history's
virtuous powers he fashioned a practice, from *A Lume Spento* through
*The Cantos,* more continuous than the usual views of his poetic
evolution (including his own) have generally allowed.

If no *virtu,* then no self; if no self, then nothing to express. Like
Stevens, Pound's life as a poet was in constant, if implicit, dialogue

with the archetypal and revolutionary American desire for radical origination in a new land ("new land, new men, new thoughts"), a desire for self-creation that Emerson thought would be realized only if we could forget history, rid ourselves of the old man of old thoughts from the old land. In order to kill himself off as an expression of history and simultaneously re-birth himself as the first man living utterly in the present, a man must "go into solitude," not only from society but also from his "chamber" – the place where "I read and write," where though no one is bodily present, "I" am "not solitary," because "I" have the unwanted company of all those represented selves who populate my books. The "I" must therefore be emptied of everything, including its literary company. And the virgin American woods, Emerson thought, is the context which might induce the necessary ascetic action, the place where "I" may escape all mediation and confront nature "face to face" – the place where "I" can say, at last, "I am nothing." With the historically layered self presumably so negated, the "I" – this urgent and almost passive emptiness which is not quite nothing – becomes a capacity for reception ("a transparent eyeball"), a hollowed-out space anxious to be filled: desire in its purest form – in Emerson, a no-self gratified, become filled up, and so rescued at the last moment from nothingness by the inflowing currents of the Transcendental Self.

Pound's effort to rethink lyric practice is inseparable from Emerson's dynamic of American desire, which in its turn is an expression of the quintessence of the immigrant imagination on its never-ending crossing of a real or metaphoric Atlantic, the immigrant who would leave "I" behind in the suffocating ghetto of a real or a metaphoric Europe (say, some small town in the Midwest), leave behind the "I" that *is* for a magically fulfilling self that we are not but would become – Vito Andolini become Vito Corleone, James Gatz become Jay Gatsby. In Pound, the Atlantic crossing is reversed and (in the trajectory of his biography) taken all the way back, from Idaho to Philadelphia to Italy. An American expatriate who left his country because he believed its cultural and economic system denied him literary selfhood, Pound took his American desire to make it new, the "nothing" that "I am," back to European ground, and in a cluster of his earliest poems figured himself precisely as a determinate emptiness of literary longing seeking writerly identity in recontact with international literary tradition, which is what he achieved in glamourous substitution for Emerson's Transcendental Self. What Pound learned very early was that the Emersonian promise of selfhood couldn't be delivered; Emerson's American woods, after all, were only natural, there was no literature there, no *selva oscura,* no Yeatsean mythological mystery. Our so-called virgin land was a nightmare to Pound precisely because of its solitude and its purity.

So, as a reverse immigrant, Pound fled the literary death whose name was natural immediacy, fled an America where he enjoyed the sorts of freedoms and comforts that classic immigrants coming to America sought. He went to Italy — his twenty-third birthday still several months off — seeking cultural life in the very period when millions of Italians from the south were fleeing their homes (such as they were) for America in the hope of improving an economic base that Pound's family had already secured, and upon which (thanks to his father's generous understanding) he could — and did — modestly draw during his expatriation. In effect, Pound replayed Henry James's criticism of America as a place whose cultural newness made a certain kind of literature improbable. James's core judgment of American society — he thought it "denuded" — signifies what, for him and for Pound, had been lost in the new world. James's solution was to drop the innocent American into the context of European experience: "one might enumerate the items of high civilization," James wrote, "as it exists in other countries, which are absent from the texture of American life until it should become a wonder to know what was left." The effect of such absence on an English or French imagination "would probably," he surmised, "be appalling." On himself and on Pound, the impact of such absence provided the energy for and often the structure of the writing they would do.

In a brief poem from *A Lume Spento,* Pound stages the predicament

of his empty American "I" gazing into the mirror of desire; he sees
"I" represented as a series of incompatible images; the denuded "I"
who *is* comes before the mirror and presumably "before" what is
represented in the mirror as the foundation of representation. But
this "I" is represented as somebody else, as the "he," the consciousness Pound would take on: "O strange face there in the glass!/O
ribald company, O saintly host!" "On His Own Face in a Glass"
stages the moment of self-awareness as a moment of some shock and
anxiety ("I? I? I?"), a moment of self-awareness in which he comes to
know that there is no self anterior to representation to be aware of
and that all the self that can ever be exists in the magical medium of
representation, in literature now envisioned, as the pilgrims and
other immigrants imagined America itself, as a mirror of transforming desire. Pound's primary poetic tone for such knowledge was
mainly confident, even grateful, as if in one stroke – the shape his
entire career would take bears heavily upon the point – he had
discovered a role to play which coordinated all of his impulses as
poet, literary historian, critic, anthologist, and translator, with this
last activity providing the cohesion which made the role unified,
lent it identity, so that he did become a self of sorts.

In the concluding poem of *A Lume Spento,* Pound represents his
soul as a "hole full of God" through which the "song of all time
blows. . . . As winds thru a knot-holed board." And in his first
English volume, *A Quinzaine for This Yule* (1908), he represents the
"I" similarly as a "clear space" –

> 'Tis as in midmost us there glows a sphere
> Translucent, molten gold, that is the "I"
> And into this some form projects itself:
> Christus, or John, or eke the Florentine;
> And as the clear space is not if a form's
> Imposed thereon,
> So cease we from all being for the time
> And there, the Masters of the Soul live on.

These early poems about poetry — so stilted, so unmodern in diction — escape mere conventionality by the extremity of their representation of the self seeking inspiration and poetic selfhood. As Pound figures it, his pre-poetic self is much less than that favorite romantic figure of self at home in the world, unanxiously dependent, self as aeolian harp awaiting the winds of nature that will stir it into music. Pound's pre-poetic self is in possession of no resources of its own. In what sense it is a self is hard to say: "Thus am I Dante for a space and am/One François Villon." But when not Dante or Villon, what then? Just who is this "I" who ceases to be when the virtuous and manly masters of his soul fill the hole of self? The self as translator, the self of no virtue, becomes a medium of the *virtu* of others, and Pound's poems, *The Cantos* most especially, become a kind of international gallery, a hall of exhibits of the originality that he lacked and that without his heroic retrieval would be locked away in a cultural dead space, of antiquarian interest only. Pound's famous avant-garde directive, "make it new," really means "make contemporary what is old." Pound is a man without a center, in whom the old masters can "live on"; his poetry is the lifeline and medium of their persistent historicity. His poetry's "modernity" would lie in its creation of a usable literary and political past, exemplary in force: a model to live by and a cultural community to live *in*.

If the absence of *virtu* is no condition to be overcome in a search for an original self of his own but the durable basis of everything Pound did as a poet — an absence of identity that he came comfortably to accept *as* his identity, a trigger of poetic production, early and late — then in one important sense Pound never really "evolved" as a poet. The numerous and dramatic shifts in style we can note from *A Lume Spento* to *The Cantos* — and not only from volume to volume but often within a given volume — are not evidence of the dissatisfied, self-critical young writer groping toward his one and only true voice, but the very sign of his voice and all the maturity he would ever achieve. The word Pound frequently used to describe this persistent mark of change in his poetic writing was *metamorphosis*, from "the tradition of metamorphoses," as he explained in 1918, "that teaches us that things do not always remain the same. They become other things by swift and unanalysable process." Pound's theory of myth was based on an attempt to explain the moment when a man, after walking "sheer into nonsense," tried to tell someone else about it "who called him a liar." The man was forced to make a myth, "an impersonal or objective story woven out of his own emotion, as the nearest equation that he was capable of putting into words."

Among the manifestations of Pound's obsession with protean energy there is his radically avant-garde idea of literature as "something living, something capable of constant transformation and re-birth"; his doctrine of the image, which asserts that in the presence of the genuine work of art we experience "the sense of sudden liberation; that sense of freedom from time and space limits; that sense of sudden growth"; and his statement in *The Spirit of Romance* that myth takes its origin subjectively, in a moment when we pass through "delightful psychic experience." In the period spanning the many stylistic changes from his earliest poems to his early *Cantos*, Pound changed not at all on the value of metamorphosis for the sort of writer (himself) who explained the process of writing to himself in his earliest poems as an experience of walking sheer into nonsense – becoming Christ, Villon, or Dante, God or a tree – a writer who would project the psychic value of his own aesthetic experience as the real value of *reading* his poems. Pound's reader would also be freed from the self of the moment, liberated into some strange and bracing identity, joining the writer in mythic experience in order to take on, with Pound, what he, like Pound, does not possess.

The unstated assumption of Pound's poetics is that his typical reader is not everyman but an American like himself, in need of what he needs – a reader, in other words, not only with no *virtu* of his own but who does not want to be fixed with a "self," a reader for whom avant-gardism, though not known as such, is the ruling philosophy of everyday life in the land of opportunity and infinite self-development. From the delightful, because liberating, psychic experience of the poet and the parallel experience of his American reader comes this projection: the reformation of literary history in his own (and America's) image via the bold antidefinition of literature as writing without historically prior and persistent identity, writing without a prior "self" to rely on, a nonidentity of sheerest possibility, an absence of essence: "constant transformation," constant rebirth into a newness of (these are equivalents) an American and a modern literary selfhood. Never mind that "constant transformation" also describes the dream of consumer capitalism, avant-garde of capitalist economics.

Metamorphosis is the unprecedented master category in Pound's literary theory. And in spite of the explicit Ovidian allusion, the theory is not Ovidian. Nor does Pound draw upon a notion of biological metamorphosis: the man who comes "before" the glass can not be traced, not even obscurely, as a surviving form in the new self (hence Pound's shocked "I?"). But if there is to be metamorphosis in any recognizable sense of the word, there must be a prior something which undergoes transformation. If the prior "something" is, as in Pound, a determinate nothing, a hole needing filling and fulfilling, valuable ("golden") precisely because of its amorphic condition, then Pound has pushed metamorphosis to the edge of its limiting boundary: the classic American dream, self-origination ex nihilo. Pound theorizes metamorphosis, a process of self-emergence, as Emerson had theorized it: on a condition of potential-for-self only, not the transformation of one self into another, a condition without a memory out of which a self might emerge that is nothing but memory, and thus – the irony and paradox of Pound's career – no self at all.

When some of his earliest poems were republished in 1965, Pound dismissed them as a "collection of stale creampuffs," a judgment that

obscures his true target, toward which he would always feel a residual and unresolvable ambivalence: the fin-de-siècle literary scene that
had energized him by lending him masks of identity. By 1908,
when he left America for Venice, those masks marked the existence
of an avant-garde solidified by its rejection of the world that young
writers had found fully in place in England and America in the last
decades of the nineteenth century. The distinction of what is called
high modernism may be that no literary movement ever had less
respect for its social situation.

The exemplary literary rejectors – Swinburne, Rossetti and the
pre-Raphaelites, the decadents of the 1890s, and the most famous
poet writing in English when Pound left for Venice, W. B. Yeats –
were isolationists of the aesthetic who desired to fashion a self-
contained world of art, not in order to celebrate the wonders of
aesthetic autonomy, but in order to win their freedom from a world
they detested and feared they could not escape. Thus the hankerings
after apocalypse, the hope that the body of all that is world and
worldly had entered its autumnal phase, those poetic landscapes
enshrouded in mists and shadows, that nostalgia for precapitalist
societies, those extraordinary investments in the magic of word
color, the newly revitalized interest in the mythological imagination
which represents the world as an enchanted place frequented by the
gods, and, most of all, and presiding over everything, the monolithic tonality of mournfulness. Hulme, surveying the scene, said
that a poem couldn't be a poem unless it was "moaning or whining
about something or other." The children of Swinburne (the young
Pound was one of them) could not achieve escape from the disen-
chanted world made by capital and its agents – those money
changers, journalists, and literary realists who were Yeats's relentless
representatives for what, in a telling gesture of aestheticist despair,
he called, in the opening poem of *Crossways* (1889), "Grey Truth," a
code term signifying all the forces against the aesthetic, particularly
the politics of democracy, capitalist economics, and science. These
are the forces opposed by "dream" ("Dream, dream, for this is also

sooth"), another key code word in the literary context of the young Pound, signifying poetry as a mode of contemplation, vision, and revery, all in the service of world-weariness turned inward, subjectivity pursued ("Then nowise worship dusty deeds"); an affirmation of the word over the act; poetry as a fragile haven off the route where history was too obviously tending.

The retrospective embarrassment Pound felt for his earlier work aside, the poems themselves taken as a whole present considerable evidence of the sort of energy for aesthetic experiment and variety that would mark *The Cantos*. Even *A Lume Spento* (1908), all by itself, is an image of the various energies at work in late-nineteenth and early-twentieth-century English poetry. The mythological imagination he recovered via Greece, Ovid, and Yeats's Celtic twilight gave Pound a nature not virgin and sensuous, a nature not natural, but bookishly mediated, alive with the sort of culture that a modernized, skeptical, and secular world was coming thoroughly to disrecognize: "By the still pool of Mar-nan-otha/ Have I found me a bride/That was a dog-wood tree some syne"; "I stood still and was a tree amid the wood/ Knowing the truth of things unseen before,/ Of Daphne and the laurel bow." Snugly alongside such bookish lyricism from the other world, a voice much in evidence in the early Pound, was the robust earthiness of Browning: "Bah! I have sung women in three cities,/ But it is all the same"; "Aye you're a man that! ye old mesmerizer"; there was also the lament of the decadent all too aware of his victimization and the lateness of his arrival: "Broken our strength, yes as crushed reeds we fall,/ And yet the art, the *art* goes on"; there was the voice that speaks through the stylish troubadour mask of Bertran de Born: "Tho thou dost wish me ill/ Audiart, Audiart"; and there was the poet who would animate genteel diction with infusions of a native diction, not directly but through the mask of another poet (Villon) who Pound thought had found a speech "unvarnished," and who came to Pound thanks to a late-nineteenth-century vogue as much for his persona as for his writing – via

Rossetti's translation. Villon, a poet "without illusion," would "revive our poetry in the midst of mid-Victorian dessication."

"A Villonaud for This Yule" bears Pound's characteristic habits as a poet: the fashioning of a poetic discourse out of pastiche and translation, one of whose effects is to root lyric impulse historically, draw it through layers of tradition, as a writing done over other writing ("palimpsest" was one of Pound's key words for *The Cantos*). Thus to write lyric was to write the history of lyric in a kind of scholarly act graced at the same time by a poet's sort of footnote – allusion – and thereby to embed lyric feeling in a long tradition, to make lyric into an emotional and intellectual "complex," to engage spontaneity with reflection. Thus to write lyric is to fashion a composite of borrowings and inspirations whose effect is to suggest that the poet's intention is to create singlehandedly a traditional culture out of his welded fragments and bring it home to his time. De Born's "borrowed lady" or, as the Italians translated it, *una donna ideale,* is also a figure of Pound's lyric practice and his desire to instigate cultural *risorgimento,* for America in particular. *Una donna ideale* is the image of the tradition – his true Beatrice – that, particularly in *The Cantos,* Pound would invent by piecing together a new writing characterized by allusion, quotation, translation, adaptation, pastiche, even original writing in another language. This new poetry would be open to the inclusion of history by way of the incorporation of half-acres of document, the brute prose of chronicle that Pound jammed into the intimate rooms of his elegant lyricism. This is lyric impulse forced to live with what the commercial enforcers of lyric taste in Pound's young manhood refused to live with: a heterogeneity of discourses often not only unlyric but positively, at times, antilyric.

In *Personae* and *Exultations* (both 1909) Pound added a new voice to his ensemble, one that threw into sharp relief the mask of the langorous and passive aesthete. *Personae,* with its Yeats-echoing epigraph ("*Make strong old dreams lest this our world lose heart*"), contains

Pound's adaptation from D'Aubigne, an anti-aestheticist mask which stresses the muscular and martial involvement of the poet who writes "From the Saddle," whose lines necessarily bear the stress and strain of the active life. "From the Saddle" may be Pound's first incarnation in the mask of the fully integrated sensibility, a lyric expression traced by the sounds of battle. Nevertheless, "From the Saddle" continues to flourish turn-of-the-century manners ("with gin and snare right near alway," "Ever on word," "Tis meet my verse"). "Sestina: Altaforte" is more direct—"Damn it all! all this our South stinks peace./You whoreson dog, Papiols, come! Let's to music!" – though it is a highly literary directness, sounding with the voice of some forceful Shakespearean hero. Gaudier-Brzeska's creative misauditing of this poem (for the repeated "peace" he heard, repeatedly, "piss") is true to Pound's macho spirit and led to Gaudier-Brzeska's sculpting of the phallic bust of Pound, with the ironic caveat that it would not *look* like Pound; the phallic bust which was the very image of the poet as red blood that Pound would later criticize in the inheritors of Whitman, not seeing it in himself, perhaps, because when he looked in the glass of his poetry he saw no self there he recognized as his own, because these masculinist masks were just that, masks.

But they were masks of critical point, yearning portraits of medieval vigor. Here is Pound's unusual, because for once positive, connection with mass culture – the popular romance fiction of his day; here is his implicit criticism of his own decadent manner and a high culture whose neurasthenia was being medically reported on in the magazines of the day and would be definitively dissected in "The Love Song of J. Alfred Prufrock." In his "Ballad of the Goodly Fere," Pound adopted a dialect voice out of Robert Burns in an effort to savage the conventional, whispy Christ of the herd mentality with an antithetical "man o' men was he," a man like the seafarer and Ulysses ("Wi' his eyes like the grey o' of the sea") – a man of the deed ("They'll no' get him a' in a book I think . . . No mouse of the

## Ezra Pound

scrolls was the Goodly Fere/But aye loved the open sea"). Pound's vitalist Christ was a criticism not only of the virtually disembodied mainstream representations of Christ that had infuriated him, but an attack (like Frost's) on the bookish flight he saw everywhere in contemporary poetry – a critical image not only because of His masculinity but also because of the sound of His speech; no sophisticated ennui there.

By title and by vocal attitude, "Francesca," one of the poems Pound placed toward the end of *Exultations,* forecasts the mode that preoccupied him in a volume that would prove to be a turning point, *Canzoni* (1911), which caused Ford Madox Ford to roll on the floor in didactic laughter – a response that made a decisive impact on Pound's style, or so Pound said. *Canzoni* was saturated with medieval colors from Dante and Cavalcanti: poem after poem was a hushed adoration of a lady of ladies (*donna non vidi mai*), Pound's own version of Beatrice enfolded in a light not of the sun: "A splendid calyx that about her gloweth/Smiting the sunlight on whose ray she goeth." Apparently Ford thought that Pound had captured his Neoplatonic vision all too well, in a poetic manner also "not of the sun." Pound took the point to heart – and would pass it on to Yeats in another and similarly significant act of literary history.

Beginning with *Ripostes* (1912) and then *Lustra* (1916), Pound managed to reform his phrasing to a prosier (though elegant) mode while forsaking conventional decorum. He began to write a poetry that could live up to the theoretical principles he and Hulme were forging in tandem. The impulse to write lines like "Guerdoned by thy sun-gold traces" or phrases like "eke the Florentine" would be purged. But in "Francesca" Pound had already begun to break that habit, had already managed to produce a voice at once plain (by the standards of educated conversation), formal, and elevated – a "curial" voice that he would come to rely on for the numerous lyric passages that stud *The Cantos* and that provides striking contrast to his self-conscious masculinity. Thus, "Francesca":

> You came in out of the night
> And there were flowers in your hands,
> Now you will come out of a confusion of people,
> Out of a turmoil of speech about you.

And in *Canzoni* itself there are other vocal presences, including a satiric one, which would bloom in *Lustra* and beyond:

> O woe, woe,
> People are born and die,
> We shall also be dead pretty soon
> Therefore let us act as if we were
>       dead already.

If it is the case that the poetry of *Canzoni* is more various than the poet of *Canzoni* (and Ford) would allow, it is also true that the dominant mood of the volume is sustained by Pound's visionary portraits of the Beatrice-like woman who is the model of self-generating originality which Pound praised in the male poets he most admired, and which he learned, from his glimpse in the glass, that he could not claim for himself. His adoring tone is not for some imagined ineffectual angel, placed on a pedestal because (according to ancient fantasy) she is safe nowhere else, but for the female representation of a power of self-possession and independence that underwrote his basic values in politics (anti-imperialism, individualism) and in poetics (the autonomous genius, the active soul). This visionary woman will reappear in numerous passages of *The Cantos* as a goddess from out of ancient myths, brought back to life, in Pound's meditations, as a sudden new visitor to modern Italy, a breakthrough of the gods:

> And the cities set in their hills,
> And the goddess of the fair knees
> Moving there, with the oak-wood behind her,

## Ezra Pound

The green slope, with her white hounds leaping about
her . . .

The awed tone (Canto 17) of one who has been gratuitously blessed,
privileged with the ultimate surprise, is the mark of Pound's relation
to visionary women in *Canzoni* and *The Cantos*. But the difference
between her earlier and later appearances is important. In *The Cantos*
she stands not alone, as she does in *Canzoni*, a pure presence vulnerable to Ford's ironies – Ford was Pound's Mercutio – but as an
element in an integrated complex, a lyric moment of praise placed in
a poetic texture thick with many other things, most of them not
lyric. She is an element in a complex writing who is protected from
skeptics by her unprepared-for appearances and quick disap-
pearances. In *Ripostes* (1912) she is present briefly in a Dantean
metamorphosis ("Apparuit"), a change from ordinariness ("Thou a
slight thing") to visionary splendor ("I saw/thee. . . . then shone
thine oriel and the stunned light/faded about thee"). And she is
present powerfully by her absence in the volume's most riveting
poem, "Portrait D'Une Femme," a picture of the culturally privileged but dessicated female of no force, pathetically dependent, a
collector of objects of aestheticist delight and utter inconsequence
("Idols and ambergris and rare inlays"), not an independent power of
light that stuns the light of the sun but a metaphoric Sargasso Sea.
The poem's opening and scandalous first line ("Your mind and you
are our Sargasso Sea") horrified at least one famous genteel American
editor: "I sent them a real poem, a modern poem, containing the
word 'uxorious,' and they wrote back that I used the letter 'r' three
times in the first line, and that it was very difficult to pronounce,
and that I might not remember that Tennyson had once condemned
the use of four s's in a certain line of a different meter."

Pound's deliberate antilyricism in "Portrait D'Une Femme" is the
vehicle of his narrative intention to tell a story, implicated in the
details of useless junk that clogs a sensibility afloat, of a self without
a center; not a trashed female antithesis of his manly seafarer, but a

figure of the aesthete within that he would exorcise in its male incarnation in his literary farewell to London, *Hugh Selwyn Mauberly.* "Portrait D'Une Femme" is also, and most importantly, a riposte in form as well as in theme: a concentrated narrative that exorcises bad lyric and all its sentimentality with this kind of conversational piquancy:

> You have been second always. Tragical?
> No. You preferred it to the usual thing:
> One dull man, dulling and uxorious. . . .

The distance Pound traveled between *A Lume Spento* and *Lustra* can in part be measured by the titles of those volumes: the first in the self-pitying mood of the fin de siècle ("with quenched tapers"); the second in the worldly and interventionist mode of the social criticism that he would increasingly be loath to segregate from the project of his poetry ("Lustrum: an offering for the sins of the whole people, made by the censors at the expiration of their five years of office"). *Lustra* contains roughly two kinds of poetry: one borne by an insouciant plainness of antilyric voice, direct in syntax and satiric in intent, with the object of heaping hostile criticism on the bourgeois order that has no use for what Pound called "the serious artist." This voice is funny but often tiresomely insistent in *Lustra,* marking poem after poem with the (even then) conventional postures of bohemian scorn out of the garret: "Will people accept them?/(i.e. these songs). . . . Their virgin stupidity is untemptable. . . . " Or this: "Come, let us pity those who are better off/than we are. . . . " The second kind of poem, with ancestry in *Canzoni* (though in plainer syntax), presents the adored vision of female *virtu* ("She passed and left no quiver in the veins"), now grounded in the earthier poetics implied by "The Study in Aesthetics," an anecdotal reflection set in Sirmione. And Pound's choice of the Italian "Sirmione" rather than the Latin "Sirmio," which he favored in *Canzoni,* tells us that his literary reveries with tradition are feeling the gravity of contemporary life.

Even as he turned out small poem after small poem and a shocking number of pages of prose, Pound was all along – perhaps as early as 1904, while a student at Hamilton College – working himself up to writing a long poem of epic size, "long after" (Pound speaking) "mankind has been commanded never again to attempt a poem of any length." He apparently began work in earnest on this poem sometime in 1915, published his first three "cantos," as he called them, in *Poetry* in 1917, only soon thereafter to suppress them and began anew. After an initial volume appeared in 1925 as *A Draft of XVI Cantos,* gatherings of cantos were published with regularity, to the end of Pound's life, including the infamous *Pisan Cantos* in 1948 and two volumes, in 1955 and 1959, written in the insane asylum. The least taught of the famous modernist texts, the collected volume, *The Cantos of Ezra Pound* – one hundred and seventeen cantos' worth – appeared in 1970 and has been reprinted ten times as of this writing, this latter fact strong testimony on behalf of our continuing fascination with the high modernists, including this one whose major work is widely assumed to be unreasonably difficult, often pure gibberish, and, in its occasionally lucid moments, offensive to most standards of decency.

Just what kind of literary work he was writing Pound had trouble deciding. He was keenly conscious of his epic predecessors and often glossed their intentions as his own: to give voice to the "general heart," to write "the speech of a nation" through the medium of one person's sensibility. Yet for all his classic desire and expressed contempt for romantic poetry, Pound was also marked by its contrary aesthetic: "the man who tries to explain his age instead of expressing himself," he writes, "is doomed to destruction." In Pound, the poetics of *The Odyssey* and *The Divine Comedy* are complicated by the poetics of *The Prelude* and *Song of Myself:* refocused by Pound in the lens of Wordsworth, Whitman, and Poe, *The Divine Comedy* becomes Dante's "tremendous lyric."

Classic ambition and romantic impulse would surface constantly through the long publishing history of *The Cantos.* An "epic is a poem including history," Pound wrote in 1935, in the midst of a decade during which he was writing cantos that "included" history and chunks of the historical record with stupefying literality: redactions of Chinese history in Cantos 52–61, extract after extract from the writings of John Adams in Cantos 62–71. In 1937, in *Guide to Kulchur,* he declared (with a nod to Kipling) that his long poem would tell "the tale of the tribe," but in the same book he also described *The Cantos,* with analogy to Bartók's Fifth Quartet, as the "record of a personal struggle." Then, in the middle of the journey, in 1939, he struck a new note, this one neither epic nor romantic: "As to the form of *The Cantos:* All I can say or pray is wait till it's there. I mean wait till I get'em written and then if it don't show, I will start exegesis. I haven't an Aquinas-map; Aquinas *not* valid now." And with that nostalgic glance back at the cultural context of his beloved Dante, Pound approached the clarity he achieved in 1962 in his *Paris Review* dialogue with Donald Hall.

With over a hundred cantos done, he gave Hall a definition – antidefinition, really – of the poem's form that marked it "modernist" in strictest terms. Not Homer or Dante, but Joyce and Eliot stand behind Pound's search for a form "that wouldn't exclude something merely because it didn't fit." With this gesture Pound declares the classic concern of aesthetics for the decorous relationship of genre to subject matter beside the modernist point. He tells us that the literary form that can include what doesn't fit is the authentic signature of modern writing, the sign that the literature of our time has adequately taken the measure of its exploded culture.

Like Wordsworth, Pound felt himself an outsider in his society, a literary radical who knew that his poetry was unrecognizable as such by mainstream culture. As a consequence, he set himself the task (in Wordsworth's phrasing) "of *creating* the taste by which he is to be enjoyed." His project was to provide epic substance for a culture grounded in none of the assumptions that typically had nourished the epic poet: a culture no longer capable of issuing a valid rhetorical contract between writer and reader. In a culture that cannot read him – here is the motivating contradiction of *The Cantos* and much high modernism – Pound would write a poem that his culture needs to read in order to make itself truly a culture. "The modern mind contains heteroclite elements. The past epos has succeeded when all or a great many of the answers were assumed, at least between author and audience. The attempt in an experimental age" – he means socially as well as aesthetically experimental – "is therefore rash."

Rash or no, Pound persisted in epic intention because, as he told Hall, "there *are* epic subjects. The struggle for individual rights is an epic subject, consecutive from jury trial in Athens to Anselm versus William Rufus, to the murder of Becket and to Coke and through John Adams." So the poem that Pound had mainly written by 1962 found its home, not in a specific Western culture and place, as classical epics had done, but in Western culture as a whole, as the grand story of struggle, not yet won, for individual rights; and it found its strange literary form in an age of experiment that demanded he invent his own. The form he invented is at once the representation of a culture he thought to be in fragments and an offering of hope for a different kind of future, rooted in the narrative of common lineage and destiny.

Pound knew that in order to tell the tale of the tribe he needed a tribe to tell it *to,* knew he didn't have one, and in *The Cantos* – a poem without unifying epic hero or stability of cultural scene – he gave us the unlikely record of one poet's effort to create through means unclassical a new classical situation for writing. What he ended up achieving was a poem whose experimental character overwhelms all cultural and social goals except those that bear on the welfare of writers. *The Cantos* would resuscitate a community of letters for modern writers, in order that they might join a tradition of radical experimenters and their noble patrons, all those who waged their struggle for individual (largely aesthetic) rights against the grain; a tradition brought to life for an age (our own) cut off from nourishment and patronage, a home for our contemplative, but only our contemplative, life.

In this light, Pound's title, *The Cantos,* is tellingly odd. It is the nontitle of a writer who apparently never saw the need to make up his mind – who, if he could have lived forever, would probably not have endowed his experiment with a crystallizing title (like *The Waste Land* or *The Bridge*). Calling a poem *The Cantos* (and shall we say *The Cantos* "is" or *The Cantos* "are"? – to decide that question is to decide much) is like calling a novel *Work in Progress* while writing it and then publishing it under that title, or perhaps *The Chapters,* like a Renaissance sonneteer deciding to call his sequence *The Sonnets.* To publish sections of this poem, forever in progress, with the words "a draft of" included in the title only underscores the tentativeness of the writer's intention. Unlike all the epics we know, *The Cantos* names as its substance aesthetic form itself, without ever claiming, as Wordsworth and Whitman had in their romantic versions, the substantial coherence of a binding subjectivity.

Not that there isn't a discernible subjectivity afloat in the poem: there is, but it doesn't congeal as a "self" whose autonomous presence is projected in the autobiographical narrative of a poet's mind. For much of the way, "Ezra Pound" appears to us in the shape of a desire: as a generous capacity for reception, a virtually transparent subjectivity, a facilitating vehicle, a literary producer (in the theatrical sense of that word, a gatherer of artistic forces), a man, by his own account, of no *virtu,* an absence of selfhood, a hole, a mirror for others. This tissue of masks, this incessant scholarly quoter – translator, alluder, medium of pastiche, tradition's own ventriloquist – this poet as anthologist, poet of the specimen, patron and exhibitor of styles, heroes, and cultural contexts which are given space in the literary gallery and curriculum called *The Cantos,* is an active and empathetic memory trapped in the dead present of his culture, casting a long lifeline into the past (as tradition's own lifeguard) in order to rescue by transmitting tradition, and in so transmitting bring his own culture back to life again.

*The Cantos* approached as if they were written by a poet-without-a-self unveil themselves as a vast texture (text, textile, interweaving) of discourses lyric, satiric, narrative, dramatic, and nonliterary (historical, epistolary, technical); Pound's influential idea of the heterogeneous image (an "intellectual and emotional complex in an instant of time") writ very large; an immense vortex; or, in the perfect metaphor from the discarded first canto (drafted in 1912), a "ragbag," best form of all for a poet who didn't want to exclude something merely because it didn't fit; the form of a poetry by and for the culturally homeless.

And so the centrality for *The Cantos* of those storied modernist metaphors drawn from the visual and spatial arts: like *montage,* a stark juxtaposition that yields its significance in some third, unnamed thing to be construed (imagined, created), by an active reader in the process of interpretation, whose own imaginative life will be the force which brings Pound's cultural hope to realization, and who is charged with voicing the poem's otherwise unvoiced vision, with making the diagnosis, distributing Pound's medicine; a reader who appreciates Pound properly and therefore earns his own entry into the community of letters by transforming himself from passive consumer in the culture of capital into resourceful, self-reliant free agent; Pound's critic become the reader as modernist, comaker of *The Cantos,* and coworker in the enterprise of culture-making. And of course the metaphor of *collage,* surrealist version of the ragbag, a composition whose diverse and incongruously placed fragments – drawn from all manner of media – asks us (as does montage, but now on the scale of the entire work) to take the thing as a whole, not as a narrative but as a form hung in space, in order to "view" it in its entirety. Under the pressure of these metaphors, *The Cantos* become a difficult structure of fragments signifying not the imitation of fragmentation by means of fragmentation but some missing total vision (or the desire thereof), whose presence in any given canto must be supplied by an engaged reader. So read, *The Cantos* emerge as a vision of social and cultural health sporadically in evidence and constantly threatened by the historical process; a vision of the free individual gathering himself against history's gloom of diseased economics; a vision contemplated and disseminated by those who must read Pound in a thickening contemporary cultural darkness that is almost complete. *The Cantos* may be the clearest example we have of the doubled character of Pound's literary desire, to pursue aesthetic innovation for the purpose of instigating social change, a poem whose unparalleled formal sumptuousness – a cornucopia of literary texture – calls forth those mediators who would join Pound's life-long experiment in cultural hope to a world of possible readers.

"And then went down to the ship/Set keel to breakers, forth on the godly sea. . . . " That is how *The Cantos* begin, in a strange world modified by gods, with Pound translating from the eleventh book of *The Odyssey,* the descent into the underworld. Assuming the mask of an epic hero already written, Pound voyages, "Heavy with weeping" (the tone is elegiac, the subject is cultural loss), to a place of darkness, dimly lit with torches, for a colloquy with the dead, the prophetic Tiresias in particular. Ezra Pound, Odyssean poet, makes his descent into the West's literary underworld in order to conjure the ghosts of writers past in a poetry of reading. Homer's hero summons the dead with the ritual blood of sacrifice; Pound, with the blood of scholarly poetic labor, would summon Homer via a Latin translation made by Andreas Divas in the Renaissance, period of classical recovery; he presses his Latin Homer through the alliterative strong rhythms of Anglo-Saxon poetry and then into modern English, thereby producing the effect of a triple translation for the benefit of the modern English reader, an illusion of three literary traditions simultaneously present in culturally mixed traces of diction and proper names, a palimpsest, writing over writing for a period – his own – which Pound hoped would also be a time of cultural recovery.

The first of *The Cantos* begins the project of a new *risorgimento* as if it were already in progress: the first word of the first canto is *and*. We are offered a stylistic exhibit of heroic endeavor, by a poet-patron, toward the end of which the stylistic exhibitor himself comes forward, breaking out of the mask of Odysseus. In an abrupt comic descent from the heroic decorum of his tone and diction, Ezra Pound speaks – "Lie quiet Divas" – so revealing himself in that moment as a haunter of libraries and old bookstores – in the dramatic fiction of Canto 1, a man pouring over a rare book – searching for the traces of a usable tradition, and finding them in the text of Divas's translation.

In the eleventh book of Homer's epic, Odysseus' youngest companion, Elpenor, asks Odysseus to provide him proper burial, lest he restlessly and forever wander the earth's surface, and he requests a memorial so that he may enjoy an afterlife in his culture's collective memory. Just so does Pound grant Divas, another unhappy ghost, similar (if imagined) requests in order that Divas may "lie quiet." And Pound's autobiographically aggressive translation of Homer's epitaph for Elpenor ("*A man of no fortune, and a name to come*") links him to Elpenor and Divas both, and to a literary history that merges ancient, Renaissance, and modern cultures in an overarching triplet rhyme of tradition-making, the point of literary history being its own transmission; the immortality of writers depending on other writers who remember long.

Pound, a bibliophile and cultural genealogist, gives the citation as a kind of epitaph: "I mean, that is Andreas Divas,/In officina

Wecheli, 1538, out of Homer." Divas and Wecheli (the bookmaker),
those, too, are names of heroes in the commemorative world of *The
Cantos,* heroes as significant as Odysseus. For one more line and a
half Pound returns, now in his own voice — the spell of recovery is
broken — to the Homeric narrative, then (as it were) flips the pages
to the back of the book that Wecheli made, this time quoting the
Latin of Georgius Dartona of Cyprus, whose translation of the
Homeric hymns was bound in with Divas's work: some enamoured
phrases about Aphrodite ("thou with dark eyelids"), who was as-
signed the defenses of Crete, phrases whose Latin will be strange to
the modern reader, but much less strange than the idea they contain,
absurd to the modern mind (Pound knows this), of art active in the
world, beauty in defense of the city. At the end of Canto 1 Pound
comes forward as a voice among old books, trying to breathe life into
voices he feared had been silenced by his culture. In that act, he
creates a voice of his own.

> Two mice and a moth my guides —
> > To have heard the farfalla gasping
> > > as toward a bridge over worlds.
> > That the kings meet in their island,
> > > Where no food is after flight from the pole.
> > Milkweed the sustenance
> > > as to enter arcanum.
>
> To be men not destroyers.

That is how *The Cantos* end, with Pound writing lyric notes: on the
forms of his confusion ("M'amour, m'amour/what do I love
and/where are you?"); on his regrets ("Let the Gods forgive what
I/have made/Let those I love try to forgive/what I have made"); on
his econo-aesthetic obsessions ("La faillite de François Bernouard,
Paris" — Bernouard, unsung, unknown in poetry until this moment
in *The Cantos,* a contemporary version of Wecheli, a hero in the
cultural struggle for *risorgimento,* a French bookmaker who went

bankrupt printing the classics and who functions here as an incarnation of history's truth, Pound-style: the destruction of the honorable by a dishonorable economic system that will not permit the valuing of beauty and beauty's patrons). Notes, too, on his unceasing hatred for the human costs of war and the cold-blooded calculation of the secure-from-battle ("the young for the old/that is tragedy"); notes on his sustaining confidence in the liberating power of the image as the bedrock of personal redemption, aestheticist life-preserver of Pound's youth coming in handy at the end of a life of failed larger design ("For the blue flash and the moments/benedetta"); notes on his grandiose ambition ("I have tried to write Paradise"), his anchoring modesty, his disavowal of ambition ("Do not move/Let the wind speak/that is paradise"); notes on his cultural deprivation, having to go it, as Dante did not, without a Virgil-like teacher for his guide ("Two mice and a moth my guides − "). All his notes are the verbal condensation of desire, and desire, the gathering ambience of *The Cantos*, become palpable, the real subject of this last collection, *Drafts and Fragments* (1969).

In this final fragment of the final canto (117), a collage representative of virtually everything Pound thought about in *The Cantos* as a whole, the striking note sounded is not in some final revelation for poet and reader but in the variegated sounds of the poet's voice − in Pound's tonal agility, his compression of a range of vocal attitudes: the desperate old man, speaking painfully in the dark, sometimes in the curious mixed tones of prayer and imperative; sometimes in gentle self-directive; sometimes in fragments of amazement ("That I lost my center/fighting the world"; "That the kings meet in their island/where no food is after flight from the pole"); sometimes in desire's timeless infinitive ("To have heard the farfalla gasping/as toward a bridge over worlds"). Fragment follows fragment, in a poem heavy with sharply etched perceptions and feelings freed (largely) from reason's habitat of correct English syntax: a poem of reason undone, and in its unravelment of reason displaying the constituents of a mind trying to strip itself of the authoritative power of utterance it used to command (half-wanting to fail, still desiring authority), wanting to enter the realm of the unspeakable with the Monarch butterflies in need of no food – those kings that are figures of the soul entering the last mystery. The final line is the one with which Pound (according to his lover, Olga Rudge) wanted to end *The Cantos,* a line impossibly poised in tone and form, hung between yearning and self-confident imperative: "To be men not destroyers."

Between the first and the last of *The Cantos,* in a cluster which occupies the virtual center of the entire work – approximately fifty lie on either side of it – fall the Chinese and American history cantos (52–71), a section nearly one-quarter the length of the complete cantos, and presenting the one continuous stretch of writing to be found in *The Cantos of Ezra Pound;* a chronological span recounting some five thousand years of Chinese history, from 3000 B.C. through the eighteenth century A.D., mediated for America by the French Enlightenment (when Chinese texts began to be translated), an era in European thought that eventually passed formatively into the social theories of John Adams and the founding fathers.

There's a point to Pound's history, but the point is not easy to grasp because his history is told in a rush of names, dates, references, and events presented largely without explanation or narrative connection. The effect is one of relentless obscurity, which was perhaps Pound's intention: to rub our noses in the fact that we have been cut off from the sources of what he imagined to be social vitality, that we have no tradition, that we need to make another Odyssean journey back to another cultural underworld, one not Western, and that we can do it, but it will take scholarly work. Such work itself would, presumably, be salutary, a sign that we are recovering (in both senses of the word), for in doing the work that Pound asks, we begin the process of self-healing. And if enough of us who do this work of recovery will only disseminate its findings, we shall be on our way to cultural and not just personal healing as the active readers whom Pound needs in the corporate effort to make the bridge between the isolated island of the modern world and the mainland of cultural history. The payoff will be a renovated economics, with justice for all, and a renovated language in which the word will bear the right name. Like an honest currency (in Pound that means an imagist economics), the word will not go the way of abstraction because it will be ligatured to real goods extant. And economics and poetics alike will be underwritten by a benevolent totalitarian (Confucius being a more perfect totalitarian than Aristotle; Mussolini, the hopeful modern instance), who protects money and words, properly ligatured, from manipulation by usurers, gun manufacturers, the fantastic international Jewish conspiracy, and other corrupters, financial and aesthetic, real and imaginary.

So do the Chinese and Adams cantos work in theory; in practice, and by the measure of Pound's aesthetic, they are a literary disaster. The aesthetic and the great majority of cantos insist on heterogeneity in texture, voice, and form; the Chinese and Adams cantos present a homogeneous voice of didactic intent. The aesthetic and the great majority of cantos insist on fragments and the surprising and delightful juxtapositions of montage which invite creative reading; the Chinese and Adams cantos progress by a principle of deadly smooth continuity that puts the reader into the passive position of a student listening to a lecturer with no dramatic talent. The literary project of *The Cantos* is modernist, but cantos 52–71 fulfill no one's idea of modernist writing, or even, perhaps, of interesting writing.

The Chinese/Adams cantos fail because they lack the vivid presence of cultural poverty that motivates Pound's project for redemption. They give us a portrait of the poet comfortable in his views, speaking without duress from nowhere. But at their most riveting *The*

*Cantos* evoke as their true speaking subject, however minimally, the presence of a writer – *The Cantos* are "about" a writer as much as they are "about" anything – a writer engaged in struggle, working against the grain, under the inspiration of the muses of memory, those muses being his only hope in a culture without memory; as in Canto 1, for example, where, at the end, we finally see Pound, book in hand, meditating on ancient ideals of heroism and beauty from a place where those ideals are not honored. Or in Canto 2, where Pound fictionalizes himself, Whitman-like, as a brooder at the seashore, a man for whom all mythologies of the sea are simultaneously present, from Homer to Ovid to Picasso, but with no mythology of his own to be at home in. "And" – the linguistic sign of Pound's consciousness, eager to bind together – here in Canto 2 becomes the sign of a mind which says "and" because it cannot say "because" – because it cannot trace a logical path to its leap into Ovid's *Metamorphoses,* the presiding cultural exhibit of canto 2.

"And by Scios": Pound becomes a first-person participant in the story of the kidnapping of the young Dionysus by sailors who would sell him into slavery (not knowing who he was). The episode retold from Ovid is a story whose chief characters, in many variants, dominate *The Cantos,* a story of money lust and mythic power: poetry turned against and vanquishing greed (usually the story ends badly in *The Cantos,* but not here); Dionysus is unleashed, and Pound in attendance, awestruck, retelling the consequences for the ears of worldly power ("Fish scales on the oarsmen," "Arms shrunk into fins"): "And you Pentheus, had as well listen . . . or your luck will go out of you." Canto 2 concludes with a return to the brooding poet in his place on the shore. With his vision lapsed into the desolation of the present, and the Ovidian memory fading fast, now only an after-image mediating his experience of the sea, Pound presses Homer's epithet of the wine-dark sea through Ovid's Bacchus ("wave, color of grape's pulp"); Pound, a writer whose detailed and life-endowing memory of literary tradition unsettles him for life in his own world.

Can these, or any of Pound's literary exhibits, make our dry cultural bones dance again? Can his specimens of cultures past make any difference? Do Pound's heroes from ancient and Renaissance worlds (forerunners all of *Il Duce?*) translate as our heroes, or do they best remain where they are, exemplars for his imaginative life, beacons in his struggle through cultural darkness? In his last canto Pound says, "I have tried to write Paradise": a line whose force lies not in the vision glimpsed, or even in the vision glimpsed-and-then-lost, but in the effort of writing a Paradise that can be lived only in the act of writing, sustained in and by a writing that cannot sustain it for very long. The quintessential fact about Pound's paradise is that it cannot be culturally transported outside *The Cantos*. The most moving (if implicit) image of *The Cantos* is that of a writer working mightily at the retrieval of the West's great cultural highs, who believes that if he can only talk eloquently enough, incessantly enough, about what he loves, the subjects of his love will spring to life before him, talked back to life – if only he does not lose heart (as so frequently he does), lose vocal energy and intensity (this, too, is part of the image) – and in so doing remind himself and us where we all are.

One of the strong, comically pathetic moments of *The Cantos* occurs in the *Pisan* group when Pound admits defeat and in the same breath tries to build out of defeat's humble gifts a new paradise. If *Il Duce* is the summation of the heroic tradition, then what can Pound save of tradition with "Ben and la Clara *a Milano*/by the heels at Milano"? And he answers in Canto 74:

> Le Paradis n'est pas artificiel
> but spezzato apparently
> it exists only in fragments unexpected excellent sausage,
> > The smell of mint, for example,
> > Ladro the night cat

And the reader's equivalent, the unexpected excellent literary sausage of a broken paradise, lies in scattered but numerous moments of

individual elegance, sudden interventions of Pound's virtuosity in
the midst of his historical labor of recuperation; as in Canto 13,
where he presents in doctrinally constrained dialogue the Confucian
ethic and social ideal — a canto intended to make a point about
order, personal and public, and who underwrites it:

> If a man have not order within him
> He can not spread order about him;
> And if a man have not order within him
> His family will not act with due order;
> And if the prince have not order within him
> He can not put order in his dominions.

Pound assigns those lines to Kung himself, the man whose authority
stems from the wisdom that cannot be questioned, an oriental voice
drawn through Western timbres of biblical propheticism: the constant Poundian conjunctive ("and") now marking unshakable certitude ("And if a man," "And if the prince," and you'd better believe
it). And we shall hear that supremely self-possessed voice again,
whenever Pound feels his doctrinal oats. But in the midst of this
canto about the origin and dissemination of right political authority,
dictatorial power, we watch the poet in pursuit of something else,
like a bloodhound after the irrelevant detail, in a long aside off the
doctrinal tract, seduced by the unfolding, self-pleasuring movement
of his own conceit; the familiar Poundian conjunctive now marking
lyric momentum:

> And Tian said, with his hands on the strings of his lute
> The low sounds continuing
>       after his hands left the strings,
> And the sound went up like smoke, under the leaves,
> And he looked after the sound. . . .

Within the doctrinal program of Canto 13 these lines move with a
grace that passes beyond the reach of doctrine; they are the unex-

pected and unexpectable gift of cantabile, for no ends beyond the singing itself.

Elsewhere – strikingly so in the Malatesta group (Cantos 8–11) – Pound's minor beauties engage major preoccupations, not as food for isolate aesthetic indulgence but as medium of historical work. Cantos 8–11 concern the exploits of an obscure fifteenth-century Italian professional soldier of fortune, Sigismondo Malatesta, a complete political cynic with a singular passion for art and artists – just the sort of passion for which Pound will forgive anything (and with Malatesta there is, apparently, much to forgive), a type of the Poundian hero who achieved what he achieved "against the current of power" and found his truest expression of selfhood as patron par excellence, in unswerving devotion to the building of the Tempio Malatestiano in Rimini: Malatesta, in other words, as figure of the poet Pound would be in *The Cantos,* building in the Tempio, as Pound would build, a "little civilization," part pagan, part Christian.

Pound's method in the Malatesta group is cagily documentary: he quotes heavily from chronicles, letters, legal documents, papal denunciations; inserts his own retelling, sometimes as on-site narrator, in recreation of scenes for which no documentation exists. These cantos take the shape of a boiling polylogue, some voices friendly, most not, to Sigismondo's person and desire; they give off an ambience of thickest treachery, of men (including Sigismondo) willing to do anything – he for the love of art, they for the love of power. The arrangement of the documents is dramatic: Pound's purpose is to conjure his obscure hero (Canto 8 opens with incantatory rhetoric), to show him in the act of emerging from corruption, his voice freeing itself, soaring, somehow uncontaminated; a voice elegant, dignified, gracious, lyrical, and promising violence, a man whose passion rescues him even from the evil that he does. The strength of Pound's showing lies not in the narrative of Sigismondo – its confusions overwhelm even Pound – but in the rhetorical effects he manages in honor of his hero. Pound loves the man, and his love creates a

verbal habitation that insulates him from the garbage of his circumstances. We know not Malatesta but Pound "writing Malatesta" —
not "of" or "about" Malatesta, but writing Malatesta as in "writing
poetry;" or "writing Paradise," or in this translation of one of Malatesta's letters concerning what he would do for Piero della
Francesca:

> So that he can work as he likes
> or waste time as he likes
> (*affatigandose per suo piacere or no*
>    *non gli manchera la provixione mai*)
>                    Never lacking provision.

The prose meaning of Pound's English captures the prose of Malatesta's Italian, but with its arrangement into a versified parallel,
like two lines of poetry with a full caesura at the end of each line, the
translation adds an eloquence beyond the touch its of prose sense.
Pound's translation becomes a stylistic index, the verbal maneuver
that directs us by dint of its phrasing alone to the generous soul of
Malatesta. And the sandwiched Italian original proves Pound's fidel-
ity of translation, his capacity for living transmission:

> With the church against him,
> With the Medici bank for itself,
> With wattle Sforza against him
> Sforza Francesco, wattle-nose,
> Who married him (Sigismundo) his (Francesco's)
> Daughter in September,
> Who stole Pesaro in October (as Broglio said
>              "*bestialmente*"),
> Who stood with the Venetians in November,
> With the Milanese in December,
> Sold Milan in November, stole Milan in December
> Or something of that sort,

*Ezra Pound*

> Commanded the Milanese in the spring,
> The Venetians at midsummer,
> The Milanese in the autumn
> And was Naples' ally in October, . . .

From this swamp of political confusion, this comic litany of the months and seasons of byzantine betrayal – spoken, no doubt, in some smoke-filled backroom – comes a line from another level, elevated in syntax and tone, with a Latin phrase at the end (like an anchor of final authority) telling us what Malatesta did – the Latin working for Pound (as languages other than English often did) as some talismanic discourse, the facilitator of magical transcendence from politics to the plane of art: "He, Sigismundo, *templum aedificavit.*" "He, Sigismundo" – a phrasing repeated often in the Malatesta group – not only clarifies just who it is among these obscure political actors that Pound is talking about, but adds the sound of awe, like an epitaph which registers the shock of the memorialist, that in the midst of all this, he, Sigismundo, did what he did: "In the gloom, the gold gathers the light against it."

In his introduction to the *Active Anthology,* Pound says that experiment "aims at writing that will have a relation to the present analogous to the relation which past masterwork had to the life of its time." He insists, "without constant experiment literature dates." He means that literary experimentation is the response to the challenge, posed by social change, that writers come to terms with a new world. The implication is that the true history of literature is the discontinuous nonhistory of experiment, a series of modernist revolutions (what Pound means by "masterwork") in evidence across the ages, whose relations to one another lie not in content, form, or value, but in the incomparable fact of radical originality – radical as in "root"; originality as in deriving from an "origin": a literature

231

rooted in an origin, the origin here being the writer's salient historical situation. The severe discipline of a modernist aesthetic relegates
"literature" as such, or "literariness" as such, to the status of empty
concepts, because no writer who would be modern (original) in any
age (rather than the voice of some other time) has anything to lean
on. Original writing (the essence of which is that it has no essence)
proceeds, as always, in the dark, driven by difficult questions the
answers to which are never known in advance: What is it like to be
alive now? What strange new forms has human being assumed here,
in this place? Would we, if we could, do some social experimentation? New World writing – the project of an "American" literature
– is the exemplary moment of modernist literature.

Pound thought Eliot insufficiently moved by the experimental
spirit. Of Eliot's modernist benchmark, "Tradition and the Individual talent," he wrote: "This kind of essay assumes the existence of a
culture that no longer subsists and does nothing to prepare a better
culture that must or ought to come into being." If Western culture,
as Pound told Donald Hall, is the struggle for individual rights,
beginning with jury trial in Athens, then ever since the late eighteenth century we have been living in an age of revolution for
individual rights in relation to which Eliot's "existing monuments"
of literary tradition can have no organic significance. Pound thought
"existing monuments" a contradiction, thought we needed "something living," and might have sought (he would have been stunned
by this suggestion) support from Emerson for his political reading of
the course of the West: the necessity, as Pound put it, to respect the
"peripheries" of the individual.

The chief sign of the times, Emerson wrote in "The American
Scholar," is the "new importance given to the single person. Everything that tends to insulate the individual – to surround him with
barriers of natural respect, so that each man shall feel the world is
his, and man shall treat with man as a sovereign state with a sovereign state – tends to true union": he meant, tends to just community. Emerson thought the revolutions of democratic change he was

witnessing had implications for revolutions of cultural freedom, the individual and national rights of intellect and imagination. "Our day of dependence, our long apprenticeship to the learning of other lands, draws to a close. . . . We have listened too long to the courtly muses of Europe." Or, in the equally clarion call from the opening paragraph of "Nature": "Why should not we have a poetry and philosophy of insight and not of tradition . . . ?"

Emerson, in the optative mood, spoke on behalf of the American cultural achievement he hoped would come to pass, an aesthetic birth that would, in Pound's words, bear a relation to its present which past art bore to the life of its time. Pound's criticism of Eliot sounds suspiciously like the criticism of a nativist leveled against an expatriate, who in fleeing his country has also fled Emerson's challenge to American writers (whether here or abroad) to resist the seductions of Old World culture, to make the cultural journey over the Atlantic to America, to come home, not in order to embrace the American imagination but in order to create it.

But Pound, like Eliot, was a reverse American immigrant, an unlikely ally of Emerson, who seemed all along to have *intended* to seek out those courtly muses who inspired no revolutions on behalf of any individual. Emerson probably had Longfellow in mind when he wrote the following, but the implied stricture seems to fit Pound even better: "I ask not for the great, the remote, the romantic; what is doing in Italy or Arabia, what is Greek art, or Provençal minstrelsy; I embrace the common, I explore and sit at the feet of the familiar, the low." Pound's theory of experimentation is in the American grain, but his practice in *The Cantos*, his pamphleteering of the 1930s, his Rome Radio broadcasts during World War II – are they not betrayals? Had not Pound written, in the outrageously entitled *Jefferson and/or Mussolini:* "The heritage of Jefferson . . . is HERE, NOW *in the Italian peninsula* at the beginning of fascist second decennio, not in Massachusetts or Delaware"?

Perhaps, though, the failure was less Pound's than Emerson's, whose visionary essays of the 1830s and 1840s on the future of the

American writer, who would be nourished in experimental freedom by an original culture, do not come close to comprehending what would become the crisis of the modern writer, whose classic situation in the age of revolution is one in which he feels himself irremediably outside, in uncertain relation to the culture of his time. Pound in New York, in 1910, on the eve of decisive expatriation, gathers his data for his first and most sustained critical meditation on American culture ("Patria Mia"). He reflects upon life in a democratic culture and concludes (in effect) that there has been no improvement in the situation of cultural deprivation Emerson had observed in the 1830s. He leaves America, confirmed in his judgment that we are a people committed to the exigencies of the practical life and the cash nexus; with a sense that the cost of a new land was severance from the cultural past of Europe, a loss evidenced by the dry imitations of English verse he has read in the organs of the literary marketplace; and with a belief that the marketplace is the instrument of amnesia, the great barrier to the past, which would seem to ensure, for those who did not take Pound's expatriate option, the permanent triviality of American writing. For those like Pound, who would not or could not write to market demands – for all writers of modest middle-class means (or less) – America's post-aristocratic culture could offer only perennial anxiety about economic survival; the choice of the literary vocation was a choice for poverty and the contempt of mainstream society.

The exciting new culture Emerson had prophesied turned out to be mass culture, engineered by a culture industry feeding its commodities to democratic man, not a culture, as Emerson had hoped, organic with the life of the ordinary man. Pound, not alone among modern American writers, believed that the American common man was of no literary interest except as he might serve as the object of the ridiculing satiric gaze.

Far from being the expression of an American who had forsaken his culture, *The Cantos* are the work of an American experimenter standing at cultural ground zero. This experimenter is a man not unlike Henry James's archetype of the American, who works himself furiously up to cultural snuff — the archetypal modern as major autodidact of no cultural patrimony, who by sheer effort of discipline acquires all there is to know, and whose typical vocal posture before the great European cultural treasures is one of stunned awe; who will address Homer, Ovid, and Dante, *talk* to them in worshipful apostrophe, speak their names as only an adoring American could speak them, as the names of gods; an American who will find certain moments in these writers so excellent that he will repeat them over and over in *The Cantos,* as if he were recording them in a notebook of the most important quotations of great writers I have read. For all its complexity, *The Cantos* often resembles the book of wonders of a precocious American student.

By the measure of the ambitious desire to create culture that moved their writing, *The Cantos* are a failure. They do not engender (or recover) a unified vision or a single narrative, rest upon no stable foundation of concepts, offer no odyssey of character; and for these failures we probably should be grateful. *The Cantos* "are," not "is." *The Cantos* narrate, quote, translate, dramatize, sing, and rant — as literary montage and collage they invite readers to supply the missing totality that would make sense of all the fragments; but what is missing, or only subtly present, is not some deep-seated story that binds all the pieces together into a social whole, but the writer in the act of trying to make sense of his circumstances. In Wallace Stevens's words: "the poem of the mind in the act of finding / What will suffice." It may be that there is a sense in which every age is an age of experiment, and that all writing proceeds in the dark in an effort to find the socially companionable form, but the modernist believes (in this believing is being) that he proceeds in a darkness apparently total. Dante and Milton had the cultural gift of the Christian map: Joyce, Eliot, Stevens, and Pound believed that their cultures had little to give, that they were living in a time when all the stage sets (again Stevens's figure) were being struck (*being* struck: they were witnesses to various dissolutions). They found that the privilege of living in an age of revolution was more than matched by the burdens of modernist culture; they found that they could take nothing for granted; that every thing would need to be reimagined.

The world of *The Cantos* is close to the world of the later Yeats, who saw the destruction of the great country house as the socially symbolic moment of modernism's inauguration: the end of the politically and socially privileged class and all the artistic life (in all senses) that it ensured and supported (in all senses), the end of the writer's security, the underwriting of his vision blotted out in social upheaval. Adrift in a new world, Yeats is left with his memories, and Pound, passionate American reader of the classics, is left with the desire for memory within a new social system — secular, democratic, capitalist — that has no use for the past and offers no structural support for its artists, whom it does not believe can defend its cities. And it is much worse for Pound, because unlike Yeats he never saw the gracious old American estate, which is also cultural matrix — there is no American experience of this; we have no exemplary Coole Park for memory to cherish in the lineage of our American cultural blood, no Coole Park which, in unforgiving recollection, can be the measure of modernist loss. Unlike Yeats, Pound nurses no delicious and bitter nostalgia (no return-pain), unless we choose (as I do) to credit his longing as a paradox of nostalgia — a New World desire to return to the cultural home he never had.

In the notorious *Pisan Cantos* (74–84) the poet as modernist steps forward, holding back nothing. Written in a military detention camp in Pisa at the end of the war and awarded the first Bollingen Prize for Poetry in 1949, to the shock and anger of at least half the English-speaking literary world, these poems, as well as any in the modernist tradition, figure forth the modernist writer as the quintessential outsider. Now in prison, which is just about where the modernist has always thought he was, literally old, which is what modernist poets often feel even when they're young (as if they had never experienced vaulting zest for life: culturally dessicated from the start, Prufrocks all – a figure Eliot invented as an undergraduate), an old man without a country whose subject now is openly himself incessantly in conversation with himself, in elegiac remembrance of writers ancient, Renaissance, and contemporary, friends all, the literal ones also now all dead: Ford, Joyce, Yeats "to earth o'ergiven"; and talking his favorite opinions: how economic justice can be insured through just distribution and reform of the money system; how to collar the "buggering banks"; the role of the "yidds" in the world's exploitation; the cattlelike nature of the "goyim"; the death of Mussolini and the failure of fascism; the desire to build the ideal city; Pound, an old man quoting his favorite phrases, poetic and political, and then quoting them again and again; remembering his earlier cantos, alluding to the heroic figures therein; quoting his own lines, especially the one in the first canto about losing all companions: all this talk as if (Robert Frost's phrase) "the talk were all" – and it is.

*The Pisan Cantos* are jail-talk from solitary confinement (who at Pisa could Pound talk to?), jail-talk gone about as far as the modernist can take it. In the saying of his memories, in their linguistic retrieval and preservation of cultures past (especially the cultures made by writers, recalling what they wrote and sometimes what they did), Pound projects an image of the modernist writer working from the shards of tradition and frustrated political obsession, but not working them up into a new culture – placing them, instead, side by side, as he counts the losses. Pound-the-modernist is a writer in extremis because extremity is his norm – a writer who creates in his experiment a poem precisely adequate to the cultural circumstances of a man, unlike Homer, without a story to tell.

No one will take Pound, after what he has revealed, as hero or moral guide. The Pound in the *Pisan Cantos* is the best answer to the Pound who venerated heroes and thought Mussolini would underwrite economic justice and the independence of the individual. *The*

*Cantos* are a poetry full of heterogeneity to the point of chaos, an indescribable mixture whose ingredients of anti-Semitism and fascism are not of the essence because, in this experiment, nothing is of the essence. The most typical moments of *The Cantos* are those which defy the expectations of typicality: like the moment when out of nowhere we hear a black man speak (blacks in *The Cantos* appear as "coons," "niggers," and "negroes") and we learn that Pound has been done (by this black man) a risky act of charity — against regulations, he has been spoken to, and, more, has been built a box upon which to set his typewriter: "doan you tell no one/I made you that table," words that will be repeated throughout the *Pisan Cantos,* in the same way that phrases from the literary giants are repeated, until Mr. Edwards-who-made-the-box assumes the status of Sigismondo-who-made-the-Tempio. Mr. Edwards takes his commemorative place with Malatesta because, like Malatesta, he achieved what he achieved against the current of power. (What Mr. Edwards calls a "table," Pound calls a "box"; Mr. Edwards is an imaginative writer of another order.) He, Mr. Edwards, *boxum aedificavit.* And the significance of this act of patronage and charity for the whole of *The Cantos?* Only that a poetry which was written with no encouragement from its culture, and with no possibility of gaining cultural centrality, was helped along its way a little by a patron of the arts who couldn't read it, and who could have had no intention, surely, of helping this particular poem come to life and to print.

# 6

## T. S. ELIOT

T
S. ELIOT grew up knowing he was privileged and obligated. One of his biographers, Peter Ackroyd, remarks that "the Eliots were the aristocrats of nineteenth-century America (family motto: *Tace et fac*), part of that rising mercantile class which offered moral leadership to those who came after them; their self-imposed mission was to administer and to educate": to educate by leading and administering; most of all, to educate. The poet's grandfather William Greenleaf Eliot left the Harvard Divinity School in order to establish the Unitarian faith in the frontier town of St. Louis, Missouri, in 1834, where he founded a church and (as Ackroyd puts it) "three schools, a university, a poor fund, and a sanitary commission." His father, Henry Ware Eliot, grew wealthy from the proceeds of the Hydraulic-Press Brick Company, of which he was president. His mother, Charlotte Champe Eliot, was (one wants to say "of course") a poet, some of whose verses were published in newspapers; most of which were pasted into her scrapbooks.

Social versus cultural responsibility, striking business prowess versus aesthetic sensibility: in America, these historically opposed domains of male and female influence were the heritage of the twentieth century's most famous and powerful taste-determining (recently much abused by the academy) man of letters. Thomas Stearns, a chip off the old family block, became a poet, a literary critic, a stalwart at Lloyds of London and Faber and Faber, a Nobel prize winner, and, in the peak years of his fame, the author of a prose of heavy concern (the cultural equivalent of his grandfather's sanitary commission).

Not one of the major American poets with whom he might be compared could claim Eliot's kind of family background and expectations (in his case, unhappy patrimony), and only Frost could compete with his fame. But even Frost finishes a distant second, except in the continental United States, where he finishes in a dead heat, as Eliot's opposite, the shining example of nativist resistance to the international modernist, the man from St. Louis, who came to sound like an Englishman, in contrast to the man from San Francisco, who cultivated a Yankee voice both in writing and in person. Frost and Eliot: foremost literary actors in a country that features numerous excellent ones. With Eliot's cultural charisma and force, with the mystique of his poetry, with the career that was undergirded and sustained by an amazingly successful series of landmark essays (one after the other), big boulders in the stream of twentieth-century literature which no one could afford to ignore – with this reputation, this image, none could compete.

The man-of-letters-to-be stepped forward early, as the boy-of-letters, age eleven, when he wrote and illustrated at Smith Academy in St. Louis fourteen numbers of a weekly magazine, *The Fireside,* containing "Fiction, Gossip, Theatre, Jokes, and all interesting." He entered Harvard in 1906, began publishing poems in *The Harvard Advocate* the following year and regularly thereafter. In 1909, Eliot joined the editorial board of the *Advocate* and added book reviews to his repertory. In other words, the patterns of his literary life were pretty much fixed in his undergraduate days.

In his junior year (1908), Eliot enjoyed a transformative literary experience that radically revised the shape of his early poetry. He read Arthur Symons's *The Symbolist Movement in Literature* and a new world was suddenly opened to him. Rimbaud, Verlaine, Corbière, and, most of all, Jules Laforgue presented him with an unconventional way of standing in the world of literature. Sentences and phrases in Symons's chapter on Laforgue will leap out at readers (even those only casually familiar with Eliot's early poetry) as a preamble to "The Love Song of J. Alfred Prufrock," a poem unimaginable in the landscape of American and English verse in 1908. Here is Symons on Laforgue:

> "The old cadences, the old eloquence, the ingenuous serious-
> ness of poetry, are all banished"
> "the sickly modern being, with his clothes, his nerves"
> "it plays, somewhat uneasily, at disdainful indifference"
> "there is in it all the restlessness of modern life"
> "it is part of his manner not to distinguish between irony and
> pity, or even belief"
> "He composes love-poems hat in hand"
> "how much suffering and despair, and resignation to what is,
> after all, the inevitable, are hidden under this disguise"

After reading Symons, a few months later Eliot read the complete poems of Laforgue, and he became himself. Laforgue did for him, as he would put it years later, what no "single living poet in England or America, then at the height of his powers," could do: "point the way to a young poet conscious of the desire for a new idiom."

"The Love Song of J. Alfred Prufrock" was written in part during Eliot's senior year (1910) and completed the following year in Europe. In 1910–11, he had as possible outlets in America for his new poem (excepting the *Advocate*) only the mass-circulation magazines whose values and commercial function Pound was mercilessly dissecting in "Patria Mia" even as Eliot composed his early masterpiece. Eliot understood that in 1911 "Prufrock" was unpublishable. He committed it to his notebook and then seems to have given up on it. In the fall of 1914, in London, he met Pound, who read "Prufrock" (by then three years in manuscript). Pound promptly sent it on to Harriet Monroe, whose newly founded *Poetry* was presumably the sort of place intended for things like "Prufrock." But Monroe sat on it, and only after hard prodding by Pound (she wanted an upbeat ending) did she publish the poem, in June 1915.

Before his Laforgian conversion, Eliot was writing some poems that might have appeared in Richard Watson Gilder's *Century* magazine; with "Prufrock," he burst upon the avant-garde scene and became a presence to reckon with. The poem would shortly inspire work as independently brilliant, and important, as Pound's "Hugh Selwyn Mauberly" and Stevens's "The Comedian as the Letter C." Eventually, "Prufrock" would become a performance for the high school textbooks, the most recognizable voice in twentieth-century literature and the implicit definition of modernism, the embodiment of a self-conscious style that poets in Eliot's generation (Hart Crane, William Carlos Williams), and after, would need to learn to reject if they were to chart their own course.

Symons's chapter on Laforgue describes the shell of "Prufrock," the gestures and the poses, and it explains all there is to know about the Laforgian imitations that Eliot chose not to preserve, and the one he did keep for his first volume ("Conversation Galante"). Even the title of Eliot's first book, *Prufrock and Other Observations* (1917), is a Laforgian deflation of conventional lyric piety: coolness, objectivity, and analytic precision, not the gushing nonsense of popular poetry, the title says, were to be the marks of the new poetry that Hulme and Pound would polemicize into existence in the London where Eliot moved in 1915, a poetry whose tone and texture would implicitly function as criticism of the lyric styles it would replace. A "modern" poem was to be an observation recorded, not a feeling expressed.

The now legendary and too familiar, but in 1915 historically fresh and strange, opening simile of "Prufrock" implicitly announces a revolution against poetry as Eliot's readers would have known it from the nineteenth-century lyric norms preserved in what passed for contemporary poetry in Eliot's youth. In the opening lines of the poem, a stock lyric subject is aggressively reversed by a poet interested, as a poet, in the hospital operating room, and that old poetic evening, with its soft, subjective tone, opens onto odd subjective terrain ("like a patient etherised upon a table"). Who sees evenings in this way? Whose sick love song is this? In "Prufrock," Eliot seizes upon the studied wit and artificiality, the subterfuges and shocks of Laforgue's antiromanticism, in order to enter the lyric world again, but on new (in historical context), antipoetic terms. The layered gestures of irony, indifference, and tiredness, the (self)-mock-heroics of the persona, the projected face of neurasthenia — all of these Laforgian mannerisms are not ends but strategies for the slyer reclaiming of inward space, lyricism in the company of the relatively new science of anesthesiology.

So "Prufrock" is a poem of feeling and sensibility masquerading as an observation, delivered, famously, as a dramatic monologue without auditor, in rhythms that forecast a voice of search and longing, teased out over a career which, by *Four Quartets,* is a much scrutinized public text: search and longing in the cadences of incantation, waiting for grace, but often, especially early, but late too, encased in embarrassment (no, he is neither Saint John the Baptist nor Prince Hamlet), weariness and fatality ("I grow old . . . I grow old . . . "), and hesitation, always hesitation, on the verge of acting, not acting ("Do I dare . . . ?"). What poem in the English canon proceeds so insistently through the crippling interrogative? The rhythms speak desire of apocalypse, but the tones, the sound and sense of the startling rhymes, the grandiose allusions that diminish the self be fore memories of the past, the lacerating self-consciousness, especially in the company of women, all play from the interior the muse of despair. "Prufrock" is the first major showcasing of Eliot's persona, the voice that simultaneously hopes and retreats, wanting new life ("Let us go then"), but instead waking, the effect of ether now worn off, into a death of consciousness ("human voices wake us, and we drown"); wishing for power, but believing in its impotence (lacking the "strength to force the moment to its crisis").

But "Prufrock" is most of all a drama of literary anguish, a writer's drama, played through the mask of a character (like the poet himself) who is well-born, prim, even prissy, in self-dialogue, telling himself that a walk on the wild side is just what he needs as the proper prelude to really letting go of all that he knows as himself, in order (like a hero from the later fiction of Henry James) to relinquish himself to a life of impulse and instinct ("I should have been a pair of ragged claws"), sex and violence appearing as the other domain of a consciousness at some level barely human, buried but faintly stirring, and titillating. The gestures, the manners, and the desires that find speech, the poem itself – this is perhaps one of Eliot's strongest and most characteristic effects – are all glimpsed as if from an emanating point the other side of the poem and language, from a subjectivity that sees itself, defines itself, as oppressed, threatened, and hurt by language, a self that nevertheless sees the world through language: as in "streets that follow like a tedious argument / Of insidious intent"; as in "the works and days of hands / That lift and drop a question on your plate"; as in "time" itself experienced as the permission of "a hundred visions and revisions" and (fatal rhyme-word) "decisions" revised. The central act of choice for this self is the literary act of rewriting. The eyes "fix you in a formulated phrase," the phrase punctures and pins him to the wall. Traditional texts (always looming) pressure and get inside the voice, capturing its rhythm, turning it into someone else's writing, diminishing and debunking its puny urges. The famous alienation of "The Love Song of J. Alfred Prufrock" is grounded in a young man's fear of impotence, sexual and literary (what could possibly, for him, be the difference?). Eliot's poetry, from the start, gives off whiffs of decay and death. "Prufrock" is the first in his series of portraits of the artist as the old man of youth.

The celebrity of "Prufrock" has obscured the virtuoso variety of performance in Eliot's first volume. "Prufrock" is the work of a sensibility that has pared itself out of existence, but in "Portrait of a Lady" and "La Figlia Che Piange" the dramatist enters his play. These are the poems of a writer who enjoys seeing himself in dramatic light, so much the better to luxuriate in his manipulative power and take pleasure in his own dramatizing sensibility, his self-consciousness as arranger, producer, director, god of his imagined world, not indifferent to his creation, but a specially privileged character within – he alone, T. S. Eliot, there, in literary space, free, who felt himself free nowhere else.

"Portrait" is part narrative and part character sketch, featuring slices of reverberating dialogue, a poetry, as its title suggests, inspired by Henry James, and it is partly a self-portrait of the writer with vampirelike relations to real life (a late Jamesian theme here), which he needs to convert into material for composition (composition alone having the power to compose him): the vampire who knows but cannot change himself, who must compose (suck blood) at any cost. He says to himself: "You have the scene arrange itself – as it will seem to do –;" "Well! and what if she should die some afternoon, . . . die and leave me sitting pen in hand. . . . " This vampire-writer has a knack for the distilling comic phrase: "We have been, let us say, to hear the latest Pole/Transmit the Preludes, through his hair and finger-tips"; he takes satiric relish in the democracy of the newspaper, with all manner of data placed side by side; he has an eye for the new ethnic details of Boston circa 1910:

An English countess upon the stage.
A Greek was murdered at a Polish dance,
Another bank defaulter has confessed.

With its ruling subjunctive tense and correlative moods of yearning and emptiness, the director (in "La Figlia") becomes his actors in a strategic confusion of pronouns ("I" becomes "he," "he" and "you" become "we"), and the dramatist speaks lyrically, thereby undoing the fiction of self-possession that belongs to writers who choose the dramatic mode. To what extent does this observer want to stay outside, under the cool control of his reason? Or is his reason a repression of a desire to give himself, blessedly to lose himself? The virtuosity of performance in Eliot's first book is a mark of his literary prowess, but it is also a mark of uncertainty and struggle in a writer who has not yet found a mastering voice, because he does not yet know who he is.

And the satiric performances in *Prufrock and Other Observations* only reinscribe the problem: "The *Boston Evening Transcript*," "Aunt Helen," and "Cousin Nancy" are exercises, studied and flat, sporting unsurprising, pro forma ironic contrasts. The poetic voice sounds self-possessed, but there has been no challenge; Eliot dominates his material too easily. Only in the last of the satiric group, "Mr. Apollinax," does he let us inside his imaginative process in a kind of poem (topical satire) that would ordinarily prohibit revelations of this sort.

In "Mr. Apollinax," mythic sexual energy is set against effete contemporary social material ("Priapus in the shrubbery" against "the teacups"). This time ironic contrast provides the framework, not the substance of the poem. A few years later Eliot would begin reading *Ulysses* in manuscript, and would find, as he thought, a "method" for writing significantly in a world where frameworks are hard to come by honestly. "Mr. Apollinax" is his first, and perhaps independent, stab in that direction, a comic evaluation of a desiccated society from the perspective of an anciently rooted yet still possible vitality. This satiric poet finds personal urgency in his memory of myth, urgency that seems not yet clearly understood by himself: the surprising nexus of myth, sexual force, contemporary emptiness, satiric judgment — the heterogeneous poetic substance, really, of *The Waste Land* — is here handled in nascent form. And in the center of the poem is an extended conceit, hard to figure into the poem's satire but easy to figure into the work that will come: coral islands and a worrisome death by drowning, a death that may not be the end, constitute elements of a complex image that allures as its unfolds, unfolds perhaps because it allures, pursued by a poet who may have no choice but to pursue it:

> His laughter was submarine and profound
> Like the old man of the sea's
> Hidden under coral islands
> Where worried bodies of drowned men drift down in the
>   green silence,
> Dropping from fingers of surf.

The title of Eliot's first volume appropriates the naturalist rhetoric of Zola and the prestige of late-nineteenth-century positivist science, so much the better to wage cultural war: to kill off and bury the enervated spirit of lyric that ruled the scene in Eliot's youth in England and America. Eliot and his modernist company succeeded in securing an avant-garde space for a different kind of poetry and an aesthetic culture of experiment. But in the meantime, genteel poetic practice continued, and continues, unabated in the mass-market magazines and in the popular anthologies featured in the mass-market bookstores, a poetry for American poetry-lovers who do not read Pound, Eliot, and Stevens, less and less of Frost, and rarely in the English canon.

In mass culture, revolutionary modernist literature succeeds in establishing itself as a separate culture, hostile to mass consumption and the values of mass consumption, and, in the same act (ironic revolution) reestablishes its kinship with the great tradition ("tradition and the individual talent"), which, more and more in the context of modern America, seems equally separatist and hostile to mass, democratic man – his needs, his training, his ideals. With hindsight, modernist literature takes on a traditional cast, and traditionalism, in our context, looks adversarial. Yeats would not have been surprised.

Against this background of Eliot's youth, the notable thing about the group of poems made up by "Preludes," "Rhapsody on a Windy Night" (these two written in the "Prufrock" period), and "Morning at the Window" (written shortly after his move to London) is the novelistic character of their patterns of imagery, a poetry of realist texture – inspired by Baudelaire – which anchors itself in the lower echelons of society, in urban scenes of the down-at-the-heels, the grungy, the unsavory. In its time, this is also the kind of poem (like "Prufrock" but in a different register) that proclaims itself against Poetry with a capital letter. Broken blinds, newspapers blowing down the street, faint stale smells of beer, dingy shades, furnished rooms, yellow soles of feet, soiled hands, vacant lots, a dress torn and stained, a spring broken and rusty, a cat licking rancid butter, body parts but rarely whole bodies – such are the defining images of a scene strolled through and brooded over by a consciousness alternately repulsed and hallucinated by what it takes in, a consciousness willing to let in all that the standard lyricism of its time had excluded from poetry, but a consciousness, nevertheless, whose own lyric needs for transformation and transcendence remain incorrigibly romantic (in Eliot, a lyric self always lurks). Laforgian and Zolaesque conversions are useful; they bring surprising literary change to the domain of poetry. Eventually, though, another kind of conversion will come to seem necessary, one that lyric writing can long for but cannot itself accomplish.

Three events set the shape and texture of Eliot's everyday life through the publication of *The Waste Land* in 1922. In 1915, he decided to move to London; in the same year, he met and married (in rapid succession) Vivienne Haigh-Wood; in the month they were married, *Poetry* published "Prufrock." Thanks to "Prufrock," Eliot entered the avant-garde with a splash, as a writer of such originality that, on the basis of this single poem, he was established as the new poet to watch, a tone-setter. But *The Waste Land* brought him out of the alluring literary underground for good, where Pound remained as a writer's writer, to the riveted attention of the literary world at large. *The Waste Land* made Eliot at once the towering poet of modernism and its public face, the figure to whom those who cared (and those who did not care) for modernism would need to pay attention, an awesome image, idolized and detested. Very quickly, *The Waste Land* ceased to be a poem to be read and became a phrase to be intoned, the essence of a perspective and an attitude, the signature of a lost generation: in other words, a cultural event that got beyond Eliot's intention and control. The scandalous success of the poem, the reams of commentary it has spawned, its centrality for the teaching of modern literature, all have had the double effect of making Eliot a major force in world literature while obscuring the specific narrative of his life and poetry. More than any other figure of literary modernism, we have tended to know Eliot – and, consequently, to like him or dislike him – as a reputation.

Marriage to Vivienne Haigh-Wood brought his much agonized over condition of virginity to an end, and marriage plunged them both into chaos. They suffered endless emotional and physical troubles, the former promoting the latter, but they supported each other unstintingly and selflessly. He took devoted care of her during her hard times; she was a fiercely loyal supporter (and keen reader) of his writing, a great believer in his talent, who did all she could to gain him the time that he almost never had to write poems.

They suffered collapses; more than likely, no change of circumstance could have saved their life together. Nevertheless, their circumstances were damaging. Eliot's family was wealthy but did not approve of his choice of career. His parents had expected him to return from his graduate studies in England, philosophy dissertation in hand, ready to assume a position at a distinguished American university. But he wanted a career in writing, not in teaching, and, like Frost, knew that London was the capital of the English-speaking literary world, the place to be. The early London period of the Eliots

was marked by a steady stream of requests to St. Louis for understanding and financial aid. Eliot, Vivienne, Pound, and Bertrand
Russell all wrote. Vivienne, for one, did not stand on pride: she told
Charlotte that she was darning her husband's underwear. Eliot's
father and brother responded with frequent, though modest, gifts.
And Eliot spared himself not at all: he taught at night (at jobs that
often entailed immense commutes); he steadily wrote reviews for
philosophy and literary journals that paid; he became assistant editor
of the *Egoist* (a position which required, in addition to the usual
dreary chores, that he write, anonymously, when sufficient copy was
not at hand, almost entire issues); he produced a huge number of
still mostly uncollected essays; he took on a regular job at Lloyds
(which meant that his evenings were reserved for editing, writing
essays and reviews, and personal correspondence) – all the while
conceiving of himself as a poet whose budding reputation and promising future he was squandering, here and there finding the time to
do what he believed he was meant and most needed to do. And so
the leitmotifs of Eliot's correspondence of the period: too much
work, too little time, too little money, too nervous, too tired to
write poems – in Vivienne's phrase: "that inexorable pile of work
piling up against him." He "dried up" (his phrase); he "collapsed"
(his word); she collapsed.

Eliot's views of what "literature" ought to be and how it ought to
function were influenced in large part by his reading, and they were
expressed on numerous celebrated occasions in critical writings that
span his career. But these views were also driven by the economically
constrained life he felt forced to lead in London – and "forced" is half
right and half wrong. "Right" because it would be difficult to
imagine anyone, with foreknowledge, choosing the misery in which
he lived; "wrong" because Eliot believed that the life we get – he got
– was a matter of desire, if not choice: "everybody gets the kind of
life he wants," as he put it to his brother in 1916.

From all manner of sources Eliot knew the romantic claim that
poetry was radically different from all other kinds of writing: it

presumably resisted utilitarian manipulation, it was autonomous, a unique thing working only for its own ends. Despite declaring himself to be against romanticism on various occasions, he tended to accept these staple propositions of literary theory in the romantic mode, especially in his early career. But the truth of the theory that authentic poetry has no function in the world of profit and loss he learned from experience. It would not feed him and Vivienne or pay the rent, unlike, say, editing, or writing for the popular press, or teaching literature at night to working-class people who taught *him*, to his delight, that they too took a disinterested view of literary experience, they too valued it for itself. The autonomous nature of art, his art in particular, had economic effects in life, his life. Other kinds of writing might pay the rent – Frost and Pound had tried their hand at fiction, because with fiction you might get lucky – but poetry of the high modernist moment, Eliot's poetry certainly, was economically hopeless, which, of course, it was supposed to be (he got the life he wanted).

And so the more his time was eaten up by economically necessary pursuits, the less time he had for writing poems (exactly the life he wanted!), the more deeply special those moments became, because they opened up an alternative space of consciousness, another level of living. Of the likelihood of pay raises at the bank, Eliot said (at the time he was also lecturing at night), "at my present rate of increase of salary I can reasonably look forward to a time when they [the lectures] will be unnecessary, and I shall be able to spend *all* my spare time exactly as I please. When I can earn all the money I need out of one thing, and be able to read and write in the rest of my time without thinking of the financial reward of what I do, then I shall be satisfied." His conception of his poetry ("my own serious work," my "independent writing") was virtually forced upon him by the literary work he did to help sustain his and Vivienne's existence. In this personal setting, the famous description of the poet's self-sacrifice in "Tradition and the Individual Talent" – "What happens is a continual surrender of himself as he is at the moment to something which is more valuable" – tells the story of Eliot's need to enter into the poetic process in order to achieve a new life beyond the struggles of "himself as he is at the moment," the man who is trying to get by, transcended for "something" – what exactly is it? – "which is more valuable."

After securing a position at Lloyds, for a time (it will be brief), on his own testimony and that of the one best able to corroborate it, Eliot, as Vivienne put it, "*writes* better, feels better and happier and has better health when he knows that money (however *little*) is assured, and coming in regularly – even tho' he has only a few hours a day to write in, than when he has *all* day – and nothing settled, nothing *sure*." A couple of weeks later, in another letter to her mother-in-law, she wrote: "not one of his friends has failed to see, and to remark upon, the great change in Tom's health, appearance, spirits, and literary productiveness since he went in for Banking." Eliot's father, naturally, approved: his son had finally taken on real work and had confined to his "spare time" – his son's phrase – the useless activity of writing poems. Naturally, his father's emissary, Tom's conscience, also approved. He had gotten the life he wanted, or was supposed to have, a difficult distinction at best.

Like Stevens, Pound, and Frost, Eliot was a modern American man, with all the problems that the world imposes upon one who chooses to become a poet. Eliot, too, was a full-fledged citizen of the bourgeois world, a modern writer in a sense that Yeats was not. Yeats had fired away at similar social enemies of poetry, but from a position that the American modernists could not assume, with memories of a hospitable aristocratic (Anglo-Irish) past, a real Coole Park become a Coole Park of the mind, a bitter but delicious nostalgia that was poetically productive, a memory which no American could share.

The modern American poets (Stevens is the exception: he would never lift a finger on his own literary behalf) cultivated literary schizophrenia: they pursued poetry as an alternative culture yet worked mightily to make their poetry and themselves, as figures of

the poet, important, influential, and, in a word that Eliot never
shied away from, *powerful*. In the process of composition, a poem
was to put one on another plane of existence, beyond the reach of the
reason that reigned in the culture of capital. Once in public, however, Eliot did all he could to make his writing an "event" in that
very culture ("event" is his word). An Eliot poem, as he knew when
barely thirty years old, was and always would be a rare thing. He
early knew himself as a man who would write little. He would
therefore cultivate a mystique: isolation, detachment, an enigmatic
persona. At the same time, he would cultivate his connections in the
world of letters, and when he came with a poem, he would come
with a thing literally *remarkable,* a happening, something to be
discussed and debated but never ignored.

Before 1922, the year of *The Waste Land,* even before 1920, the year
of his first critical book, *The Sacred Wood,* Eliot had decided — this
writer known for one poem and a handful of strong essays — that he
could become a force in English letters. He believed himself on the
verge of assuming literary power, more than any American had ever
enjoyed in England, with the possible exception of Henry James.
His first critical book would need, therefore, to deliver "a single
distinct blow," so that his criticism, like his poems, could also
become an instrument for wielding "influence" and "power" (his
words) in the literary capital of the English-speaking world.

The essays collected in *The Sacred Wood* project a unified and
supremely self-confident voice; at times, as Eliot saw in retrospect, a
voice shading into solemnity and pomposity, a tone and persona
precisely the reverse of Prufrock, hiding that side of himself. Here is
the man, the voice implies, who knows literary history since Homer
with the detail and ease of an elder statesman of letters (in fact, the
essays of *The Sacred Wood* were written by a young man between his
twenty-eighth and thirty-second years, not that well schooled in

literary history, who had worked up his knowledge for the occasion). And the composure never cracks. At his most winning, Eliot writes sentences of luminous insight and agile wit that seem to demand to be copied out because they embody a literary wisdom – often much more than literary – which, the voice implies, will prevail.

The essays possess vocal unity but not the intellectual unity of the systematic thinker: it is easy, but pointless, to hunt for and find contradiction in *The Sacred Wood* (it has been done). One of the purposes of Eliot's dissertation on F. H. Bradley seems to have been to undermine the classical project of philosophy. He told his class-mate Norbert Weiner that in order to stay inside the boundaries of common sense one would need to avoid taking any theory to its conclusion – an act which always violates our experience – and to avoid consistency. Eliot never had any use for Emerson; he took the side of Josiah Royce against William James, the side of the theorist of community against the Emersonian celebrant of free-lancing indi-vidualism; but in his approach to literary criticism he was himself a case-by-case pragmatist who avoided "foolish consistency." Thematic recurrences in the essays seem to well up from an inductive engage-ment with particulars, seem never to be imposed, and perhaps that is why his major themes and ideas are so compelling. He gives us the impression (this, perhaps, his shrewdest rhetorical effect) that his ideas emerge naturally, that they come because they must, not be-cause he wants them to.

The pragmatic spirit of the literary critic is matched and moti-vated by the cosmopolitan character of Eliot's sources: Laforgue and the French symbolists, Charles Maurras, Remy DuGourmont, Paul Claudel, the Elizabethan and Jacobean dramatists, Dante, Donne and the Metaphysical poets, T. E. Hulme, Pound, Henry James, Ford Madox Ford, and, later, when he no longer felt it necessary to muster the weapons of antiromanticism, he recognized a kindred spirit in Coleridge's definition of imagination ("the balance or recon-ciliation of opposite or discordant qualities"). But it was yet another Harvard presence of Eliot's undergraduate years who bent his atti-

# T. S. Eliot

tudes in antiromantic directions, and who encouraged him to look
to French thinkers, well before those encounters with Hulme and
Pound, which confirmed but did not shape him. Irving Babbitt's
*Literature and the American College* (1908) now reads like a primer for
T. S. Eliot's thought.

In the late 1920s, Eliot would pen his distance, writing, in effect,
that Babbitt's neohumanist "inner check" of restraint turns out to be
grounded on nothing but the individual's own innerness. Nevertheless, much of Eliot's social and literary criticism, from beginning to
end, assumes both Babbitt's classical values and their animus toward
Bacon and Rousseau, and everything those cultural gods of modernity have come to represent. With Babbitt, he stands against human-
itarianism and the enthusiasm that all men are worthy of a promis-
cuous sympathy and benevolence; against the belief in the kingdom
of man through the interventions of science (the religion of "progress"); against the rule of impulse ("one impulse from a vernal
wood"); against the "inordinate exaltation of the individual," the
democratic spirit, the "pedantry of individualism," and the "free
play of one's individual faculties." He stands *for* discipline, constraint, and the ideals of community; *for* tradition and classical
literary values that stress impersonality and the universal life (as
opposed, in Eliot's dark imagery from Dante and Bradley, to the
prison of self); *for* the muses of memory over those of inspiration and
genius. And, always, Eliot believes in the social centrality of literary
experience: in Babbitt's words, "that golden chain of masterpieces
which link together into a single tradition the more permanent
experience of the race." The golden chain of masterpieces (an inspiration here for the future author of "Tradition and the Individual
Talent") invites not "servile" but "creative imitation," a "balance" of
the "forces of tradition and the claims of originality." Finally, in the
language of Babbitt, we see the return of the poet's paternal grandfather, William Greenleaf Eliot: social obligation in attendance of
the "minds and characters of future citizens of a republic." Now mix
in the authoritarianism of Maurras, and the Eliot who would declare

himself in 1927 "classicist in literature, royalist in politics, and anglo-catholic in religion" is virtually formed more than a decade before he will make the much quoted declaration that Babbitt himself had urged him to make, in the "open."

The major ideas of *The Sacred Wood* are the major and often recurrent ideas of Eliot's career (they will set the foundation of the New Criticism): (1) the *integrity of poetry* ("a poem, in some sense, has its own life," and note "in some sense," a qualification usually ignored by his formalist inheritors); (2) the need to cultivate awareness of *literary tradition,* not as a repository of rule-bearing repressors, harsh father-figures, but of "masters" who persist as "living forces" of inspiration and historical community (Eliot always speaks negatively of the tyranny of the dead, the canonical standard); (3) the value of *unified sensibility* and the need for its recovery, a sensibility that he finds in Dante and Shakespeare but not in Massinger and Milton, who mark its breakdown, whose intellects are not "immediately at the tips of the senses"; (4) the celebration of *dramatic form,* for its power to express social variety, and (5) the kind of *dramatic character* (absent in modern drama) which delights in seeing itself in dramatic light; (6) the *music-hall artist* as an inspiration for modern literary form, a figure for the potential recapturing of the organic ideal of the performer-artist integrated with a performer-audience; (7) the need for a *framework* – stabilized habits of response, a "culture" evident in the overall "preparedness," the receptivity of an audience, a "temper" which a writer does not create but assumes as a basis of his rhetorical contract with his readers; (8) the value of inheriting a *literary form* ("no man can invent a form, create a taste for it, and perfect it, too": Eliot, unlike Wordsworth and Pound, was an unhappy, a reluctant experimentalist); (9) the ideal of *impersonality* ("The progress of an artist is a continual self-sacrifice, a continual extinction of personality").

But for all his avowed classicism, Eliot stands, as a poet, closer to Blake than to his beloved Dante: "He was naked," he says of Blake, and exposed to the "dangers to which the naked man is exposed" –

"formlessness" in particular. In his brilliant phrase for Blake, he became the creator in *The Waste Land* of an "ingenious piece of home-made furniture," more in the romantic and the American grain than he wanted to be, or could admit, desiring "a framework of accepted and traditional ideas," but never (like Dante) in confident possession of it. In his essay on Blake, we come up to the edge of "Gerontion" and *The Waste Land*. Eliot, like Royce and Santayana, is critical of the sweeping modernist tide (perceptualism, hedonism, imagism, the poetry of fragments, "odds and ends of still life and stage properties"); he struggles against the tide, but is at its mercy nevertheless. He did not want to stand between Dante and Blake, but that's where he found himself, and that is his drama.

Most of the poems in Eliot's small second volume were composed between 1917, when *Prufrock and Other Observations* appeared, and 1920, a period that also saw the publication of a number of his most provocative essays, including "Tradition and the Individual Talent," "Hamlet and His Problems," and a piece about Henry James: three essays that give us discursive entry to the poetic obsessions which propelled him, especially in "Gerontion," into a literary territory hostile to critical commentary, a poetry virtually alien to the generalizing power of ideas.

In James's fiction Eliot saw the expression of the sort of sensibility he found and admired in Dante, Shakespeare, Donne, and certain Jacobean dramatists; a tradition interrupted, so he thought, around the time of Milton, who represented both a major divergence and a major (damaging) influence throughout the eighteenth and nineteenth centuries; a tradition resumed by the French symbolists, James, and (he hoped) himself. What went wrong around the time of Milton? Was the problem primarily literary or social in nature? A literary breakdown caused by a social breakdown? Eliot liked to hint at theories (particularly the latter one, because he believed that a healthy literature could not be written in a sick society), but he never argued for or even asserted an explanation with any detail or clarity. He would suggest teasing theories of a Fall, but nowhere in his work does he speak of a lost social Eden. Around 1920, Eliot was piecing together (making up) a tradition (like an ingenious piece of homemade furniture) of integrated sensibilities (the writers he was most drawn to), and, at the same time, feeling a ruling desire to become part of that tradition, to join that company in beloved literary community.

As the modern representative of this tradition, James is "a mind so fine no idea could violate it," the "last test of a superior intelligence" being its "baffling escape from Ideas." The point is to avoid, somehow, thinking with the intellect (as if it were autonomous) because ideas, once abstracted from the totality of the healthy personality, became Ideas, and "run wild and pasture on the emotions." The writing of James represents, not a fusion of equal portions of "idea" and "feeling," but a capacity for generating thought, as a derivative, from the irrational matrix of personality. But once abstracted from a whole within which the distinction between idea and emotion cannot arise, then ideas ("Ideas") in themselves will take on a malevolent life of their own: they will reenter the personality in violent fashion, in a kind of rape – or, in another of Eliot's figures, as preyers on emotion, dessicators, vampires at the throat of personality.

*Hamlet* (and its title character) presents the problem of dissociated sensibility from the other end. The play represents a different kind of violation of personality, with Shakespeare unbalanced and his emotions become autonomous, preying on his ability to create rational design, to conceive and develop an "objective correlative," a "set of objects, a situation, a chain of events" that, once given in literary form, will evoke emotions adequate to and expressive of the object, the situation, the event; the emotion and its correlative should ideally be interdependent, another image of the wished-for wholeness which *Hamlet* presumably does not achieve. This failure to produce an objective correlative in *Hamlet* results in the expression of feeling in excess of everything. *Hamlet* is characterized by an "unmistakable tone" (like a distinctive person? a distinctive literary style?), tantalizing (the "'Mona Lisa' of literature") but impossible to localize in any quotation, or set of quotations, or any action. The play fails, thinks Eliot, except that toward the end of his essay he indicates that this presumed lapse in Shakespeare's dramatic power may be something more interesting: an experience any person of sensibility has gone through and then (usually) repressed. This terror of excess, these feelings exceeding everything, this shock of finding out that what it means to be human is to experience feelings corresponding to nothing in the world. Eliot would rather have been like Henry James than the Shakespeare of *Hamlet,* but he didn't get his wish. He was, instead, an "unmistakable tone," difficult to localize, a style, a literary presence, Mona Lisa–like, impossible to shake from consciousness once he has been encountered.

In this context, "Tradition and the Individual Talent" is less a pronouncement about the nature of literary history than it is an expression, in literary-historical language and analysis, of Eliot's desire for community-in-history: the desire to "surrender," to yield "himself as he is at the moment to something which is more valuable," a process of "continual extinction of the personality." By "personality" Eliot means something we possess painfully, in isolating individuality; and those who have a personality know what it means to want to escape it. By "extinction" he means the death of *that;* the "something which is more valuable" is not a no-self but a self-in-historical-community. "Community" meant for Eliot, in 1917, the literary tradition since, and proceeding from, Homer. In the following well-known passage, change "order" to "community," change "novelty" to "self," and Eliot's vision of organic mutuality, his social hunger, is clear. "The necessity that he shall conform, that he shall cohere, is not one sided; what happens when a new work of art is created is something that happens simultaneously to all the works of art which preceded it. . . . the existing order is complete

before the new work arrives; for order to persist after the supervention of novelty, the *whole* existing order must be, if ever so slightly
altered. . . . "

Like his first collection of poetry, Eliot's second features considerable
tonal range, although such range is again obscured by a lead-off
poem ("Gerontion") whose familiar sound marks it as both a relative
of "Prufrock" and a forecast of the over-voice of *The Waste Land,* the
poem for which "Gerontion" was to serve as preface until Pound
convinced Eliot not to use it. "Gerontion" is daunting and unrelen-
tingly intense; other poems in the volume are satirical and playfully
humorous, or satirical and not especially playful or good-hearted;
still others are written in French (playfully and otherwise: an exercise that helped him to get over a dry spell).

"Burbank with a Baedeker: Bleistein with a Cigar," an instance of
Eliot's satiric intention going for mock-heroic effects, defines American Jews as exemplary degenerates of contemporary culture, the
invaders of Venice. The debunking allusive context of high culture,
Shakespearean moments from *Othello,* and the glance at Byron's
Venice at the end of the poem, cannot contain the extended expression of repulsion in the middle of it, where Eliot sounds driven to
the edge, full of rhetorical savagery, in a virulent rhetoric for which
no objective correlative is possible, in excess of everything except
anti-Semitism. The Jew, materialism, is the death of art, a note not
definitive of modernism in the Eliot/Pound mode, but involved
with it.

The Sweeney poems take allusion into another dimension. In
"Sweeney Erect" Eliot hears the urgent imperative of tradition,
which he may not be able to answer ("Paint me a cavernous waste
shore/Cast in the unstilled Cyclades"); he experiences the memory of
the Homeric past surging into consciousness, virtually taking it
over: "Morning stirs the feet and hands/(Nausicaa and Polypheme)."

In "Sweeney Among the Nightingales" he transforms his allusive technique into an interpretive principle, a way not only of evaluating the present, but of understanding the present as an expression of the past, not so much diminished as it is luridly continuous, gross realist texture undergirded by mythic narrative. Allusion is the acknowledgment of the presence of the past; allusion says cultures are haunted.

"Gerontion," the strength and fascination of Eliot's second volume, is the poem which joins "Prufrock," *The Waste Land,* "Ash Wednesday," and *Four Quartets* in establishing the major poetic episodes in the narrative of Eliot's career and life. In method and tone (though not in range of materials) "Gerontion" could certainly have been a preface to *The Waste Land.* In this poem, Eliot enacts a central proposition of "Tradition and the Individual Talent": he is "aware that the mind of Europe – the mind of his own country – a mind which he learns in time to be much more important than his own mind – is a mind which changes, and that this change is a development which abandons nothing *en route.* . . . the difference between the present and the past is that the conscious present is an awareness of the past in a way and to an extent which the past's awareness of itself cannot show."

It is the mind of Europe that Eliot, in "Gerontion" and *The Waste Land,* surrenders himself to, because he believes it to be more valuable than his private mind, and in so surrendering enters a literary community of long historical duration, as the "conscious present." This consciousness attaches epigraphs to its poems (in a language not necessarily English: the mind of *Europe*) and tends to express itself in associative leaps (embodied in the discontinuities of collagelike formations) – leaps that defy logic and chronology because the "conscious present" is aware of the past all at once, as a totality, not as a linear series of events. Allusion for this kind of consciousness is not a simple literary strategy, a knowledge of the past manipulated in the present by a writer dispassionately distant from the past, but a mode of consciousness whose nature is historical. However difficult it may be to grasp the rationale of the allusive network in "Gerontion," or the reason for the particular jumps that this consciousness makes in this poem, the art of Eliot here and in *The Waste Land* is to make us feel that all the allusions and associative jumps are inevitable.

And who is this speaker? He is ("of course" one wants to say; this is Eliot's world) old, self-dramatizingly so: "Here I am, an old man in a dry month"; he is a stranger to the world of heroic action; he evokes the Jew once more in a dehumanizing rhetoric; he yearns, via Blake, for "Christ the tiger" to consume him away, into a new life; he desires Christian communion but cannot help himself from evoking delicious pre-Christian pagan parallels, via Henry Adams — another guilty, self-styled, cold man fascinated by the displays of lusty spring below the Mason-Dixon line ("In depraved May, dogwood and chestnut, flowering judas"). And the memory of Adams in the fecund South somehow (we don't know how) leads into the swift internationalist evocations of character weirdly at play, participating in some black mass full of vague sexual innuendo, with Eliot's verbs doing precisely perverse work ("Mr. Silvero/With caressing hands . . . Hakagawa, bowing among the Titians . . . Fraulein von Kulp/Who turned in the hall, one hand on the door"). Then follows the major passage on history as an overwhelming woman, confusing, full of brutal ironic reversals ("Unnatural vices/Are fathered by our heroism") and the impossibility, in this poem, of separating the public flow of history from the private disasters and humiliations of an unhappy sexual alliance: the mean self-lacerations ("I have lost my sight, smell, hearing, taste and touch:/How should I use them for your closer contact?"), and the futility ("What will the spider do,/Suspend its operations. . . . "). Eliot's famous sentences about "surrender" and "the mind of Europe" do no justice to the thick specificity of his mind's interaction with that larger entity, or to the surrender that does not extinguish his individuality, or to the thinking that he does through his nerves, the artful illusion sustained in "Gerontion" that his mind is never violated by Ideas.

The job at Lloyds of London brought the Eliots some security, but their tranquility was short-lived. The family psyche quickly resumed its precipitous downward course; the marriage became a disaster. Eliot's overly taxed daily work life – he was at it virtually all of his waking hours – did not permit him much contact with his self-conceived, deepest core of identity as a poet. After his doctors recommended a three-month rest away from home and all work, he took off, ending up in a Swiss sanitarium. He got his rest; he got his vacation; and by the end of his break from home and London, all the while apparently not thinking of his poetry as "work" in the sense that his doctors must have meant the word, he found that he had almost begotten *The Waste Land*. The breakdown was just what he needed. I say "almost begotten" because he also needed Pound's midwifery. It is not probable, given the evidence of the poems written before and those written after, that *The Waste Land* would have assumed its modernist collage form, sporting such sharp and brilliant discontinuities, had Eliot not sought Pound's reaction and had Pound not been willing (but Pound was Pound) to wield a wicked and unerring editorial red pencil. That, in brief, is the personal narrative behind the poem which probably led Eliot to describe it, long after its appearance, as a "personal and wholly insignificant grouse against life; . . . a piece of rhythmical grumbling."

The literary narrative is more familiar, and more devious. *The Waste Land* is the fullest working-through of the impulses, and the voice of those impulses, driving Eliot's major early work, a poem that needed to be written after "Prufrock" and "Gerontion." Its formal and spiritual inspirations are complex and difficult to discriminate, but nevertheless in rough presence they are clear. James G. Frazer's *The Golden Bough* and Jessie L. Weston's *From Ritual to Romance* are the anthropological sources Eliot names in his notes to the poem, the books that gave him stories of ritual pagan religious practices – hints, as he took them, for literary form and a possible narrative of redemption (personal and collective, a distinction not much admired by Frazer, Weston, and Eliot). Frazer and Weston were sources for a deep structural underpinning of *The Waste Land* that, thanks to Eliot and a number of his explicators, have been made too much of (both the sources and the deep structural underpinning). Whatever else they are, the notes are the work not of a personal grouser but of a socially responsive interpreter intending to set his own work in "significant" light.

Eliot's reading of *Ulysses* constituted another major inspiration and culminates in his essay "'Ulysses,' Order, and Myth" (1923), the most important early, if indirect, critical reflection on *The Waste Land*, in which he saw Joyce's book as the expression of a need for "method" that he imagined to have given more shape to *Ulysses* (and to his own poem) than really obtains. This essay gives us not the slightest glimpse of the inventiveness and surprises, the unpredictable leaps and changes, that mark both *Ulysses* and *The Waste Land*. Joyce's continuous manipulation of a parallel with *The Odyssey* and Eliot's use of Weston's anthropological narrative or of several classical literary texts, are alike in tact of deployment, lightness of structural presence, and the gentleness with which deployed structures do not control their respective deployers' imaginations, or the unexpected and unexpectable vivid particulars of texture that cannot be dominated by structure, or indeed other methods of prereading and prewriting. The main point of Eliot's essay is that the present is an opaque fragment unless set inside the framework of a classical literary narrative which will restore the context of significance, the fragment-redeeming whole. There is no understanding except through the lens of literature; Wilde would have approved. Together with his notes to the poem, the essay on Joyce sets in motion the solemn traditional take on High Modernist experiment, often to the detriment of that experiment.

And, finally, the essay "The Metaphysical Poets" (1921), is an elegant summary of Eliot's critical preoccupations to that point, an indirect anticipation of the vast literary-historical ambition of the epochal poem he would publish the following year. In light of that essay's argument, the history of poetry in English, the main current of authentic poetry, as Eliot believed, interrupted around the time of Milton, would find its grand resumption in *The Waste Land* thanks to the unified sensibility of this proper heir of Dante, Shakespeare, and Donne. Of course, Eliot never said that publicly, maybe never said it privately, even to himself. But given the drift of his critical and poetic writing to 1922, that was what he desired, personal grouse or no personal grouse: On the one hand, modesty of ambition and, on the other, grandiosity.

The notes to *The Waste Land* are prefaced by a paragraph that begins, "Not only the title, but the plan and a good deal of the incidental symbolism of the poem were suggested by Miss Jessie L. Weston's book on the grail legend." And he adds, "so deeply am I indebted, Miss Weston's book will elucidate the difficulties of the poem much better than my notes can. . . . " Anyone familiar with Frazer and Weston, Eliot concludes, "will immediately recognize in the poem certain references to vegetation ceremonies." The statement is unremarkable in its demands. If you wish to understand the poem, it says, you will need to read other books first. Yet in his essay on Dante of 1929, he would say that "genuine poetry can communicate before it is understood," implying that "understanding" might not be our primary way of deriving pleasure and even significance from "genuine poetry"; and, indeed, Eliot's aesthetic always seemed less in favor of understanding than it was in favor of entering, through poetry, reading or writing it, another and rarer level of experience, a substratum of feeling shut off from the purity of reason. In Eliot, a romantic always lurks.

Readers of Milton (the younger Eliot would have detested the comparison), to cite only one spectacular example of difficulty, have long known the problem. The fact that Milton leaned hard on the Bible and other widely known Western classics makes a difference, but not a difference in kind. (Joyce leaned on Homer, but *Ulysses* persists in its strangeness.) Milton and Eliot not only make reference to other texts, those texts are taken in, or perhaps "make an invasion" is the way to put it, become part of the complex weave of their writing, in the case of *The Waste Land* the poet being almost perfectly covered by a canvas crowded with allusion, quotation, and pastiche. Eliot's poetry, like Pound's and Milton's, is a poetry of reading (for writer and reader alike), and – again like Pound's, but not like Milton's – a poetry of reading that could take for granted no fit audience, however small. Who among Eliot's readers, at the time of publication, could pick up on the allusions to Shakespeare *and* Virgil *and* Weston, particularly when the allusions to central writers are not necessarily to central moments or lines in their texts? Maybe none, probably not even Pound or Joyce. The notes were necessary, first of all, because the printer demanded more pages in order to fill out a signature for the book version of the poem. But they were also aids necessary to all readers; they comprise Eliot's tacit admission that he would need to introduce and train his readers in his curriculum of cultural literacy in order to make them ready to grasp his diagnosis of cultural disease.

Somehow, Eliot would refer to the tradition and teach it all at once, although "the tradition" is not correct, since it would be difficult to know, on the basis of what he quotes and alludes to, from Virgil to Verlaine, Buddha to F. H. Bradley, Webster to Weston, of just what this tradition could possibly consist, if not of Eliot's fabrication: a piece of ingenious homemade furniture, Blakean through and through. His tradition is (never mind all his schooling) the idiosyncratic imagination of an enthusiastic autodidact, trying, like Pound, to impart his treasure to readers (not a readership) who haven't the foggiest, and in the main do not care. (Autodidact may be another word for American.) *The Waste Land* represents the bizarre case of an unorthodox writer, leaning hard on his personal odyssey as a reader, his education be damned, trying to invent orthodoxy – precisely the literary situation that Eliot would castigate a few years later in *After Strange Gods,* a text written after his conversion, when he, no longer a free-thinking agnostic, could go after celebrated modern writers and suggest that no coherent community (i.e., no real community) could accept them or, for that matter, too many "free-thinking Jews."

In *The Golden Bough* and *From Ritual to Romance,* Eliot read of certain vegetation ceremonies, the rituals of fertility cults of very wide geographic distribution (the lure of a "universal" story), dating back to 3000 B.C. or more, some of whose practices and symbols survive in the Tarot cards, are represented in numerous medieval quest romances, and in, and *as,* Christianity itself (whose presence in *The Waste Land* is always in tandem with pagan myth). It is a basic narrative of the birth, fruition, decay, and death of nature – the autonomous cycle of seasons unknown – and a parallel and symbiotic narrative of human fertility, the waste and regeneration of the land and the loins, the latter process being represented in a ruler, a king of semidivine origin, who is himself representative of the life principle and is subject to the vicissitudes of declining sexual powers, death, and rebirth; the life principle periodically endangered; the fate of king, community, and nature indistinguishable; the fate of king and land nevertheless subject to control in the ceremonies described by Frazer and Weston: a community empowered by itself to save itself.

The basic narrative, its rituals and symbols, provides, Eliot says, "the plan" of his poem: plot, intention, design, and the attendant values of "the plan." Knowledge of the plan is useful if we are going to grasp Eliot's historical consciousness, his playing against the anthropological plan with contemporary characters, situation, and dialogue (the living theater of the plan). The counterpointing and the setting up of diminished and truncated (and sometimes comic) contemporary parallels constitutes "the mythic method" of the poem, which other writers could learn from Joyce, Eliot thought, and would need to follow, as if *Ulysses* were a scientific model, if they would write in a form appropriate to the modern world, and if they were to control – give order, "a shape and significance" – to what he called, in the essay on Joyce, "the immense panorama of futility and anarchy which is contemporary history." He meant contemporary history viewed and evaluated from the prospect provided by "the plan" – or at least he should have meant that.

Milton leaned on the Bible and on all those who had read it or had absorbed its myths without necessarily reading it, not having to read it because they lived in the culture of the Bible – these readers comprised his potential readership and gave Milton a chance at cultural centrality and immortality. Eliot, by leaning on still rather obscure texts in anthropology, would appear to have had no chance to make *The Waste Land* a readable text outside the modernist coterie. Nevertheless, *The Waste Land* has achieved a certain diminished centrality by finding a readership of insiders, other poets whose careers were in part formed by negative reactions to the poem or what they thought the poem stood for: Hart Crane, William Carlos Williams; a movement of antiformalist poets in the 1950s and 1960s; and, most crucially, university readers, academic literary critics and the generations of their students who were taught what they needed to know in order to avail themselves of the insider's pleasures; they were taught not only Frazer and Weston but the classic texts of the Western literary tradition, the university being perhaps the last place where those texts may be systematically and rigorously read. As the keeper of what are called canonical texts, the university has become what Eliot would never have approved of for his idea of a healthy society: the cordoned-off preserver of literary culture, the institution that unavoidably puts at the margin what it preserves; the literary department, in other words, as upscale bohemian enclave, site of the last serious readers of the major literature of the West. "Alienated readers" is understood.

For all those so armed with special decoding devices, the poem, beginning (obviously now) with its title, becomes a radiant series of organic fragments, survivals or traces, in a minor key, of ancient ritual and deep persistent myth. In its first section, "The Burial of the Dead" (an echo of the Anglican burial service), are found the imagery from the desert, the brown fogs of Dickens and Robert Louis Stevenson, the stony rubbish, the dead tree, and the dry stone which gives no sound of water; the references to the Tarot cards, and particularly the reference to The Hanged Man, figure of a dead God, a Christ-like being who may be reborn, but which the fortune-teller cannot find, and the gruesome but thematic humor of the planted corpse beginning to sprout. In the second section, "A Game of Chess," are counterpointed scenes of marriage, impotence, and abortion; in "The Fire Sermon," variations on the theme of infertile love, and again the brown land, the river "sweating" oil and tar (a startling figure of the perversions of nature, human and otherwise); in the fourth, the ambiguous "Death by Water," the title itself as reference to a central nature-cult ceremony of rebirth; and, lastly, in "What the Thunder Said," are the references to Gethsemane, the journey through the desert, the approach to the chapel perilous, and the anticipation of life-renewing rain. With the aid of Frazer and Weston, *The Waste Land* reads as an ironic quest-romance, filtered through a modernist aesthetic of collage whose effect is to deny narrative progression and change and to insist on a nightmare of temporal simultaneity.

The pleasures of knowing the plan, pleasures attendant upon structural understanding and getting the real story – secret allegory, decoding, riddle-solving, secret translation – are never the pleasures of texture, sensuous pleasures of aesthetic encounter, delights of the surface – values of reading *The Waste Land* that have, oddly, receded over time, that familiarity has not enhanced. It is the pleasure of the *plan,* the primacy of structure, that has been enhanced over time. It is hardly possible anymore to read the poem without passing through scholarly mediation: the explanations of anthropological sources, the fixing of literary sources, echoes, allusions, and their skillful annotation. No university reader can do otherwise, or would think of doing otherwise, or maybe should do otherwise. The cultural centrality of *The Waste Land,* as *the* pessimistic expression of the lost generation, is the centrality that critics and scholars, with Eliot's boost, have made. Yet the plan, though it underlies the poem, does so faintly and obscurely, tactfully so, despite all the academic labor to make the plan "obvious," an unavoidable structural presence in constant control of the details of the surface. And the elucidated literary allusions and quotations also now sit there "obviously," as if Eliot had written his poem standing up, notebook in hand, in front of his library shelves, yanking off the proper texts, putting in the telling quotations.

*The Waste Land* made by scholarship is largely cold and willful – an image of Eliot that the anti-Eliot movement in poetry and criticism, from the fifties through the seventies (it seems to have recently tapered off) was happy to seize upon in efforts to write and promote a new antiformal poetry (as though Eliot's work were not a formal oddball) and to promote the reputations of Hart Crane, William Carlos Williams, Wallace Stevens, and the romantic literary tradition, broadly defined, back to Spenser, that the young Eliot at times, and his inheritors in the New Criticism very often, had trashed. The countertrashing of Eliot and the New Critics helped to refocus our vision of literary history, reinstating movements and figures necessarily excluded by Eliot's and his New Critical inheritors' notion of authentic literary tradition. The countertrashing, so richly deserved, was also useful.

In any effort to encounter a more immediate incarnation of *The Waste Land* we might be helped by what Eliot said about Ben Jonson in *The Sacred Wood:* "Though he was saturated in literature, he never sacrifices the theatrical qualities – theatrical in the most favorable sense – to literature or to the study of character. His work is a titanic show." *The Waste Land,* quintessence of modernist experiment, a poem loaded with learning and "literature," is never sacrificed to "literature."

By "theater" and "theatrical," Eliot intended several things: first, the literary form he thought best suited down through the eras to meet, engage, and capture the life of the writer's times (the historicality of theater); second, a writer's literary self-consciousness of being *in performance* while writing, seeing himself in a dramatic light, in the act of creating himself as a character; third, a music-hall show, a series of entertainments, or the music-hall performer himself, represented for Eliot best by *her*self, Marie Lloyd, the entertainer whose death moved him to cultural mourning in a short essay published in the year of *The Waste Land,* in which he extols her organic genius, that special connection she activated with her audience, whom she led to discover and know itself as contributing, on-site artist in support of her (in several senses) *living* art.

*The Waste Land* as theater is attested to by Eliot's own recorded performance and by the frequency with which it turns up as a text for readers' theater on college campuses – persuasive testimony to the poem's dramatic character and possibilities, with its five parts functioning as five separate shows, replete with characters from all classes, language "high" and "low," jokes, dialogue, playlets, gossip, sex, popular and operatic song (something for everyone) – "and all interesting." *The Waste Land* is a titanic variety show (a *satura,* a mixture) offering the pleasures of the theater, pleasures independent of deep structure and myth, analytic intellect, or literary knowledge, pleasures one need not be an insider to enjoy and that cannot be excited by attention to "plan" and "mythic method."

One of Eliot's notes in particular, however, throws up an insuperable barrier to the experiencing of such various pleasures. It is the note on Tiresias which states that Tiresias ("I, Tiresias, though blind, throbbing between two lives"), who makes his initial (overt) appearance in "The Fire Sermon," is "the most important personage in the poem, uniting all the rest." Various figures, Eliot says, "melt" into one another; "all the women are one woman, and the two sexes meet in Tiresias. What Tiresias *sees*, in fact, is the substance of the poem." This note does the same kind of texture-obliterating (melting) work that Eliot's comments on Weston, Frazer, and "the plan" had already done. Once again we are encouraged to plunge below the surface, so variegated, to a deep structural principle, by definition homogeneous, essential, and reductive. Whether via Weston, or whether via Tiresias-the-unifying-voice, the poem's presumably presiding consciousness, we come to the same place, where all theater and theatricality, all particularity, vanishes into thin air. No music hall that operated on such principles would last for more than a night. We are not entertained; we are bored when all the women are one woman and all the men one man.

The misleading (and self-misled, if Eliot believed it) note on Tiresias is useful if taken to suggest a less reductive principle of reading, the author's helpful hint for encountering his poem's aesthetic (sensuous, vocal) cohesion in the face of a collection of fragments that might seem unifiable only at the level of deep structure (unity apparent to intellect, not ear or eye). The note on Tiresias, so understood, becomes an instrument for the unveiling of *The Waste Land*'s persistent vocal presence, a presiding but not devouring voice that intones the poem's opening lines, a voice authoritative, prophetic, elegiac, moral, and, via "Prufrock" and "Gerontion," always soul-weary: "April is the cruelest month." This voice, so strongly "written," quickly disappears in "The Burial of the Dead" into characters like the insomniac Marie, the fortune-teller, Madame Sosostris, and the unnamed joker who madly teases Stetson about his blooming corpse — disappears, that is, into "speech," the conversational rhythms of contemporary characters; then into the formal dialogues, the diptych that comprises most of "A Game of Chess"; then into the music, bawdy and stately, that appears in "The Fire Sermon"; then, transformed, as the voice which sings the formal lyric of "Death by Water" and drives the incantation of "What the Thunder Said."

# T. S. Eliot

This persistent voice, this would-be voice-over, this voice that would stay above and outside, giving moral perspective, delivering judgments dour and covert, in effect falls inside, becoming itself frequently a subject of waste when, for example, toward the end of its introduction of the first dialogue in "A Game of Chess," we suddenly find it inside the suffocating interior it describes, falling from its perch, the safety of the simple past tense, down into the entrapment of the present participle and the room of desiccation: "Staring forms/Leaned out, leaning, hushing the room enclosed." Or, in other telling moments, when we feel the rhythms of the voice-over duplicated as the rhythms of the unnamed man who fails in the hyacinth garden; or when the persistent vocal presence is spoken *to*, made a sexual offer, *made* a character, in effect, by the proposition of Mr. Eugenides; or when, in perhaps as telling a moment as we will find in the poem, the voice-over becomes another of the walking urban dead, lured by the mandolin playing in a workers' pub on lower Thames Street, a pub adjacent to the splendid church of Magnus Martyr, adjacent institutions neither of which he can participate in. The mandolin sounds in his mind in tandem with the music of Ariel, heard by Ferdinand in *The Tempest*, Shakespeare's late play of transformation and redemption. This voice-over, this contemporary Ferdinand (searching for his Miranda, in this poem of numerous failures of love), this head full of echoes and memories of rebirth, who will not himself be reborn, does not go into the pub he wants to go into, where, or so he imagines, life is not lived in the mind: pub and church, side by side, an image of the unified, organic community for which Eliot longed. This lyric moment from "The Fire Sermon" (257–65) is perhaps the most telling in the poem because it incarnates, in a plain-styled diction, the driving desire at work in *The Waste Land*: to get out of the waste land. Desire so framed – the passage sits virtually at the center of the poem – is critical desire. The problem is not being able to come to terms with the modern metropolis, whose scene provides the details of the poem's setting, the debilitating context for a shape-changing urban stroller in the financial district, trying to forget the profit and the loss, a consciousness that would preside over the waste land with moral clarity, but more often than not finds itself losing its authority, becoming resident within. Eliot does not find his "Miranda," that "something which is more valuable" to which he would sacrifice his "self."

But the immediacy of this voice is not the immediacy of sound by itself, cut off from intellect. It is the immediacy of a total sensibility that takes in the London scene all at once as sensuous datum (of mainly repulsive detail) and as object of knowledge. This is a mind that looks at the world and does not think, London is "like" Dante's *Inferno;* this is a mind that looks at London and *sees* Dante's *Inferno;* a mind that imagines the sexually indifferent typist and doesn't think, "In Oliver Goldsmith it would have been different" (Eliot counts on us getting the difference), but more importantly cannot experience the real except through literary mediation; as a literary voice yielding itself constantly to other literary voices; a mind that looks at "life" and sees "literature" in action. The experience of voice in this poem is dramatically concrete, like the experience of a playgoer who, through the medium of the actors' voices, gains access to a presiding mind that functions as the "conscious present," and "awareness of the past in a way and to an extent which the past's awareness of itself cannot show," a mind not *with* a perception, but *as* a perception, "not only of the pastness of the past, but of its presence." But this presiding consciousness, heterogeneous and impure, this "conscious present," this head full of memories of literature and ancient ritual, is also the conscious past, in a way and to an extent which the past, as past, could never be conscious – that is, as an awareness of the present from the point of view of the past.

*The Waste Land* is finally a traditional poem, not because it looks like any poem that was written before it (it does not), but because its experiments in form, its splintered negotiations of a poetic consciousness in full flight from subjective stability (escaping its personality), make sense only as they engage and revivify traditional writers in ways that those writers could never have imagined or desired, in a world that those writers did not imagine. *The Waste Land* is not a monument of literary history. It is an image of literary history itself in the act of undergoing difficult transformation, abandoning, as Eliot put it in "Tradition and the Individual Talent," "nothing *en route.*"

We can see *The Waste Land* conceived as its anthropological substructure, a "plan" now not so obscure; or *The Waste Land* as sensuous embodiment and narrative of a voice constantly reincarnating itself in surprising tones, characters, and in other writers; shattering its substantial unity; or, better, *The Waste Land* as some deep-set plan contacted only through particulars of texture. And as one more version, this one suggested by terms from (for young man Eliot) the new art of moving pictures and the newly revolutionized art of painting: "montage" and "collage," recently deployed by critics to characterize the poem's surface (that is, "aesthetic") impact.

In *The Waste Land,* Eliot, a man of his aesthetic times, created a kind of painting in five panels, which must be grasped by the mind's eye all at once, as a spatial form, taken in as if the poem were a single complex image, not a work to be read through time, from beginning to end, but a work to be "seen" in a glance. This version of the poem can be contacted only by readers of veteran status who know the allusions like the back of their hands, who have read the poem so many times, in frustration and pleasure, that, in effect, they hardly need a text because they have made themselves into viewers. *The Waste Land,* so encountered, becomes the literary equivalent of a work of analytic cubism, a series of layered "planes" transparent to each other, whose overall effect is the fracturing of the traditional literary unities of time (1922), place (London), and continuing, binding representations of character (many of them sordid and neurasthenic).

Eliot's experiment does not welcome questions about when, where, and who. And it constantly overrides the distinction between real and representation. So that contemporary London (the poem's "real," the poem's "present"), Baudelaire's Paris, and the scene of *The Inferno* stand co-presently in "The Burial of the Dead"; so that lovers from *The Aeneid* and *Hamlet* stand in co-presence, as if they all existed in the same space with contemporary couples in "A Game of Chess," the panel of couples; so that *The Tempest,* Spenser, and Marvell provide gestures of love side by side with various contemporary enactments of the flesh in "The Fire Sermon," where Buddha and Saint Augustine speak, side by side. The old unities are replaced by what an active reader must bring together in a reconciling glance: not, finally, the past and present in ironic juxtaposition (though such juxtapositions stud many local textures of the poem), but past and present, "literary" and "real," in immediate painterly presence, a wall of pictures, a horror of simultaneity for a consciousness that knows too much and for which freshness of experience is impossible. In lines from the first of the *Quartets:*

> If all time is eternally present
> All time is unredeemable . . .

But the metaphor of spatial form does not quite hold all the way. In the fifth and final section, time leaks ominously out of space, painterly panel becomes narrative, and the fixed and repetitious seem about to undergo change. A key Shakespearian moment ("Those are pearls that were his eyes") is worked and reworked consciously in the poem's voice-over and unconsciously in characters who say it, not because they know Shakespeare (they do not) and enjoy displaying literary sophistication, but because the line must be spoken, because this longing for transformation must be felt. Section five, then, is seen through a veil of hallucinatory rhetoric: Gethsemane, the road to Emmaus, the whirlwind tour of exploding European capitals, and the approach to the Chapel Perilous, where the grail-quester might ask the right question, so much the better to facilitate redemption of land and impotent king, so that we might live in a new world, forgetting "the profit and the loss" (Eliot's sole but insistent political gesture, his revulsion from the world of capital.) The tone is apocalyptic; some revelation, the much longed-for change is at hand, but what is it that lurks just over the horizon?

Eliot ends the poem in the mode of a desire (half-fearful) expressed just a year before *The Waste Land* appeared by Yeats in "The Second Coming," a desire revisited several years later by Frost, most notably in "Once by the Pacific." "Someone had better be prepared for rage" is how Frost puts it, and Yeats would have agreed. Eliot is prepared for rage and hopes for salvation. Like Yeats and Frost, he defines his modernity in *The Waste Land* as that intuition of being on the verge of upheaval – the breakup, the smashing, and the sinking of a whole era: not the new, but the verge of the new, for better or for worse. Probably, these writers fear, for worse.


Ezra Pound knew another *Ulysses:* a book, he believed, "presumably as unrepeatable as *Tristram Shandy;* I mean you cannot duplicate it; you can't take it as a model." Pound's *Ulysses* is a a liberating force, the spirit of invention and a spur to the imaginations of succeeding writers to search out the springs of originality: make your own world, make yourself. So Pound's Joyce is the figure of modernist artistic selfhood, incarnating itself in a distinctive, virtuoso style, itself constantly reimagined in *Ulysses,* almost from chapter to chapter. Joyce the artist, then, as the exemplary instance of the radical individual, repeating not even his much less someone else's form, a figure of freedom in a world of various tyrannies (artistic, economic, social), the high modernist inventor as political hero whose motto is, and must be, *non serviam;* the figure of Joyce: the anarchic self, trusting in nothing.

But a "model" is precisely what the young Eliot took Joyce's book to be, a display of narrative method which he thought had the force of a "scientific discovery," a form to be assented to and a paradigm to work within. Young Eliot, the reluctant experimentalist, the unhappy individualist, thought he had found in *Ulysses* reason enough to give up his adventures in form. For if Joyce was the founder of a new literary tradition, then Eliot might become the new Shakespeare, working infinite refinements on a form given to him, bringing to culmination what had existed, so it goes, in Joyce, in a cruder state. Writers who came after *Ulysses* should be members of the literary community of *Ulysses,* finding their literary individuality inside the Joycean form, which makes possible variant and original selves, variations within a norm, without subverting the communal ground of variation.

The reasoning sounds familiar because it is. The reasoning, which his teacher Josiah Royce would have admired, is the foundation of Eliot's literary and social thought, early, middle, and late. "Tradition," "existing order," and the "supervention of novelty" were the terms he used in "Tradition and the Individual Talent." The point is to "sacrifice" yourself to "something which is more valuable," to lose one kind of isolate, disconnected "self" in order to find a self organically connected to a whole for which you do not have the responsibilities that would devolve upon its inventing God and sole sustainer.

Early on, the terms are literary, but in hindsight they teasingly suggest a great deal more than literary selfhood inside a magnificent community comprised of "the whole of the literature of Europe from Homer" to the present, Joyce having revived Homer for the literary present. The early literary essays, like many of his later major prose pieces, are expressions of Eliot's desire for relation inside an ideally cohesive culture. The poetry, in the meanwhile, "Ash Wednesday" and *Four Quartets* not excluded, is an expression of the actual, Eliot's life inside an incoherent and resolutely secular culture. *The Waste Land,* in this perspective, is not the mourning of an absence of values but the staging of a consciousness overwhelmed by fragments of literary forms and values as well as religious frameworks and values, a consciousness disheartened but nevertheless fascinated by a jumbled world of cultural variety that it tries to hold together in a single glance, a world in which everything is in play but nothing takes root, nothing commands, except the twin foci of Eliot's contempt: the profit and the loss and the casual sex, which is our fate, which is what Tiresias foresees.

Although his concern for literary form and the embracing social form he called a "framework" is in evidence before *The Waste Land,* after the publication of that poem, and while critics were debating its mood, meaning, and problematical unity, Eliot moved insistently in the direction of exploring "framework," the form of forms for writers and other wandering pilgrims. His literary essays continue to speak of the advantage to the writer of a "coherent traditional system of dogma and morals," "allegiance" to "something outside," and the necessity for an alternative to the vapidity of the "inner voice" and the climate of liberal opinion. But these essays (for example, "The Function of Criticism," 1923; "Dante," 1929; "Religion and Literature," 1935) move boldly out of the aesthetic arena when they argue that the writer's deepest relation to something outside, his union with that something, is "unconscious" or (in an intriguing phrase) "mostly unconscious." "Form" and "framework" acquire highly specific content: tradition, region, family, parish, community and the gathering terms, Christian society and Christian culture, are the key words of value in the later Eliot, the signs of a doctrinal context that give clarity to the struggle evident in *Four Quartets* but never resolution, and never sectarian narrowness.

The intention driving Eliot's later career – I mean all that he did after he joined the Church of England in 1927 – is public, socially involved, intellectually activist. Eliot, editor and intellectual, founded *The Criterion* in 1922, and for seventeen years thereafter worked to nourish a mostly conscious cosmopolitan culture, rooted in diverse national ground but unified beyond the borders. In the early 1930s, he turned to the theater, because he wanted "to have a part to play in society as worthy as that of the music-hall comedian," because, though he never said it explicitly, he wanted to be the Marie Lloyd of high-modernist literature. His career in theater is a would-be farewell to the social disdain of high-modernist coterie. The modest Broadway success of *The Cocktail Party* thrilled him for more than reasons of financial gain (which was not negligible); he would have loved *Cats;* he packed a basketball stadium at the University of Minnesota with a lecture on criticism. These were some of the significant external signs of a conscious will to join and sustain "something which is more valuable," but to live at a "mostly unconscious" level.

Eliot's later major social criticism – *After Strange Gods* (1934), *The Idea of a Christian Society* (1939), and *Notes Toward the Definition of Culture* (1948) – is controversial for its harsh disposal of central modern assumptions and pieties (liberalism, secularism, and democracy; the latter mere rhetoric, he believed, veiling financial oligarchy), for its counterstatement of a Christian religious framework, and for the anti-Semitism of a much cited passage in *After Strange Gods.* In the jargon of our day, Eliot believed "multiculturalism" to be a contradiction in terms if intended as a description of any given and genuine culture and a banality if intended as a description of the human world, the world being obviously full of cultural differences. In *After Strange Gods,* Eliot argued that culture could neither exist nor persist except in small, out-of-the-way pockets, free from the impact of modernization, close to the soil, and, particularly in the United States, free from the influx of foreign races, far from New York City (let us say, in and around Charlottesville, Virginia). In *The Idea of a Christian Society* and *Notes,* he dropped his nostalgia for rural life and made no hostile references to Jews.

Eliot's anti-Semitism in *After Strange Gods* is exactly what it seems to be, but it is something more when set in the context of the Israeli experiment in society and the troubles in Northern Ireland. "Anti-Catholic," "anti-Islamic," and "anti-Semitic," in such contexts, miss a significant point. Efforts to establish and sustain a cohesive culture and society ("cohesive" is redundant in Eliot's analysis, a synonym for "real") are bound, at a certain level, to be exclusionary, to desire "cleanliness," ethnic, religious, or both, and to be hostile to self-differentiating elements ("dominant," in the realm of culture, is another synonym for "real"). Such efforts need not be violent and xenophobic, though the Israeli and Irish examples, mild as they are alongside some others in the twentieth century, remind us that violence and intolerance often attend the projects for cohesive culture. Eliot worked in *The Criterion* for a cosmopolitan effect because he believed that national cultures need constant transfusions from outside in order to stay vital; he cherished above all a multicultural world, cultures differently and deeply rooted. But he feared that liberal and secular modes of thought and U.S. cultural imperialism would obliterate that diversity, would homogenize the world's cultural texture, and he had contempt for societies that by intention or thoughtless drift might become multicultural. Eliot clearly could not admire the multicultural diversity of the United States, and did not believe that such diversity could become a "culture" in any sense of the word that he understood. On Eliot's behalf it may be said that the charge of anti-Semitism leveled at *After Strange Gods* is spurious in the context of his traditional analysis of what culture is, and that the jury is still out concerning the American experiment in diversity. In a couple of places in the poems, and in several places in his published letters, "anti-Semitic" is an accurate description – and that, too, needs to be acknowledged if we are to get on with the projects of literary criticism and literary history, which do not require that writers be models of decency.

Eliot's much desired, "mostly unconscious" relation is to culture conceived as "habitual actions, habits and customs, from the most significant religious rite to our conventional way of greeting a stranger." Culture, as the "blood kinship of the 'same people living in the same place,'" is an expressive totality, a "way of feeling and acting which characterizes a group throughout generations." Culture, in other words, is necessarily mostly unconscious. Inside culture, behavior constitutes belief, and behavior is mostly not chosen. The "individual," thoroughly enmeshed in and dependent upon the group and its traditions, is released into "individuality"; the "individual" is permitted by "tradition." In such a vision, and it *is* a vision (recalling his early vision of literary totality and tradition), the necessary values are conservation, stability, and resistance to change – values to be managed and cultivated by the culture's intellectuals (in a Christian culture, the community of Christian elite who presumably mediate the pattern laid up in heaven in its relation to actual society). It was Eliot's hope that culture would have no use for the cult of personality, would not encourage the artist to nourish his alienation, his deviance, and his differance, would not permit itself to be a proving ground for avant-garde thought and expression, would not desire to position its artists and intellectuals as agents of social change, much less revolution. Eliot never lived in such a cultural place, which exists, for him, only in the ideal projections of his prose. He was doubtful that the real world could be so transformed, but thought it important, nevertheless, to imagine, argue, and work (in his prose life) for a world so transformed.

The major poetic episodes in Eliot's career after *The Waste Land* include: "The Hollow Men" (1925), in effect, an epilogue to *The Waste Land;* "Ash Wednesday" (1930, with sections published over the three previous years), his initial and still major expression of Christian commitment; the opening of his career as verse dramatist with *Murder in the Cathedral* (produced and published in 1935); and the crowning achievement both of his Christian turn and his poetry after *The Waste Land,* the four meditative poems that appeared in collected form in 1943 as *Four Quartets* ("Burnt Norton," 1935; "East Coker," 1940; "The Dry Salvages," 1941; "Little Gidding," 1942). The site of *Four Quartets* as a meditative venture, its constraining cultural ground, is precisely the cultural place that Eliot had excoriated in his prose, the actual culture he lived in ("No place of grace"), not the one he dreamed of in *The Idea of a Christian Society.* The essential themes and tones of *Four Quartets* are sounded in "Ash Wednesday": resignation and fear in the context of encroaching age; crippling self-dialogue and the plea, the prayer for patience, humility, and deliverance; sumptuous and pressingly sexual memory and the desire for the ascetic life – all, and always, in the tone of the pilgrim requiring transformation, waiting for grace.

"Burnt Norton" was a gift, grace from the literary gods, an accident that grew from some discarded fragments of *Murder in the Cathedral.* Only with "East Coker" did Eliot hit upon an intention for a suite of four poems for which "Burnt Norton" would provide a model of structure in five parts – or movements, as his musical metaphor would demand – sections to be repeated and varied in ensuing poems, so much the better to achieve an effect of spatial form periodically interrupted by an effect of temporality. In the thematic expression of his musical shape: constricting order, suffocating enclosure, suddenly opened and redeemed by a surprising infusion of grace; meaningless flow, one damned thing after another in the shifting world, suddenly punctuated and thrown into perspective by a fixed presence, a center, the endlessness of flow becoming elegantly geometric. In the language of his master metaphor, consciousness seeks to be "at the still point of the turning world," a reality that human kind can bear (at best) only in rare, ecstatic doses. The Reality is Incarnation, neither flesh nor fleshless; the fixed Presence, ever-present, is Christ, who may be sought, occasionally contacted, ever-present but mainly not present.

Because *Four Quartets* follows *The Waste Land,* its fate, despite all the literary pyrotechnics of the earlier poem, is to seem even more literary, a poem that requires knowledge of the earlier poem if its place in Eliot's inner journey is to be grasped in proper context. In addition, because of its open personal references to its author as a literary man in the middle of the way, and just because this man, when he writes and publishes it, is the leading man of letters of his time, who is making substantial references to *The Waste Land* (the third movement of each of the poems, with one exception, is a retrieval of the scene of *The Waste Land*, without the technical difficulties), it is assumed that the reader of course knows who he, T. S. Eliot, is – knows his fame, has long sensed his ambition for high place in literary history, knows about the conversion of 1927 to the Church of England. Despite its relative ease of access, *Four Quartets* is a poem for a literary insider who (the final limiting factor) is no reflex secularist.

The structure of the *Quartets* consists of an initial section which presents the sort of large view of things that tends to be called "philosophical." In each of the poems the problem is time itself: in "Burnt Norton" evoked abstractly; in the others, with concreteness, in the styles of lyric meditation and biblical prophecy and the imagery of generations, natural force, and miraculous eruptions of spring in winter (the rise and fall of houses, the great brown god of the Mississippi, "spring time/But not in time's covenant"). The initial section is then broken by extra spacing, the indication of a leap to a passage of visionary memory whose object is personal. The second sections begin with a lyric of cosmological vision, followed by a reflection and elaboration again personal, this time concerning the trials of a poet in grave doubt about all that he has accomplished. The third sections (with the exception of "Little Gidding") are revisitations of waste-land scenes; the fourth are all doctrinal in weight, Christian allegorical lyrics of agonized (never complacent) tone. And the concluding sections deal with the question of poetry itself – the nature of its language and values. As a whole, the *Quartets* present an alternation of voices lyrical and discursive, the expression of a writer who must always be questioning the worth and place of his expression. Underneath everything, the persistent vocal substance is meditative, the tone is measured, stoically at peace, the voice of a poet trying to care and not to care, trying to sit still.

# T. S. Eliot

The unresolvable tension of *Four Quartets* is that Eliot, a reluctant experimentalist, who wanted to (but did not) inherit viable traditional form, who wanted to (but did not) bury isolate selfhood in a community ("which is more valuable"), who could not finally hide his life entirely in Christ, nevertheless committed himself in this poem to the most uncompromising implications of avant-garde aesthetic. Knowledge of the past, he tells us, imposes falsifying pattern onto the present, falsifying because "the pattern is new in every moment/And every moment is a new and shocking/Valuation of all we have been." Knowledge of one's craft, likewise, imposes falsifying pattern. The triumph of literary form and language is its radical mimesis of the new and shocking moment. It is a triumph over literary history, over the falsity of received pattern, over convention. What we have already perceived, yesterday's perception caught in yesterday's poem, is yesterday's triumph — good only for yesterday and who we were yesterday. Today we are dumb, and every effort to write and live freshly is necessarily a "raid on the inarticulate/With shabby equipment always deteriorating."

Yesterday's equipment is shabby, and so is yesterday's self. Shabby but comfortable, comfortable but a lie. Old men, or older men, as he should have written (the *Quartets* were composed between his forty-seventh and fifty-fourth years), would rather not be explorers. They would rather repeat themselves as writers, repeat themselves as selves. They would rather repeat than create; rather not chance possession because they do not wish to bear any Reality, or be borne by it. The courage to "make it new" as a writer is not a metaphor: it is Eliot's path to regeneration.

The other side of Eliot is never avant-gardist, is the very antithesis of the spirit of the avant-garde. The two sides coexist, always uneasily but always through necessity, in Eliot's writing, life being a truncated travesty if imagined otherwise. I refer, of course, to his commitments to tradition, literary history, the past. The urgent way to put it is the best way: his life, and ours, with the dead. Not the dead letters of texts, but those familiar, compound ghosts haunting texts. Here, at last (in an echo of Pound's "The Return"), he contacts Joyce's great orthodox theme. And this is how he says it in "Little Gidding":

> We die with the dying:
> See, they depart, and we go with them.
> We are born with the dead:
> See, they return, and bring us with them.

That is Eliot's grandest expression of communitarian vision, the voice least likely to be heard in the modern secular and liberal state.

*The Waste Land* will remain the singular aesthetic event of modernist poetry in the English language; and its stance, however we construct it, seems one we can live with because, however we construct it, it seems one that suits our sense of ourselves. But Eliot after *The Waste Land* will continue to be another matter: an event unabsorbed because, in the context of advanced Western values, it is unabsorbable.

# EPILOGUE

W HAT IS THE FATE of the artist in modern society and culture? The role of art in a world shaped by the economics and ethos of the commodity? Books about modernist literature obsessively raise and fret over those familiar questions because the writers themselves did so. And upon those questions, writers and critics of modernism have achieved well-known consensus. The role is alienated and constantly critical, and the fate of the artist is dire. As one of Don DeLillo's characters remarks in *Mao II* (1991), a novel that plays out the endgame of modernist consciousness, the modernist writer is not only a necessary outsider, he should also be an outlaw, a hunted outlaw, the target, even, of assassination, because he represents, should he get his way, the undoing of the order of things. From Pound to DeLillo, the question of the writer is unavoidably political.

The central paradox of the classic modernist writers is that the adversarial stance they typically took, the kind of experimental writing they typically did – in so many words, what made them, in *this* world, original and famous – would become, in the transformed world of their desire, unnecessary and even unimaginable. Had T. S. Eliot been able actually to live all his life in the "community" of desire he projected in his later prose, he would never have written *The Waste Land.* He could not have written it. There would have been no fragments to shore against his ruins; there would have been no ruins.

With frequent brusque lucidity, Pound put on display the key value terms in the modernist lexicon: *originality, creativity, individuality, freedom*. Pound's radical point is that these terms are synonymous, and that, together, they comprise the index of an authentic selfhood of which the artist is both rigorous champion and superb representative, and of which the artist's culture is rigorous and superb denier, marginalizer, and (Pound feared) destroyer. In DeLillo's novel, Pound's fear is completely realized: in the culture of the commodity, now reinforced and doubled in the electronic society of the image, the prized value is repetition, not originality: Campbell soup cans, coke bottles, and pictures of Marilyn Monroe – so much the better to consume our soup, our coke, and our Marilyn. Andy Warhol becomes the ambivalent god of this culture (dreadful mirror, parodist, and cynical sustainer), and he is therefore the discomforting genius of DeLillo's novel and, more, the discomforting *genius loci* of the contemporary West.

The agreement, from Pound to DeLillo, is this: that the human equivalent of the commodity is now fully in being. We now witness the well-lubricated production of the faceless mass man, who happily unburdens himself of any inclinations toward free will and independent thought, who *wants* to lose his name and signature. "The future belongs to crowds," writes DeLillo. The future belongs to the total authority of the totalitarian father in the mold of Hitler, Mussolini, Mao, the Reverend Moon, the maximum Ayatollah Khomeini.

DeLillo's champion of the self is a reclusive novelist, Bill Gray, who has lived in hiding for years, and who, in the book's last pages, expresses his profoundest desire, to avoid consumption by his culture: "He wished devoutly to be forgotten." Bill's style of speaking tends toward the subversive indirections of his deadpan manner. His straight talk is rare and therefore all the more riveting when it comes. The single subject of Bill's sincere manner is his own creative process, which he passionately evokes on several occasions as antithetical to the world of repetitions and human automatons. He tells us that writing is the "pure game of making up," the "lost game of self." The style of his book, the swing of his sentences, is the shape and style of a selfhood that does not preexist the book. I write, therefore I am.

But if writing the book marks the writer's potentially pleasurable awareness of his emerging self, it also provides him with his central political principle of freedom, whose extinguishment he witnesses all about him. In the dynamic of creation, the book becomes the site of freedom's emergence, the image of its victory for the individual over the totalitarian principle, not identified now with some exterior and much hated (easy to hate) figure of fascism, but within: the totalitarian within us all, including the novelist himself, who wants to, he confesses, but finally cannot, own and control his characters. They resist him:

> Even if I could see the need for absolute authority, my work would draw me away. The experience of my consciousness tells me how autocracy fails, how total control wrecks the spirit, how my characters deny my efforts to own them completely, how I need internal dissent, self-argument, how the world squashes me the minute I think it's mine. . . .
>
> Do you know why I believe in the novel? It's a democratic shout. Anybody can write a great novel, almost any amateur off the street . . . some nameless drudge, some desperado with barely a nurtured dream can sit down and find his voice and luck out and do it. Something so angelic it makes your jaw hang open. The spray of talent, the spray of ideas. One thing unlike another, one voice unlike the next. Ambiguities, contradictions, whispers, hints. . . .
>
> And when the novelist loses his talent, he dies democratically, there it is for everyone to see, wide open to the world, the shitpile of hopeless prose.

The major political assumption of the modernists is that people in advanced Western societies desire, or would desire were they sufficiently intelligent about their circumstances, the originality and freedom of an authentic selfhood; that people should want what they, the modernists, want; that the serious artist is, or should be, the exemplary individual. Wanting to make the world possible for themselves — and why shouldn't they? — modernist writers believe that everyone would be happier if only they could become artists. The world would then be a decent place. Of course, they see that all the evidence points in the other direction. Virtually nobody wants what they want. In fact, given the flow of things, the possibility of (noncommercial) art and freedom, as they envision it, will simply be rubbed out of human possibility. That is what they tend to believe. Hence, apocalypse; modernists tend to be apocalypticists. So Yeats, in "The Second Coming": the blood-dimmed tide is loosed, and what rough beast is this, slouching to be born? So Frost, in "Once by the Pacific": "Somebody had better be prepared for rage." So Eliot, in the last section of *The Waste Land:* the hallucinatory images of exploding European capitals, and the sullen and hooded and swarming hordes. So DeLillo in *Mao II:* ". . . people gathering in clusters everywhere, coming out of mud houses and tin-roof shanties and sprawling camps and meeting in some dusty square to march together to a central point, calling out a name, collecting many others on the way, some are running, some in bloodstained shirts. . . . "

In the United States, we do not target artists for political assassination. DeLillo, who is strongly sympathetic with the dying Bill Gray, is also a thoroughgoing skeptic and ironist. In response to Bill's lyrical evocation of the pure game of making up, the lost game of self, another character says, "It sounds like mental illness to me." Yet another character makes an even more telling point: "Bill doesn't understand how people need . . . to lose themselves in something larger." And Bill might have replied, "I do not want to lose myself in the glut of media imagery, or in the mindless crowd that chants its fealty to The Father. I reject your models of 'something larger.'"

The missing term in modernist thinking — Eliot stands by himself on this point — is community: something larger, something more valuable than isolate selfhood, that would include original selves, nourish and sustain them, while also nourishing and sustaining a network of connection, a wholeness (greater than the sum of selves) which the thinker of community believes makes healthy selfhood possible. But where in the secular and liberal West are the models for this to be found? Fundamentalist Muslims would teach us a lesson in seriousness, and so would those who live in monasteries and convents. In the absence of religious commitment, the choice of my modernists for radical disconnection seems right.

# BIBLIOGRAPHICAL NOTE

On the four writers I have treated in this book, and on modernism in general, the literature is vast. I have no doubt been influenced by many more critics and scholars than I can remember. I mention here only those few I do recall with vividness, whose work I know that I could not have done without.

R. P. Blackmur's *Language as Gesture* and Yvor Winters's many essays on the subject of modern poetry remain, for me, the most provocative and profound. Books by F. O. Matthiessen and R.W.B. Lewis on the James family and William H. Pritchard's *Lives of the Modern Poets* (New York: Oxford University Press, 1980), I have kept close at hand. Also consistently useful are: Roy Harvey Pearce's *The Continuity of American Poetry* (Princeton: Princeton University Press, 1961); Bernard Duffey's *Poetry in America* (Durham, N.C.: Duke University Press, 1978); and both volumes of David Perkins's extraordinarily thorough *A History of Modern Poetry* (Cambridge, Mass.: Harvard University Press, 1976, 1987). The most provocative book on modernism I have read is Raymond Williams's *The Politics of Modernism* (London: Verso, 1989).

On Frost: the three volumes of Lawrence Thompson's biography; Pritchard's superb *Frost: A Literary Life Reconsidered* (New York: Oxford University Press, 1984); and Thompson's and Louis Untermeyer's editions of the letters.

On Stevens: Joan Richardson's *Wallace Stevens: The Early Years,*

*1879–1923* (New York: William Morrow, 1986), and Holly Stevens's important editions of the letters and journals.

On Pound: the commentaries of Christine Froula and William Cookson; the two volumes of Carroll F. Terrell's indispensable *A Companion to the Cantos of Ezra Pound;* biographies by Noel Stock and John Tytell; the letters edited by D. D. Paige; Eugene Nassar's *The Cantos of Ezra Pound* (Baltimore: The Johns Hopkins University Press, 1975); and, of course, Hugh Kenner's *The Pound Era* (Berkeley and Los Angeles: University of California Press, 1971).

On Eliot: Grover Smith's ever-useful *T. S. Eliot's Poetry and Plays: A Study in Sources and Meaning* (Chicago: University of Chicago Press, 1956); Valerie Eliot's edition of the letters; Peter Ackroyd's biography, *T. S. Eliot: A Life* (New York: Simon and Schuster, 1984); and *T. S. Eliot: The Modernist in History,* ed. Ronald Bush (New York: Cambridge University Press, 1991).

# INDEX

# Index

# Index

# Index

# Index

# Index

Psychology, The, 1, 4, 22; Talks to Teachers on Psychology, and to Students on Some of Life's Ideals, 18

Jarrell, Randall, 107

Jefferson and/or Mussolini (Pound), 182, 233

Johnson, Ben, 270

Johnson, Lionel, 188

Johnson, R. U., 64

Joyce, James, xiii, 12, 13, 104, 107, 180, 216, 235, 237, 264, 266, 267, 268, 277, 278, 286; Dubliners, xiii; Ulysses, 246, 264, 267, 277, 278

Kafka, Franz, 12, 116

Kant, Immanuel, 4, 42, 53, 58

Keats, John, 5, 8, 7, 92, 94, 125, 135, 169, 184, 192; "Ode to a Nightingale," 94

Kilmer, Joyce, 79–80

Knowles, F. L., 59, 64; Golden Treasury of American Songs and Lyrics, 59

Laforgue, Jules, 240–1, 242, 243

"Latest Freed Man" (Stevens), 164

Lawrence, D. H., 136

Leaves of Grass (Whitman), 2, 16

Letters to John Bartlett (student of Frost) (Frost), 48, 50, 52, 68, 102–3, 104–5,

Lewis, Wyndham, 80, 180

Lindsay, Vachel, 70, 81

Literature and the American College (Babbitt), 255

Little Book of Modern Verse (Rittenhouse), 59, 78, 79

"Little Gidding" (Eliot), 282, 284, 286

Longfellow, Henry Wadsworth, xi, 2, 3, 49, 50, 233

"Love Song of J. Alfred Prufrock" (Eliot), 52, 210, 241–5, 248, 253, 260, 261, 263, 272

Lowell, James, xi, 2

Lucretius, 13

Lukács, Georg, 12, 13, 17, 18, 147

Lume Spento, A (Pound), 61, 191, 192, 199, 202, 203, 204, 208, 214

Lustra (Pound), 211, 214

Lyrical Ballads (Wordsworth), 83

Mailer, Norman, 104, 135; Why Are We in Vietnam?, 135

Man with the Blue Guitar, The (Stevens), 153, 158, 159, 160

Mann, Thomas, 18

Mao II (DeLillo), 287, 290

Marcuse, Herbert, 5

Marvell, Andrew, 99, 101, 276; "Damon the Mower," 99

Marx, Karl, 18, 153; German Ideology, The, 153

Massinger, Philip, 256

Masters, Edgar Lee, 70, 81

Maurras, Charles, 254

Melville, Herman, 135; Moby-Dick, 135

Mencken, H. L., xi

"Mending Wall" (Frost), 95, 96, 111, 112

Metamorphoses (Ovid), 226

"Metaphors of a Magnifico" (Stevens), 143

"Metaphysical Poets, The" (Eliot), 91, 264

Milton, John, 135, 150, 168, 235, 256, 257, 265, 266, 268; Paradise Lost, 168, 182

Moby-Dick (Melville), 135

Modern American Poetry (Untermeyer), 77, 80, 81, 82

300

# Index

# Index

# Index

Printed in the United Kingdom
by Lightning Source UK Ltd.
9407100002B